THE PLEASURE OF
YOUR COMPANY

THE PLEASURE OF YOUR COMPANY

A Socio-Psychological Analysis of Modern Sociability

Emile Jean Pin
in collaboration with
Jamie Turndorf

PRAEGER

PRAEGER SPECIAL STUDIES • PRAEGER SCIENTIFIC

New York • Philadelphia • Eastbourne, UK
Toronto • Hong Kong • Tokyo • Sydney

Library of Congress Cataloging in Publication Data

Pin, Emile Jean.
  The pleasure of your company.

  Bibliography: p.
  Includes indexes.
  1. Interpersonal relations. 2. Social interaction.
3. Social psychology. I. Turndorf, Jamie. II. Title.
HM132.P53 1985   302   85-494
ISBN 0-03-003787-5 (alk. paper)

Published in 1985 by Praeger Publishers
CBS Educational and Professional Publishing, a Division of CBS Inc.
521 Fifth Avenue, New York, NY 10175 USA

© 1985 by Praeger Publishers

56789 052 987654321

Printed in the United States of America on acid-free paper

INTERNATIONAL OFFICES

Orders from outside the United States should be sent to the appropriate address listed below. Orders from areas not listed below should be placed through CBS International Publishing, 383 Madison Ave., New York, NY 10175 USA

Australia, New Zealand
Holt Saunders, Pty, Ltd., 9 Waltham St., Artarmon, N.S.W. 2064, Sydney, Australia

Canada
Holt, Rinehart & Winston of Canada, 55 Horner Ave., Toronto, Ontario, Canada M8Z 4X6

Europe, the Middle East, & Africa
Holt Saunders, Ltd., 1 St. Anne's Road, Eastbourne, East Sussex, England BN21 3UN

Japan
Holt Saunders, Ltd., Ichibancho Central Building, 22-1 Ichibancho, 3rd Floor, Chiyodaku, Tokyo, Japan

Hong Kong, Southeast Asia
Holt Saunders Asia, Ltd., 10 Fl, Intercontinental Plaza, 94 Granville Road, Tsim Sha Tsui East, Kowloon, Hong Kong

Manuscript submissions should be sent to the Editorial Director, Praeger Publishers, 521 Fifth Avenue, New York, NY 10175 USA

INTRODUCTION

On her way to the door, Joyce paused in front of the hall mirror to fix her earrings and her hair. Everything was OK. Maybe we'll dance, she thought. She twirled in front of the mirror to see her dress swirl gently. After putting on her coat, she hurried to the party. It was being given by her boss, Edward Kohn, the director of W.N.B.W., and because this was the first time Joyce had been invited to one of his gatherings, she wondered whether she would know a soul. Before ringing his door bell, she gave her make-up the last touch-up. When the door opened, she entered clasping her handbag very tightly.

Mrs. Kohn greeted her with a fixed smile, asking her her name. "Well, Joyce," she replied, "it is nice to know you. We'll talk a little bit later, I hope. Drop your coat in the bedroom, go to the bar, have a drink and make yourself at home."

While waiting for the lime to be squeezed into her gin and tonic, Joyce looked around. There were about twenty guests clustered in groups of twos, threes, and fours. Of all the guests she knew only two: her office head, a tall man in his fifties, and a young woman from the editing division whose function in the company was not clear to her. The remaining were older than she—in their middle or late forties. Almost all the women wore long dresses. Joyce stared down at her protruding knees; she was definitely dressed too informally. "Stupid Kohn! Why did he tell me the party would be 'informal?'" she thought, looking for him. He was moving from group to group carrying drinks. As he passed near her he greeted her: "Too bad my hands are occupied. But I morally embrace you. See you soon. . . . " Glass in hand, Joyce wondered where she would go. The woman she knew had avoided her glance, and the office head was too involved to be disturbed (he was telling two female companions of a new pilot series on Arabic customs to be shot in Morocco)—not the proper time to approach him. As she stood alone for several minutes, she grew more nervous and began to feel wet beads surfacing on her forehead. Where should she go? What should she do? She finally noticed an elderly gentleman emerge from the bedroom and pass a group of laughing people on his way to the bar. With a glass in one hand and his cane in the other, he moved away from the bar and toward her area of the room, casually looking for a partner. When he spotted Joyce standing alone, he approached her with determination.

"Sorry I can't shake hands. My name is Richard Eldstone." The name and the face were familiar. In fact, his portrait was in the boss's office—he was the founder of W.N.B.W.

"Of course, I know you, Mr. Eldstone. My name is Joyce McLean."

"I *am* sorry," replied Mr. Eldstone, "but I must sit down. My hip was recently operated on and I should not stand. Come here next to me and tell me what you do."

Joyce walked towards the couch and hesitantly sat. She didn't have much choice. "As you may have guessed," she said, "I work at the station—and I like it."

"I'm glad you like it. I worked very hard making it what it is today. I wanted to do something new: commercially sound, of course, but also educational and artistic. I was young then." Mr. Eldstone then took a few seconds to adjust his posture on the couch. "It is so stupid, you know, but I have to find the exact position in which I can sit without pain."

Joyce timidly asked: "What happened to you?" She later regretted her question. For more than a half hour she got a detailed, and at the same time disorganized, account of the initial symptoms, the first diagnosis—wrong, of course—the first operation—wrong as well—the two others that followed, the shifting of doctors and hospitals, the aluminum nails, the opportunistic infection, the medicine prescribed to take care of it, the gastrointestinal side-effects of the medicine, the physical rehabilitation. Trying hard to follow the erratic wanderings of the story, Joyce interjected, "how horrible," "incredible," or simply "uh huh" and "I see," hoping they were appropriately timed. Desperate to escape, Joyce lifted her empty glass, announcing to Mr. Eldstone that she needed to go to get a refill. But just then, the host came to her and ceremoniously handed her a second drink:

"Gin and tonic," he said proudly, "I'm right, aren't I?" She couldn't repress a silent but very forceful "s***."

A few minutes later, to her relief, the hostess announced that the buffet was ready: "Come, please, help yourselves and sit at whatever table you like!"

Joyce helped her companion to his feet and slowly walked with him to the buffet. The line had already formed. She helped herself to a little bit of everything: scallops in sherry sauce, turkey and cranberries, broccoli, squash, *salade russe*, and pickles. When looking for a seat, she spotted a table with two empty chairs and took one of them. Her table companions were all strangers. One person had already started to speak about the Afghan crisis. She said hello (*sotto voce*) to her neighbor who answered with a smile but immediately turned his attention back to the speaker. Nobody had yet taken the last chair, but soon—as she might have expected—dear Eldstone hobbled over, last in the line and last to sit down. She forced herself to smile at him but then riveted her eyes on the person who had been delivering the monologue, now discovering in herself an interest in Afghanistan she had never before known existed. Eldstone had no choice but to introduce his neighbor on the other side to the mysteries of the hip bone. Meanwhile, the Afghanistan expert's monologue was infrequently interrupted by the comments or questions from one of the commensals, a news analyst for W.N.B.W. Joyce hoped anxiously that an opportunity to change table companions would develop—maybe when dessert was placed on the buffet table, but dessert did not bring any change in the seating situation, since the bartender, acting later as a butler, removed the used plates and served everybody a baba immersed in a strawberry cream. "Well, at least I've had some good dessert!" thought Joyce. When everybody stood up for coffee and liqueurs, she went to the hostess complaining of a bad headache and left hurriedly, depressed.

Almost all human beings participate in social gatherings, with relatives, old acquaintances, friends, or strangers, all for the sake of mutual enjoyment. This shared pleasure is sought at weddings, christenings, bar mitzvahs, birthday parties, bars, dinner parties, and, as is more and more the case in modern industrial societies, people meet each other in large standing receptions and at cocktail parties. There is hardly a day in their lives when people are not faced with the problems of how to enjoy each others' company. Quite often, however, people return home or resume work with a feeling of disappointment, as did Joyce. What is supposed to give them amusement, instead leaves them with a vague sense of failure. It especially seems to be the case when they return from what we will call in this book the "modern gatherings"—large receptions and cocktail parties where the participants are largely unacquainted. This sense of failure, or at least the malaise often experienced in this type of gathering, does not prevent the individuals from attending them again and again. It is as if some unquenchable thirst were driving them to reexperience the mixture of pleasure and discomfort often derived from modern sociability.

This book sheds some light on the drives which ensure the endurance of sociability in general, and of modern sociability in particular. It will also study the dynamism of both traditional and modern parties, following the chain of events which invited guests experience. For example, first individuals must prepare themselves for meeting the other guests, then they must choose partners, approach them, converse with them; all the while they must avoid the many pitfalls which are in store along the way. In making the best show of themselves, modern partygoers will be helped, more or less, by the hosts; and if guests make faux pas, they will try to erase the poor impressions that were created. If they do not succeed, they can console themselves in knowing that there will be a chance to "do better the next time." As we shall see, modern sociability provides endless opportunities to pursue identity support. But this support is never fully granted, and even if granted by one sampling of society, it will need to be confirmed by further and more representative samplings of the evanescent modern world.

Few sociologists have given their attention to social gatherings. Most have reserved their time and mental energies for studying purposeful actions and interactions in the realms of politics, business, education, the family, and the like. If they sometimes have alluded to sociable interaction, they did so only by way of illuminating their theories or findings concerning other matters, without specifically studying social gatherings themselves. Indicative of this attitude is a remark by Peter Berger, who stopped writing after having devoted one page to sociability: "We are not particularly interested in the phenomenon of sociability for its own sake . . ."[1] The same could be said of many other sociologists who either do not know how to approach the subject or think it unworthy of their attention. There are, however, a few remarkable exceptions.

The most notable exception is Georg Simmel who has written definitively on sociability. Simmel sees in sociability a pure form, or rather, the pure form of human association.[2] In his eyes, all other human associations are loaded with a nonsocial content, which conceals the social fact as such. Economics, politics, labor, educational associations, and the family are inextricably mixed with nonsocial contents and the sociologist may fail to extract from them the real object of study: society. The sociologist is in danger of becoming interested in production, exchange, war, money, schools, sexual issues, and of forgetting *society*. On the contrary, in studying sociable interaction, the sociologist finds society in its pure state, devoid of alloy. Simmel observes that in many languages the activity of socializing is called simply "to be in society," "*se trouver en société.*" In German the word *Gesellschaft* means both society and party. According to Simmel, the sociologist finds in the study of sociable behavior the basic principles of social interaction and is then equipped to understand other, not so pure forms of social behavior and association. In his study of human interaction, Simmel also formulated the basic principle of reciprocity, which is so fruitful in understanding human relations. Later, this principle was further expanded by the social exchange theorists.

As seminal as the writings of Simmel may be, they could not include the conceptual developments which occurred in the field of sociology in the last 50 years. In the analysis of sociability presented in this book, four main currents of reflection are used in combination: three belong to what can be called microsociological analysis and one belongs to a more macrosociological perspective.

In trying to understand the motivations between human interactions, no theory seems more rewarding than the social exchange theory. Individuals are seeking rewards. But they also possess attributes which make it rewarding to interact with them. Individuals are consequently led to enter into mutual exchanges of rewards. Reciprocity is the basic rule of the game. The concept of reciprocity will be used in this book to understand why people organize and attend social gatherings, that is, exchange invitations. It will be of constant help also to understand the interactions between the participants of the gathering. There are many exponents of the social exchange theory. We have chosen to follow Peter Blau in his *Exchange and Power in Social Life*.[3]

Among the rewards that individuals expect from each other one can single out psychological support and more particularly the identity support that people receive from each other. We will try to show how social gatherings are particularly suited for enabling individuals to discover who they are. This aspect of our analyses will be based on the interactive theory of the self as it was initially offered by George Herbert Mead and was further developed by various social psychologists, which can be—with much simplification—regrouped under the name of *symbolic interactionism*. We are particularly indebted to George McCall and J. L. Simmons for their book *Identities and Interactions, An Examination of Human Association in Everyday Life.*[4]

The exchange of identity support which takes place in sociable conversation is not an easy operation. It follows subtle strategic rules. It operates like a small drama in which the performers operate with caution and are careful to present to their partners the appropriate signals about who they are or at least who they would like their partners to think they are. No modern analysis of this social drama would be complete if it did not include Erving Goffman's dramaturgical approach. The various books of Goffman have been of great help in understanding the sociable interaction, most especially *The Presentation of Self in Everyday Life* and *Behavior in Public Places.*[5]

The previously mentioned theorists are of considerable help in analyzing sociability as a universal element of human experience. However, they do not pretend to consider sociability or its specific forms within the larger historical social context. At least they do not do it consciously. They describe human interaction as they perceive it. And of course what they perceive is historically situated. But this historic location is not the concern of these authors. By contrast, we have tried to link the type of sociability to the structure of the society in which it occurs. We try to show how traditional parties, like family parties, or public festivities were congruent with communal societies or at least with what remains of traditional communal ties within today's society. Formal dinner parties, garden parties, and tea parties were typical institutions of the upper classes in eighteenth and nineteenth century Europe, while large standing receptions and cocktail parties, which gather largely unacquainted middle-class and upper-middle-class individuals, are in tune with the modern, capitalistic, specialized society.

It is hardly necessary to refer the reader to any specific sociologist when trying to build the theoretical background for this broad macrosociological analysis of societal evolution. The list would be endless. Every great sociologist has contributed to the painting of this historical fresco, from Ferdinand Tönnies and Max Weber to Erich Fromm and Daniel Bell. One name should be singled out here, because this author explicitly links the conversational behavior of modern man to the capitalistic structure of today's society—Charles

Derber in his book, *The Pursuit of Attention: Power and Individualism in Everyday Life.*[6] It is the thesis of Charles Derber that the capitalistic, competitive structure of the socioeconomic system makes the individual particularly narcissistic and thirsty for attention. Consequently he or she is little capable of really exchanging with others in conversation. This could in part explain the unfinished character of modern sociability, since people who attend social gatherings are rarely ready to grant (and consequently are not likely to receive) what they look for, attention, recognition, identity support.

Several people have helped us in a variety of ways in writing this book. Some have called attention to a book or a school of thought; others have read the manuscript in one stage or another and have provided welcome criticisms and suggestions. We are glad to thank among others, David Riesman of Harvard University, Elizabeth Daniels of Vassar College, and Particia R. Jette of Yale University. Last but not least, we want to thank all the friendly hosts who invited us to so many parties, dinners, cocktail parties and buffets, where, while enjoying ourselves, many ideas were conceived and developed. Of course, the scenarios in this book are pure inventions and have nothing to do with existing individuals (except when they are explicitly mentioned).

NOTES

1. Peter Berger, *Invitation to Sociology* (Garden City: Doubleday, 1963), p. 140.

2. See Georg Simmel, *The Sociology of Georg Simmel*, Kurt H. Wolff, ed. and trans. (Glencoe, Ill.: The Free Press, 1950); see esp. pp. 40–57, 135–169, 338–364.

3. The major exponents of the social exchange theory are: John Thibaut and Harold Kelley, *The Social Psychology of Groups* (New York: Wiley, 1959); George C. Homans, "Human Behavior as Exchange," in *American Journal of Sociology* (1958, 63): 597–606; and *Social Behavior* (New York: Harcourt, rev. ed. 1974); and Peter Blau, *Power and Exchange in Social Life* (New York: Wiley, 1964). For a detailed history of the theory and an exhaustive bibliography, see John Chadwick-Jones, *Social Exchange Theory: its Structure and Influence in Social Psychology* (New York, London: Academic Press, 1976). We have mostly followed Peter Blau whose work itself rests largely on that of Homans and of Thibaut and Kelley. For a critical appraisal of the work of Blau see: Chadwick-Jones, op. cit., pp. 277–359. He writes: "(Blau's) Exchange and Power rests largely on the works of Homans and Thibaut and Kelley. The explanations Blau

offers are an extension of their basic propositions or model and any subsequent influence he has had . . . is only to be appreciated as part of the joint influence of these authors . . . the contributions of Homans have sketched and argued for a theory of social exchange. Thibaut and Kelley have concentrated on the refinement of experimental design. Blau has contributed a diversity of ideas, a wider perspective, yet to be taken up within social psychology" (op. cit., p. 359).

4. Symbolic interactionism's origin can be traced to the works of Mead: *Mind, Self and Society* (Chicago: Univ. of Chicago Press, 1934), principally. See also *Movements of Thoughts in the XIXth Century* (Chicago: Univ. of Chicago Press, 1936), and *Philosophy of the Act* (Chicago: Univ. of Chicago Press, 1938).

On Mead's social psychology, see Bernard N. Meltzer, "Mead's Social Psychology," in *The Sociological Psychology of George Herbert Mead* (Center for Sociological Research, Western Michigan University, 1964), pp. 10–31. On the successive developments of Symbolic Interactionism, read Manford H. Kuhn, "Major Trends in Symbolic Interactionist Theory in the Past Twenty Years," in *The Sociological Quarterly*, vol. 5 (Winter 1964), pp. 61–84. An anthology of texts directly and indirectly related to the theory of Symbolic Interactionism can be found in the collection of essays published by Jerome G. Manis and Bernard N. Meltzer, *Symbolic Interactionism* 3d ed. (Boston: Allyn and Bacon, 1978).

In their book *Symbolic Interactionism: Genesis, Varieties and Criticism* (London: Routledge and Kegan Paul Ltd., 1975), Bernard N. Meltzer, John W. Petras and Larry T. Reynolds distinguish between two major trends of thoughts among symbolic interactionists: that of H. G. Blumer and that of M. H. Kuhn. Though both depend ultimately on Mead's thinking, the former is more in line not only with the Mead theory, but also with his more phenomenological and introspective approach, while the latter tries to operationalize the interactive processes in a way suitable to "objective" and quantitative measurements. Moreover, Blumer's approach gives more importance to the spontaneity of the self, more specifically of the "I," in its creation and development, while Kuhn sees the self as a socially defined reality, a "Me" deterministically created by the (reference) groups to which individuals relate or of which they are members. This, however, "sacrifices the processual character of the self and the negotiated character of behavior. . ." (op. cit., p. 45). The perspective adopted in this book for the study of social gatherings is in line with that of Blumer in both its methodological and conceptual components. For an attempt at analyzing parties in the line of Kuhn, see Jeanne Watson, "A Formal Analysis of Sociable Interaction," *Sociometry* 21 (Dec. 1958), pp. 269–280.

Another interactionist who has inspired many pages in this book is Erving Goffman, whose approach is discussed below in note 5.

5. Erving Goffman, *The Presentation of Self in Everyday Life* (New York: Doubleday, 1959) and *Behavior in Public Places* (New York: The Free Press, 1963). Erving Goffman, under the influence of Kenneth Burke, assumes that when human beings interact, they try to manage or control the impressions the others get of them. We "perform" for others so that they see us as we want them to see us. However, our own approach to performances tries to avoid the appearance of cynicism that one easily gathers from Goffman's writing. We do not think that individuals play a deceptive game when they try to manage the

impressions others will receive of them. In their attempts to produce a favorable impression on others, individuals are not trying to deceive them, but to present them with what they think are correct, true images of themselves, one which is as close as possible to the real image they have formed of themselves. When Goffman writes, "Thus, when an individual appears in the presence of others, there will be some reason for him to mobilize his activity so that it will convey an impression to others which it is in his interest to convey." (*The Presentation of Self in Everyday Life* [Garden City, N.Y.: Doubleday, 1959], p. 4). We would prefer to say, 'Thus, when individuals appear in the presence of others, there will be a tendency in them to mobilize their activity so that it will convey an impression to others in conformity with the images they have formed of themselves.' A criticism of Goffman's approach can be found in S. M. Lyman and M. B. Scott, *A Sociology of the Absurd* (New York: Appleton-Century-Crofts, 1970), especially p. 20. See also Alvin W. Gouldner, *The Coming Crisis of Western Sociology* (New York: Basic Books, 1970) and H. Blumer, "Action vs. Interaction," a review of Goffman's *Relations in Public*, in *Society* 9 (April 1972), pp. 50–53.

  6. Charles Derber, *The Pursuit of Attention: Power and Individualism in Everyday Life* (Boston: G. K. Hall & Co., 1979).

CONTENTS

THE PLEASURE OF YOUR COMPANY

1
WHY DO WE ORGANIZE
AND ATTEND
SOCIAL GATHERINGS

The scene is a cocktail party in a suburb of Chicago in the late 'fifties. Gloria, a graduate student, has volunteered to participate in a study of parties. Randolph Spatowsky, her boy-friend, persuaded his mother to invite Gloria to the party. Her assignment is "motivations," that is, she must find out why there are parties. She has decided to make the problem easier by not asking people why parties exist, but rather, why they have come to this party. Entering the Spatowskys' living-room, she spotted a blonde girl, in a pink organdy dress, who seemed to be looking for a partner. Approaching her, she said:

"Hi! I'm Gloria."

"Hi! I'm Susan. Are you a friend of the Spatowskys?"

"Yes, of their son, actually. And you, How do you come to be here?"

"Well, two weeks ago I was eighteen," the blonde girl began. "And I was so thrilled when I got the invitation!"

"But why did you come?"

The girl seemed puzzled. "Well, . . . because I was invited!"

Gloria tried to impress those words on her memory: " . . . because I was invited." That must have been the motive, at least for Susan.

Then she saw two middle-aged women who were dressed elegantly and were just a little too thin—Duchess of Windsor type. As she approached, they looked at her and smiled. Encouraged, Gloria joined them, saying, "*Please*, go on with your conversation."

"Well, Miss . . . . "

3

"My last name is Rodson, but call me Gloria—please."

"Well, Gloria, I was just saying to Mrs. Lowfield that I have not been in this house for eight years. After I divorced my third husband, a cousin of Ernest Spatowsky, I was ostracized by the whole family. But two weeks ago, what did I see in the mail? An invitation to a cocktail party at the Spatowskys! I read it again and again. I could not believe my eyes."

"But, why did you come?"

"Well, . . . of course, because I was invited."

Gloria mentally wrote a second check after the motive "because I was invited," but started to become a little puzzled about the results of her scientific investigation. However, summoning up all her energies, she let her eyes sweep the room in search of a different element for her sample: a rather young man and woman, dressed in wash-and-wear suits, stood side-by-side, sipping their drinks and exchanging a word or two periodically. They will be glad to talk to someone, thought Gloria. She went to them.

"Hi! My name is Gloria. I'm a friend of the Spatowskys' son. How do you do?"

"Very pleased to meet you, Miss . . . ."

"Call me Gloria, please."

"Pleased to meet you, Gloria," said the man. "Paul and Georgette Dubost. We're new here and were delighted to receive an invitation from the Spatowskys. They seem to be the most elegant people in the neighborhood. And imagine, it is the first cocktail party we've ever been invited to!"

"And may I ask, why did you come?"

"Well, . . . you know, we were invited!"

At this point, Gloria, in spite of her polite smile, felt quite disturbed. She thought, there must be something wrong in my line of questioning. They all seemed to have different reasons for attending, yet she always got the same answer: "because I was invited." Maybe she was not asking the right question? All these answers seemed to point in the same direction: They came in response to an initiative taken by the host. Then she must ask him why he organized the party.

Ernest Spatowsky was a tall man in his fifties with a long, well-carved face and keen blue eyes that suggested energy, efficiency, and a sharp awareness. He was going from guest to guest, exchanging a few phrases with each individual or group. When he came near Gloria, she asserted herself:

"Mr. Spatowsky, what a pleasant party, and what nice people you have invited! You know, Randolph must have told you that I am a social psychology graduate student and I am wondering why people organize parties. You, for instance—Why did you launch this cocktail party?"

"Dear Gloria, you put me on the spot. I have never given much thought to it. Let's see . . . well, first, I imagine, we're having a party because Ann [his wife] and I have been invited by so many people to *their* parties; we had to invite them in return to show our gratitude. But, also, we are glad to see our friends. If we don't invite them from time to time, we lose sight of one another. Then, I think I like to make new acquaintances, and even new friends. Imagine, for just a few seconds, a society in which each individual or family lived totally separate from others, only meeting them for business. Wouldn't it be a soulless society, at best a world of busy ants? I think we would suffocate."

Gloria was furiously memorizing these thoughts. "Mr. Spa-towsky, you have made my day," she said. "What you said is great! Thanks!"

Back home, Gloria spent the rest of the night pondering Ernest Spatowsky's reflections: Free conversation is necessary to the birth of a common soul, she concluded. How could we understand one another if we did not build a common culture, a common language?

Our age has reached a degree of compartmentalization in business, administration, politics, and even the arts, that no past century has ever known. Occupations put people in touch with only a very limited circle of customers, colleagues or clients, while the rest of the world revolves beyond their contact and their knowledge. If it were not for the mechanisms or events that call people of various ways of life together, humanity would look like an immense honey-comb, divided into millions of small isolated cells. Among other social inventions, social gatherings have the function of opening the cells, of compelling the technician to meet the artist, the adminis-trator to listen to the business people, the men and women of the trades to learn from the politicians and vice versa. It is only by con-stantly associating with one another, by experiencing the repeated trials and errors produced by attempts at communicating, by ex-changing views on the economy, the laws, war and peace, the theater, music, and the visual arts, that the members of a society come to agree on the meanings of the words they use, on the values upon which to base common judgments, on common goals to promote and the best ways to reach them. In other words, only through a regular exchange of views can a common culture be born, and only then is the culture protected against the threat of being split into innumerable closed cells, or exclusive groups, each with its dialects or trade slangs.[1] The benefits are not only for society but for the individual as well. Individuals cannot function in the world or acquire a consistent perception of themselves and of the universe of which they are a part without participating in the common culture which gives to every object as well as to each person a location, a meaning, a function. Individuals must break out of their occupational jails at least once in a while, as they must escape the isolation of their family circles. The world ceases to exist, for those who are not in "conversation" with it.[2]

The function of creating a unified culture is fulfilled in part by books, periodicals, and other mass media. Officially organized conventions and meetings are also of some help. However, relatively few people are reached by these cultural tools. Few read and those who do have access to a very small sample of literary works. Fewer still participate in conventions and meetings. In addition, the impact of mass media is so superficial that, one day after an event occurs, most readers of newspapers are incapable of summarizing one-tenth of what they have read. Among the most efficient causes of a unified culture are the common but informal chats, coffee breaks, luncheons with friends, or social gatherings of various kinds. These are the moments and places where opinions about political candidates, consumer products, or the value of films and plays, are exchanged. This exchange leads to a form of social consensus, but this consensus is perpetually threatened and is constantly in need of repair.

Those responsible for suggesting or organizing gatherings help the world to remain in one piece. Most often they are unaware of the function they fulfill. However, there are cases when the hosts or the party organizers are quite conscious of their duties regarding this function: Kings, civilian and religious leaders, presidents of all kinds, and heads of families feel responsible for the maintenance of the social world, or at least, of the part of it which is entrusted to their care.

By calling their people to collective entertainment, they reinforce the unity of the group. A festive gathering reminds everyone of being a part of a larger social reality. As Emile Durkheim brilliantly explained, the "effervescence" of the celebration elevates every participant to a higher level of emotional commitment to the group, to its endeavors, and to its history.[3]

To a lesser degree a similar effervescence can also be found in private parties organized by friendly hosts who have invited friends and acquaintances to enjoy each others' company. While in these cases the hosts do not feel responsible for establishing or maintaining the political solidarity of the group, they know, however, that their personal goal—to please their friends—will be better attained if they succeed in creating some common emotion at the gathering, a feeling of being part of a celebration which transcends the daily routine. Parties are organized at Christmas time, on Thanksgiving, on religious holidays, or more simply, at the end of the week when work gives way to rejoicing. Parties are also organized for a birth, a wedding, or a birthday. In all these cases the gathering is called around an event which helps unify the participants.

Unification of all the guests and the building of a common culture are usually not the primary goals of the hosts of private gatherings, especially in the case of what we shall call later the "modern gathering," which is constituted mostly of unacquainted individuals. However, as often occurs in human affairs, when individuals pursue their own interests, they also contribute unknowingly to the fulfillment of a social need. By organizing parties, hosts help create a social dialogue even if their main personal goal is much more limited. When sending the invitations, hosts are probably mostly concerned with creating or maintaining bonds of friendship between themselves and each of their guests.

The need for being surrounded by a circle of friends is especially felt in our modern fragmented society. In the past, in the context of a more communal society, the primary ties of family, neighborhood and church were enough to create around each individual a protective ring of people ready to help in case of need. In today's fragmented and specialized world, familial ties, even if they still exist, are not sufficient to support and protect the individual. We need a network of friends in the various sectors of life. Also needed are friends to help us find a job or place to live; we need advice in our trade; essential also are friends to represent us or guarantee our debts or uphold our credit. We need friends to lend us money when the bank denies it, to serve as our executor, to collect ideas on everything and anything, from cars to Broadway shows and restaurants. We need very good friends to get advice in personal matters about which our relatives are incompetent or not objective. The development of a circle of friends occurs mostly through the exchange of mutually rewarding favors, gifts, services, which little by little create a bond of mutual trust. Once the friendship has been established, the exchange of gifts and services continues as a way of reinforcing the bond. Among a variety of possible gifts, invitations to parties are important, because they state that one's company is enjoyable and also offer us, as we shall say later, one of the most valued gifts, that is, the opportunity of getting identity support from a variety of people.

Invitations then can be considered as gifts and they possess the same dynamism that is true of all gifts, the dynamism of reciprocity. We will spend some time here analyzing the laws presiding over gift exchange, because they apply not only to the exchange of invitations—our present topic—but also to the conversational exchange which is the main activity at social gatherings and is the central topic of this book.

Gift exchange, we said, is governed by the principle of reciprocity. A gift is a favor made to the beneficiary, but it also imposes upon the receiver the obligation of reciprocating the friendly gesture. Invitations, similarly, impose upon the guests an obligation of restitution. Anthropologists and sociologists have studied the reciprocal nature of gifts and shown that this is a basic structural feature of human relations.[4] Hosts give, knowing that some day their generosity will be repaid. In accepting the gift of an invitation, the guests are conscious that some day gratitude must be shown in return. While party goers may say "thank you!" to the hosts when taking their leave, they know that words do not eliminate the duty of repayment. The words are, rather, as sociologist Peter Blau puts it, a "promissory note."[5]

Gift exchanges and invitations in particular resemble economic transactions. But they also differ considerably from the economic model. An economic transaction is ordinarily "impersonal" and does not create a link of personal nature between buyer and seller. It consists of exchanging two objects of equivalent value—object for object in barter, object or service for money in sale. The obligation between the two partners is extinct as soon as the exchange is concluded. It is a very transitory relationship. This is exemplified in the operation of the modern supermarket where no words need be exchanged between consumer and salesperson. No personal link of any kind has been created. In some societies, however, merchants and shopkeepers resent this purely impersonal interaction and insist that customers not pay immediately. A postponement creates two obligations for the customers: the first is economic—they must eventually repay; the second is of a more personal nature—in exchange for the trust that has been granted, patrons will have to show some gratitude, by becoming, for instance, regular customers of the shop.

In the case of gift exchange, the element of trust goes even further: the givers or the hosts differ from the shopkeeper because neither hosts nor givers define the nature of repayment. Both leave the terms of repayment open to the good will and generosity of the recipients. Recipients, in turn, remain "free" to return the gifts whenever and however they feel it is appropriate. It is in the nature of a gift that givers can neither demand the repayment nor determine its specific contents. To do so would kill the gratuity, the personal character, the trust which characterizes gift giving. Kenneth, an acquaintance, told me of the anger of a "friend" of his who had invited him to her house a couple of times. Knowing that Kenneth was traveling from New York to Los Angeles, the friend asked Kenneth whether he could carry a rather substantial parcel across the country for her. Kenneth was already overwhelmed with luggage and had to refuse politely. The friend angrily said. "I thought you were a friend. I have done a lot for you; can't you render me this small service?" Kenneth recognized his debt, but maintained that he had the right to determine how to "repay" it.

This freedom and this right, nevertheless, are contained within limits: if beneficiaries want to stay on friendly terms with their "benefactors," they must repay in a way commensurate to the gift. "Thus," writes Peter Blau, "if a person gives a dinner party, he expects his guests to reciprocate at some future date. But he can hardly bargain with them about the kind of party to which they should invite him, although he expects them not simply to ask him for a quick lunch if he had invited them to a formal dinner."[6]

More than likely the givers—the hosts—do not expect to be repaid in a perfectly equal manner. People always repay with slightly more or less. This temporary inequality does not disturb hosts. It leaves the exchange open, that is, in need of more gifts and more repayments. What the hosts want precisely is the establishment of a bond of friendship and trust; they are not interested in getting in return exactly the same rewards that have been bestowed upon their guests. The hosts know that in the long run the repayments will balance out. Meanwhile the bond of friendship is maintained.

For a similar reason givers may object when beneficiaries are too eager to repay them immediately. This would be interpreted as a desire to get rid of the obligation as soon as possible; an unnecessarily prompt repayment appears as a refusal of a bond of friendship that could have developed between the giver and the recipient, between the host and the guest, if only the guest had been willing. "Although an invitation to a party can be repaid any time," writes Peter Blau, "it is not proper to do so too promptly. Generally posthaste reciprocation of favors, which implies a refusal to stay indebted for a while and hence an insistence on a more businesslike relationship is condemned as improper: 'Excessive eagerness to discharge an obligation is a form of ingratitude.'"[7]

Of course, hosts expect that sooner or later their invitations will be repaid. If the guests were to ignore this repayment, the hosts would feel insulted or at least uneasy and the relationship would either fail to develop or, if it already existed, fade away. The only excuse for not returning a favor would be the impossibility of doing so. The impossibility can be either temporary or permanent. My friends, Arthur and Marjorie, told me of a gentleman who had recently come to the city. They invited him to their home several times, because they thought he was lonely or because, at times, they were in need of an unattached gentleman to complete a table. The guest was not expected to repay his debts soon since, being both alone and new in the city, he was not thought to have the appropriate facilities to organize dinners and receptions. His temporary inability to receive guests was a sufficient excuse for the delay in repaying his social debts. However, it was with great surprise that my friends learned that "the lonely gentleman" had sent around invitations for a cocktail party without inviting them. Needless to say, he was immediately cancelled from Marjorie's list of friends.

What happens in the case when it is permanently impossible for someone to return adequately an invitation? It is likely that someone in this situation will find some excuse for not accepting an invitation that cannot be matched. If, however, one accepts, then an imbalance is created between the givers, the hosts, and the recipients, the guests. If the imbalanced relationship is protracted, the hosts accumulate credits and the guests become deeper and deeper in debt. This indebtedness manifests an inequality of status which may satisfy the pride of the "generous" donor, but which will undoubtedly create in the recipient a feeling of inferiority and unworthiness.

In many societies gift giving is strictly regulated in order to protect potential recipients of excessive gifts from the impossible burden of having to extend comparable favors. No such law exists in America. However, people curb their generosity and ordinarily avoid embarrassing others by not making gifts that are too expensive. Similarly they usually either invite friends to whom they are indebted or individuals whom they suspect will be able to return the invitation. If some people are known for living on the wrong side of the tracks, or for having a small and dilapidated house, they are not invited; this avoids bringing them humiliation or embarrassment. All this, of course, is relative. Two families living in similarly spare conditions do not harm each other by exchanging invitations. This common sense rule does not stem from middle-class prejudice; it belongs to the very structure of human relations: comfortable friendships develop only between people who are not too dissimilar.

There are cases, however, in which a "superior" knowingly invites his "inferiors" with an awareness that they will be unable to repay him. Why does this happen? Several explanations can be advanced to understand a behavior which seemingly cannot result in the establishment of a friendship.

First, in an avowedly unequal society, that is, in a society in which people are born with a superior or inferior "ascribed" status, that is, a status which cannot be changed, and in which everyone accepts these status differences and considers them normal, the acceptance of gifts—of an invitation—offered by a person of superior status to an inferior does not ordinarily create distress concerning the inferior's condition. The inferiority exists whatever happens. At most, the unilateral invitation once more manifests what already exists. It is likely that the guest has already developed a philosophical attitude about it: "If I cannot do anything to improve my lower status, let me, at least, profit by it and collect the benefits attached to this necessary difference." The local medieval lord invited all his peasants to a feast at his chateau; they would drink his wine and eat his beef, and nothing was expected from them in return. Could the peasants repay the lord? How would it have been possible since his total domain over them gave him a right to claim all that they had?

Similarly, expectational differences may also exist in a modern egalitarian society, but, as we said above, they are ordinarily tolerated only if the differences are of a temporary status: the traveler who passes through a city, the newcomer in the neighborhood or the corporation, especially before one has found a house and furnished it, or the foreigner who still does not know the locale.

There is also the case of individuals who, in their desire to obtain power over other people, do not hesitate to bestow upon them gifts and invitations which they know their beneficiaries will not be able to reciprocate. The host may perhaps imagine that some kind of "friendship" will eventually develop out of this imbalanced "exchange." The guests, however, are usually aware that this will not be the case and more or less cynically accept the gifts and the invitations without any further intention of establishing a friendly relationship. In the story, "The Genial Host," by Mary McCarthy, two guests of Mr. Pflaumen, Meg and Erdman, are puzzled about one another. Both of them are regular beneficiaries of Mr. Pflaumen's "generous" hospitality. Mr. Pflaumen likes to surround himself with ambitious young people whom he invites not with the hope of getting reciprocal rewards, but for the pleasure of extending his patronage to penniless admirers. Meg and Erdman, looking at each other as they sit at Pflaumen's table for the second time, wonder, "what weakness, what flimsiness of character, what opportunism or cynicism had put the other into Pflaumen's hands."[8] People in this situation know that a moment might come when the host may present a bill and somehow demand to be repaid. When this moment comes, they will turn the host down and the relationship will come to an end, not without having provided both the hosts and the guests certain rewards.[9] The hosts will have demonstrated—at least to themselves—their superiority and the guests will be satisfied because they have drunk the sherry, eaten the caviar, met the other guests, perhaps found an employer, a business partner, or a lover. In "The Genial Host," when Pflaumen, the rich host, asks the attractive but penniless Meg to "repay" him by revealing whether she has started an affair with Erdman, Meg refuses to answer, on the ground that it is none of his business. Pflaumen can hardly conceal his anger: "At last," Meg says to herself, "you thought the bill had come in. The dinners, the letters of introduction, the bottle of perfume, the gardenias, the new Soviet film, the play, the ballet, the ice-skating at Rockefeller Plaza had all been invoiced and a line drawn underneath, and the total computed. . . . Now when you looked at it, the total was staggering, it was more than you could pay."[10] Her refusal to repay her host, that is, to give in to his curiosity, signaled the end of their relationship.

Peter Blau says that those who cannot repay their benefactors with relatively equivalent and voluntary counterfavors fall into their benefactors' mercy and become their slaves. We would like to add that, in such imbalanced situations, the gift givers, the hosts, acquire a right—a dubious one—not only to be repaid, but also to determine what the repayment will be. Instead of an equal and friendly relationship, a master–slave association is created and maintained as long, at least, as the "slave" wants to profit by the benefits of the situation. Many people may think that this exchange is close to prostitution since, in both situations, one of the partners is not free to decide what the contribution to the exchange will be.[11] A similar slave–master relationship is found within the Mafia. The lower-rank members of the organization have to show respect and allegiance to the bosses, who in turn will grant them protection. But the "Godfather" remains the one who decides when and how his protection will be repaid. The "superior" may even abstain from requiring a repayment; he continues to enjoy his power and the "inferior" is left with the permanent feeling of being in debt and with nightmarish fears about the kind of repayment that may be demanded.[12] "Pflaumen rarely gave you a chance to repay his benevolence, so that generally you were uncomfortable with him, dangerously overstored, explosive, a living battery of undischarged obligations."[13]

This seems to be an exceptional case. Most hosts would be conscious that such unilateral bestowing of gifts creates only embarrassment in their guests and either would invite only those who could reciprocate their invitations or offer commensurate favors.

There is, however, a subtle way to reestablish the balance between the host and one of his guests. Instead of frightening the beneficiary with the prospect of an undefined future repayment, the host can—in a more or less demanding way—request the repayment on the spot. Here, again, the beneficiary is not free to determine what the repayment will be. Some hosts, for instance, may invite a "special guest," expecting repayment in the form of a given performance. In that case the "guest" is not really a guest, equal to the host and the other participants. True, the other guests are also expected to contribute to the general festivity but no specific performance can be exacted from them. By contrast, the special guest has no choice; he or she is a kind of paying guest or a servant who is offered food and festivity in exchange for stories or good looks. Similarly, kings had *bouffons* they invited to their table to provide entertainment. The bouffons had no choice. A friend of mine, who is an historian, leftist political thinker, and brilliant conversationalist, was invited three times to dinner parties by a local rich businessman. The decor was lavish. The rambling country house was furnished with pieces signed by Chippendale, Adam, and Sheraton. The walls were covered with paintings by Thomas Gainsborough, Richard Wilson and Thomas Girtin, and the table was set with Wedgewood china and Baccarat crystal. A butler and two maids attended the tables. My friend and his wife—an interior decorator—had no difficulty in adjusting to the situation and delighted the host and the other guests with their wit, their knowledge, and their elegance. Their income, however, could not permit them to repay their hosts with similar splendors. Only at the second gathering did they sense that their role was a little different from that expected of the other guests. They were not expected to invite the gentle hosts in turn. They had been invited by them in order to perform and entertain. They politely refused the third invitation, and the "friendship" between the two couples ended.

Most invitations are given with "no strings attached." Hosts do not request any immediate and specific reward in exchange for their invitation. The hosts merely want to please their guests or may be returning previous invitations; the hosts also know that the present gifts will be paid back one day or another by the grateful guests. It is also known that these exchanges of invitations serve to maintain and develop the bonds of friendship without which there would be no psychological and material survival.

The guests, free of immediate requests from their hosts, content themselves during the gathering with enjoying the gifts of their friendly hosts.

At this point, the question that Gloria wanted the Spatowskys' guests to answer arises again: What do the guests themselves expect? What kind of pleasure or rewards have led them to accept their hosts' invitation?

Out of the many reasons or motives that personal experience and observation supply, some are so obvious and concrete that we hesitate to mention them: Guests hope for palatable food and drink. Should they be ashamed of their *gourmet* instincts? Each time Charles is invited by a certain colleague, he immediately envisions the delicately arranged table covered with fine hors d'oeuvres and entrees that his hosts are already busy preparing. Is Charles' expectation purely selfish, or is it not an anticipated tribute to the skillfulness and friendliness of his hosts? An old acquaintance of mine, a friendly and loquacious man, was never ashamed of showing his total and undisturbed absorption in eating and drinking, when the time for it had come at a party. One night in Rome, he was attending a buffet dinner on the terrace of a penthouse. Unattentive to the clouds floating in the red-gold light of sunset, unaware of the attractive guests around him, he busied himself going back and forth to the buffet. Indeed, he was so absorbed that he did not notice someone taking his chair away while he was helping himself, so that, when he came back with his newly filled plate, not finding his chair, he simply knelt and gave his complete reverence to the *fettucine Alfredo con tartufo bianco*. His vivid testimony to the excellence of the food caused the hostess to kneel and kiss him with delight.

All of us have attended parties during which a few guests solidly anchored to the buffet, greedily monopolize the hosts' munificence by barring everyone else from the sandwiches and petit-fours. And everyone knows that many of the guests have a tendency to slightly overappreciate the drinks offered. But the hosts rejoice: their intention was to please the guests. The guests liked what they ate and drank and their appreciation is part of the hosts' reward.

Quite often, however, the food and the drinks are not the main concern. People may go to a gathering in the hope of meeting people who may later prove useful. The young—and the not-so-young—in search of a job will not miss a party where there is the hope of meeting a prospective employer: a person in business ("I will show him my pleasant salesperson side"), a banker ("I can also calculate"), a movie director ("I have such a cute nose when seen from the right").

In the past, when newspapers were few and not readily available, gatherings of all sorts were for many a primary source of information, and to this day, we may attend gatherings for this reason. We may discover during a party information that may not be revealed anywhere else. Political candidates learn who supports whom and why, singles learn who sleeps with or without whom and spies discover who needs money in exchange for an innocent vial of microfilm. Sometimes the information we collect may not be directly useful to us but may help us to win admiration from future listeners who will think: "My, you are always so well informed!"

Needless to say, one may go to a party with the hope of finding a potential sexual partner, a partner for a night, or a spouse for life.

Many, especially those who are tied to a partner by marriage or some kind of steady arrangement, do not plan to launch a new sexual adventure. They may wish, rather, to sublimate their desires through a social flirtation. Arnold, an acquaintance, is renowned for his dogged pursuit of the prettiest woman at every gathering. When his conspicuous courting dance begins, the whole audience—his wife included—suddenly becomes wildly interested in the paintings and the china figurines.

Less conscious, but certainly a key factor in whether one accepts or rejects an invitation, is the prospect of getting social recognition. There are parties that one must attend because all those considered important within a certain network of people are likely to be there. It is necessary to remind them of one's existence whether the company is likeable or not. It can be the meeting of a high school clique, a reunion of college alumni/ae, a parish get-together, a block association party, a reception attended by everyone who is anyone in town, or even a dance to which all the most famous people in the world will pay their way.

All of these motives may appear to be very self-centered. No doubt people may be led to social gatherings by "instrumental" motives. Yes, more or less consciously, they hope to use others in order to attain their goals. But is that all? No, indeed! Quite often, if not always, people attend a gathering for the same reason for which the hosts organized it: in order to establish or reinforce bonds of friendship.

At a still deeper level, one may attend a social gathering in order to escape isolation and to get the feeling of being part of something greater than oneself. The event can be as modest as a birthday party but it is nevertheless exciting to be on the list of those selected for the occasion. The occasion could be also of larger dimensions. Early agricultural societies engaged in fertility dances which involved the whole population and many nations today promote the memory of some great victory or revolution by organizing public rallies or street dances. In both instances the individual becomes immersed into the *corsi* and *ricorsi* of cyclical movements or into the disquieting and exciting course of history. In these cases individuals are redeemed from their isolation, powerlessness, and misery.

The social gatherings that we study in this book are of less cosmic nature. They do not gather the whole nation, the whole city, or even the whole village. They are private gatherings. But even so, the individuals who attend them always feel some excitement at being part of some larger social reality. Since most individuals now pursue their daily activities in a compartmentalized, disconnected, anonymous modern world, every opportunity to become part of some kind of community—even for a few hours—is a relief and a cause for excitement. The excitement is all the greater if the hosts have succeeded in linking the party to some larger social reality or to an event which unites the participants.

Whatever the importance may be of the emotions and feelings which humans experience in festive gatherings, they do not seem to be the ultimate motive for participation in the types of gatherings we study in this book. There is still, it seems, another motive for attending them, a motive so deeply rooted that, on the one hand, it is mostly unconscious, and, on the other, it is such an integral part of the human psyche that it might not deserve the name of motive. A motive is a force that people somehow control; they can refuse to be led by it. But the need we are referring to here, the need for discovering one's identity and for getting support for this often fluid and evanescent reality is deeper than any motive.

Identity is a puzzling reality. Some individuals have a well-contoured self-image and it hardly varies through the seasons of their lives. Others are in a permanent search of their true selves. This difference comes mainly from the individual's social environment. It is a fact now fully acknowledged that human beings learn who they are from what others tell them. Social psychologists have accepted the theory of George Herbert Mead, who argues that the human psyche is composed of an "inner-forum" in which an acting, performing principle, or *I*, and a mirroring and evaluating principle—that represents others' expectations—called the *Me*, are in constant dialogue.[14] Through exchanging actions and words with others, humans learn, or rather internalize what others expect of them, given their positions and roles in life. The Me is made of these internalized expectations. Individuals then, see themselves through the eyes of others. As Harry Stack Sullivan puts it, "the self may be said to be made up of reflected appraisals."[15]

In the more static societies of the past, in which individuals operated and grew within a small and never-changing circle of relatives and neighbors, identity was well-defined, secure, and unreflected. It manifested itself in a spontaneous but peaceful certitude. Edmund Burke, the British conservative writer, opposed the eccentric, anarchical, restless frenzy of French revolutionaries to the bovine tranquillity of British gentlemen. This tranquillity, which marked the agrarian societies and more particularly the Middle Ages, was endangered not so much by the French Revolution or other revolutions, but by the surge of the spirit of individual enterprise at the time of the Renaissance. This movement of individuation, which has eventually resulted in political freedom, democracy, and a regime of economic laissez-faire, has helped and encouraged individuals to free themselves from the bonds of family, neighborhood, church and tradition. There is little doubt that modern individuals are much freer than their ancestors, but this movement of individuation has also created an ever-moving and disconnected type of society where no solid and permanent community can define an individual's identity.[16] In addition, this ever-changing world is an "achieving" society[17] where people are expected to move ahead, that is, to always produce new identities.

In a more static society individuals saw, mirrored in the eyes of others, their "ascribed" or static selves. Since the self was completely determined at birth, every other member of the community knew the others' position even before they did. Others' expectations converged so as to give each member of the community a very clear, stable and consistent view of him- or herself.[18] Modern individuals, by contrast, do not receive an ascribed status and a predetermined image of who they are or will be.[19] The various partners in life do not constitute a community and could not arrive at a consistent perception of a person's identity. Each partner sees the individual under a different angle and for the limited time of a sporadic interaction. As a consequence, modern people are in permanent quest of themselves. They ask their ever-changing partners not only "How am I doing?" but "Who am I?" The answer of yesterday is not valid today. Support is always problematic, temporary, and in need of being renewed everyday. Everyday must bring its dose of attention, recognition, support, and approval.

The opposition between the peaceful consciousness of traditional human beings and the hectic pursuit of self by modern men and women should not be taken as an absolute, but only as a relative difference. Societies of the past, as early as we can discover them, have also known their adventurers, their itinerant or sailing merchants, their upwardly mobile students and professionals, their *con-quistadores, condottieri*, and explorers. When Erich Fromm describes the Medieval individual as being all solidly bound by the permanent "primary ties" of family, community, and church, he does not mean to exclude those few adventurous individuals who, having broken with their past, their communities, and their ascribed identities, have set themselves "free" into the wide, unknown world.[20] But those individuals were a small minority. The agrarian populations, in their quasi-totality, stayed "at home"; they were miserable and hungry, but without any anxiety about who they were or should become, largely because they were not expected to be anything different from what their birth had "destined" them to be. People were invited to do their duty in the positions granted to them by Providence. By contrast, modern individuals are invited to leave home and to throw themselves into the chaotic multitude, competing with others on a merciless market for always higher achievements.[21]

This calling is made to everybody, but is not heard by all.[22] Many simply cannot answer it. They do not possess the inherited power to follow it; they constitute the lower, poorer classes.[23] Their powerlessness in turn quite often suffocates in them any desire to move up. They become resigned to their fate, unless they redirect their frustrated energies into revolutionary movements where they regain a sense of direction and acquire a new identity supported by their companions in the revolutionary struggle. As for the resigned proletarians, they perceive themselves as condemned to remain their whole lives as they are today: garage attendant, street cleaner, usher, or doorman. They find and maintain their identity not so much through their occupation, but by clinging to whatever primary ties may still link them to their relatives, their neighbors, or the members of their church. A similar attachment to the primary ties may be found at the other extreme of the social ladder; for example among the few "aristocrats," who, in the New World as well as in the Old, do not obtain their sense of self through the recognition of their personal achievements, but through their belonging to a family, which in turn makes them a member of the larger aristocratic family. Needless to say, this prestige of birth is a currency in use only in their aristocratic circle. Only in this circle are the names, the genealogies, the engagements, the weddings, the procreation of new cousins, or the death of old ones of any significance. These are the evocations which maintain the strength of the aristocratic primary ties. But they are not credentials for defining an individual in the achievers' world, which is composed of the third and largest group in today's society, the middle and upper-middle classes.

Actually, many aristocrats have become aware that they condemn themselves to progressive isolation if they define themselves only in terms of their aristocratic origin. Most of them have accepted the rules of the new game and deliberately set themselves free into the cold world of competition.

It is in the world of competition in the achieving society that the middle classes must live, not by choice, but by the very dynamics of the market. Charles Derber, in his inspired little book, *The Pursuit of Attention*, writes:

> Self-orientation becomes the consciousness of those most mobile and therefore least integrated in the community. Economically, it is expressed through such institutions as the "career," which are ways of organizing motivation and attention around the aims of the self. Particularly in the dominant classes, where prospects for mobility are strongest, careerism and visions of economic and social agrandizements become the basis of an intensified self absorption, while in the subordinate classes, where vestiges of community (such as neighborhood and church) are stronger, self orientation is less developed.[24]

The process of individuation and progressive "self orientation," which has marked the development of humanity can be accompanied by a fantastic maturation of the self, but this is possible only if individuals succeed in reestablishing satisfactory ties with others,[25] and this is far from being assured. The first impression which individuals experience when they are thrown into the competitive world is that of solitude. Whether or not the world has ever succeeded in becoming a "home" for human beings, it is not now the case for modern individuals.[26] Removed are the primary ties to relatives and neighbors. These people may still exist physically in the life of modern individuals but they are seldom competent partners in the fight that people wage for finding their true identity; furthermore the "competent" partners are not around, ready to provide support and comfort. Modern individuals have freed themselves from many ties with others, but these others now are also free of them: their attention, their recognition, their support is not automatically given, but must be pursued and conquered. Charles Derber has well underscored the link between modern individuals' "pursuit of attention" and the capitalistic, competitive world which arose with the industrial revolution.[27] It is a world where people have no value through their birth but only through their achievements. This means that they are alone,[28] unless they succeed in winning the attention of others. And since we need others to give us support in our hesitant search for identity, we are perpetually in quest of others' attention. Identity support, being no longer offered to all by the community, must be obtained as a personal gift. Like any other gift it cannot be secured except through an exchange, in this case an exchange of identity support. Sociable conversation, which is the main activity of modern sociability, is essentially an identity negotiation. And one of the main functions of today's social gatherings is to offer a time and a place where the invited guests can engage in sociable conversation. It is no wonder, as a consequence, that those social gatherings, where the main activity is conversation, are mostly organized by and for the members of the middle and upper-middle classes, the members of which are essentially the upwardly mobile, competitive individuals anxiously in search of their identity.

This book will concern itself with the ability of modern social gatherings to create the proper climate, or rather the proper stage and settings that permit participants to exchange this gift so important to modern individuals: identity support.

NOTES

1. Sociologist Alain Touraine has underscored how the absence of communication between business management and the workers at the beginning of the Industrial Revolution helped maintain and develop trade slangs. These little by little disappeared after the Taylorian revolution introduced constant intervention of the management into the workers' operations. See Alain Touraine: "Situation du Mouvement Ouvrier," *Arguments*, Janvier–Février 1959, pp. 7–15, and "Classe sociale et statut socio-économique," *Cahiers Internationaux de Sociologie*, Vol. XI, 1951, pp. 155–176.

2. "The world is built up in the consciousness of the individual by conversation with significant others (such as parents, teachers, 'peers') . . . If such conversation is disrupted . . . the world begins to tatter, to lose its subjective plausibility. In other words, the subjective reality of the world hangs on the thin thread of conversation" (Peter Berger, *The Sacred Canopy* [Garden City: Doubleday, 1967], pp. 16–17).

3. The word represents a key concept in Emile Durkheim's *The Elementary Forms of the Religious Life* (New York: Collier Books, 1961). It well describes the explosion of feelings that marks certain religious rituals. It is hardly found today in the celebration of a traditional Presbyterian, Episcopalian, or Roman Catholic service. One should have in mind a Mexican fiesta and procession, a Southern Baptist service, the encounter between Pope John Paul II and the young Catholic New Yorkers on October 3, 1979, and even a rock event.

4. See, above all, Marcel Mauss, *The Gift*, trans. Ian Cunnison (Glencoe, Ill.: The Free Press, 1954). See also: Claude Lévi-Strauss, "The Principle of Reciprocity," in L. A. Closer and B. Rosenberg, *Sociological Theory* (New York: Macmillan, 1957); Alvin Gouldner, "The Norm of Reciprocity: A Preliminary Statement," *American Sociological Review* 25 (April 1960), pp. 161–178; and more in general, the literature on Exchange Theory presented in the Introduction, note 3.

5. Peter Blau, *Exchange and Power in Social Life* (New York: John Wiley and Sons, 1964), p. 16.

6. Ibid., pp. 93–94.

7. Ibid., p. 99. Blau's quotation is taken from François de La Rochefoucauld, *The Maxims* (London: Oxford University Press, 1940), p. 73, n. 226.

8. Mary McCarthy, "The Genial Host," *The Company She Keeps* (New York: Simon and Schuster, 1942), p. 195.

9. Dennis H. Wrong, rightly states that "reciprocity is a defining criterion of the social relation itself and is never totally destroyed even in relationships of unequal power" ("Some Problems in Defining Social Power," *American Journal of Sociology* 73 (May 1968), pp. 673–681. He argues that the more powerful person may exercise greater control in some ways, but submits to the control of the less powerful in other ways.

10. McCarthy, op. cit., p. 160.

11. I remember reading in the San Francisco *Chronicle* in the late 1950s a letter to "Dear Abby" in which a fifteen-year-old girl objected to some advice previously given by the journalist. She wrote—approximately:

> Dear Abby, in your answer to "Puzzled" last Saturday you told her that a girl on a date should not let herself be kissed (especially with a French kiss). Well I don't think it is fair. When a boy has managed to get his father's car to take you around, has bought you a beautiful corsage, has treated you to a wonderful dinner, has taken you to the movies, don't you think that he has acquired the right to kiss his date?

12. It was the case of Amerigo Bonasera, the undertaker in *The Godfather* by Mario Puzo. He had never requested any help from Don Corleone and the latter had always resented it immensely: "We have known each other many years you and I. But until this day you never came to me for counsel or help . . . Let us be frank. You spurned my friendship. You feared to be in my debt." (Mario Puzo, *The Godfather* [London: Pan Books Ltd., 1969], p. 29).

Of course, in the not-so-subtle language of the Mafia, "to be in my debt" means "to be in my power" and to be compelled to do whatever is demanded.

This the undertaker did not want. Bonasera feared the consequences he would have to face if he sought Don Corleone's assistance in punishing the attackers of his daughter. The poor Bonasera was haunted by dreams in which the Don came to him with impossible demands: "Amerigo Bonasera had a terrible nightmare. In his dreams he saw Don Corleone, in peaked cap, overalls and heavy gloves, unloading bullet ridden corpses in front of his funeral parlour and shouting: Remember, Amerigo, not a word to anyone and bury them quickly" (ibid., p. 47).

In spite of his fears, however, Bonasera was compelled to give up, that is, to accept the Don's "friendship." After a long hesitation, Bonasera said: "Be my friend, I accept." Don Corleone put his hand on the man's shoulder: "Good," he said, "you shall have your justice. Some day, and that day may never come, I will call upon you to do me a service in return. Until that day, consider this justice a gift from my wife, your daughter's godmother" (ibid., p. 31).

13. McCarthy, op. cit., p. 143.

14. See George Herbert Mead, *Mind, Self, and Society* (Chicago: University of Chicago Press, 1934), esp. Part III, "The Self," pp. 135–226. Mead was himself influenced by the Kantian conception of the I, as a transcendental principle and by William James, especially by his theory of consciousness as a "stream," as opposed to some kind of static reality. See William James, *Psychology: The Briefer Course* (New York: Harper Torch Books, 1961), p. 43. For a short description of Mead's Theory of the Self, of the I and the Me, the Inner Forum, and so on, see G. J. MacCall and J. L. Simmons, *Identities and Interactions* (New York: The Free Press, 2d ed., 1978), pp. 51–55. The idea that the self is the result of a dialogue with others is not an invention of Mead and social psychologists. We read in Hegel's *Phenomenology of Mind*: "Self-consciousness exists in itself and for itself, in that, and by the fact that it exists for another self-consciousness; that is to say, it *is* only by being acknowledged and 'recognized.'" G. W. F. Hegel, *The Phenomenology of Mind*, trans. J. B. Baillie (London: George Allen and Unwin Ltd., 2d ed. rev., 1949; 1st German ed., 1807), p. 229.

15. Harry Stack Sullivan, *The Collected Works of H. S. Sullivan* (New York: W. W. Norton, 1964, Vol. I, Second Part), p. 22. See in general the whole Lecture I, entitled "Basic Conceptions," pp. 3–29. H. S. Sullivan combined Freud and Mead in his "Interpersonal School of Psychiatry," which sees the self as the result of an interactive process.

16. The contrast between communal societies of the past and associational modern societies is a theme that runs through the whole literature of sociology. Each author stressed this or that aspect of the contrast, each using his or her own frame of reference. Ferdinand Tönnies, in his *Gemeinschaft und Gesellschaft* (1887), opposed the folk-society of the past and the rational, organized associations of the industrial world, the first being more natural and the second more artificial. Similarly Georg Simmel in his *Metropolis and the Mental Life* (*The Sociology of Georg Simmel*, Kurt H. Wolff, trans. [Glencoe, Ill.: The Free Press, 1950], pp. 409–424) opposes the emotional and human character of past rural societies to the calculating climate of the large modern metropolis. Emile Durkheim in his *Suicide* (trans. Spaulding/Simpson [Glencoe, Ill.: The Free Press, 1951]) distinguishes between the comforting compactness of tradi-

tional communities and the impersonality of the modern society which compels the individual to be self-oriented if not selfish. The whole sociology of Max Weber is an analysis of the process of rationalization, through which society passes from traditional and communal types of association to an institutionalized, collective calculation of ends and means. The topic has been touched upon by almost every sociologist or social philosopher since then. Particularly rewarding are the writings of Jacob Burckhardt *The Civilization of the Renaissance in Italy* (New York: The Macmillan Company, 1921), and of Erich Fromm, who comments on Burkhardt's ideas and develops them further in his *Escape from Freedom* (New York: Rinehart & Co., 1941) where he opposes the medieval and the post-Renaissance societies: "What characterizes medieval in contrast to modern society is lack of individual freedom. Everybody in the earlier period was chained to his role in the social order. A man had little chance to move socially from one class to another, he was hardly able to move even geographically from one town or one country to another . . . He was often not even free to dress as he pleased or to eat what he liked. . . ." Humans were not alone or isolated: "In having a distinct, unchangeable, and unquestionable place in a social world from the moment of birth, man was rooted in a structuralized whole, and thus life had a meaning which left no place and no need, for doubt. A person was identical with his role in society; he was a peasant, an artisan, a knight, and not an individual who happened to have this or that occupation. The social order was conceived as a natural order, and being a definite part of it gave man a feeling of security and of belonging. There was comparatively little competition. . ." (pp. 41–42). Fromm then shows how, after the Renaissance, humans progressively severed their ties to the small communities and were sent alone into a hostile world. Humans' temptation then is to give up their newly acquired freedom and take refuge in totalitarian ventures like fascism and nazism. Among many others, see also: Daniel Bell, *The Coming of Post-Industrial Society* (New York: Basic Books, Inc., 1973), and *The Cultural Contradictions of Capitalism* (New York: Basic Books, 1976), where he writes that today's society "is not integral, but disjunctive; the different realms respond to different norms, have different rhythms of change, and are regulated by different, even contrary axial principles" (p. 75). Kenneth Keniston, in his book, *The Uncommitted, Alienated Youth in American Society* (New York: Dell, 1965) sees the contrast between the two types of societies as continuing today in the coexistence of "two non-overlapping spheres— a public sphere whose demands are primarily cognitive, and a private sphere, which remains the proper arena for feeling, devotion, faith and reverence . . ." (p. 250).

17. See David C. McClelland, *The Achieving Society* (Princeton, N.J.: D. Van Nostrand Co., 1961).

18. Kenneth Keniston shows how in a communal society the education of youths was an unconscious and spontaneous process: "Society merely demands that men continue to be what they are, which is what they were born to be. Self definition is a function of social definition. Merely to grow up in a community is to have most of the central questions of selfhood answered automatically; child-rearing is so neatly geared to specific adult roles, that the question of

"who am I?" cannot arise as a conscious question. The only problem is how to raise the young so that they will fit." (Kenneth Keniston, op. cit., pp. 250-251).

19. To anthropologist Ralph Linton is attributed the making of a distinction between the ascribed and achieved statuses and roles. The first are those which individuals inherit. The second are those they are invited to devise for themselves and attain. The first are predominant in a static and communal society. The second are typical of an achieving society that encourages its members to improve their original statuses. See Ralph Linton, *The Study of Man* (New York, D. Appleton Century, 1936), pp. 113-129.

20. The idea of achievement was already present in the mind of the ancients and Erich Fromm does not deny it. He refers to Aristotle: "Happiness, which is man's aim, is the result of 'activity' and 'use'; it is not a quiescent possession or a state of mind." To explain his concept of activity, Aristotle uses the Olympic Games as an analogy. "And as in the Olympic Games," he says, "it is not the most beautiful and the strongest that are crowned, but those who compete (for it is some of these that are victorious) so those who act win, and rightly win, the noble and good things in life" (*Ethica Nicomachea*, W. D. Ross trans. [London, New York: Oxford University Press, 1925], 1102a), pp. 17-24; Erich Fromm, *Man for Himself* (New York: Rinehart, 1947), p. 25.

21. With the beginning of capitalism, according to Erich Fromm, competition becomes the rule of the game: "Each individual must go ahead and try his luck. He has to swim or to sink." (*Escape from Freedom*, p. 61).

22. Max Weber in his book, *The Protestant Ethic and the Spirit of Capitalism* (New York: Charles Scribner's Sons, 1930), has pointed to the spiritual affinity between the Protestant (Lutheran first, then Calvinist and Puritanical) notion of the Calling and the craving for success which is part of the Spirit of Capitalism. Erich Fromm, in a similar vein, writes: "The individualistic relationship to God was the psychological preparation for the individualistic character of man's secular activities" (*Escape from Freedom*, p. 109).

23. In a previous book, I have argued in favor of a qualitative (versus purely quantitative) definition of the lower class. According to this view, the lower class is made of those who do not have the power to participate in the competition for achievement and upward mobility. They are "blocked" at the subsistence level. They either do not produce any surplus which would permit saving and investment (capitalistic or educational) or if they produce a surplus, it is taken away from them (the Marxist view). See Emile Pin, *Les classes sociales* (Paris: Spes, 1963).

24. Charles Derber, *The Pursuit of Attention: Power and Individualism in Everyday Life* (Boston: G. K. Hall, 1979), p. 93. Before C. Derber, Erich Fromm had observed that modern man is in search of "fame," which is another way of interpreting his search for identity: "The underlying insecurity resulting from the position of the isolated individual in a hostile world tends to explain the genesis of a character trait which was, as Burckhardt has pointed out, . . . characteristic of the individual of the Renaissance and not present, at least with the same intensity, in the member of the medieval social structure: his passionate craving for fame. If the meaning of life has become doubtful, if one's relations

to others and to oneself do not offer security, then fame is one means to silence one's doubts" (*Escape from Freedom*, p. 49).

25. Erich Fromm, and many others, dream of a society which would permit relationships of mutual recognition, respect and love among its members. Fromm in his *Escape from Freedom* rejects the temptation of fascism, and suggests new forms of industrial democracy. Until satisfactory forms are found, however, we think humanity will find refuge either in the private sphere or in compensatory institutions, like voluntary associations, clubs of all sorts, and in the sociable conversation of social gatherings, which offer a symbolic representation of the unity of a society that has become fragmented. See below, Chapter 3.

26. As well developed by Peter Berger, Brigitte Berger, and Hansfried Kellner, in their book *The Homeless Mind* (New York: Vintage Books, 1977).

27. However, he may have the tendency to concentrate his criticism excessively on the capitalistic world. The process of individuation, as we said, started much earlier, and can be seen as a causal factor of capitalism, more than a consequence of it.

28. Many authors have underscored modern individuals' need for community, for instance, Robert Nisbet in his *Quest for Community* (New York: Oxford University Press, 1955). But whatever communities humans will be able to rebuild they will not be according to the pattern of past societies. Once the self has been liberated, it cannot be satisfied with a simple reassertion of the "primary ties" (Fromm). Even if an effort is made to restore a link between the economic function and the political decision-making process, individuals will be faced forever with the task of defining themselves in a world that will not do it for them.

2
RECOGNITION AND
IDENTITY SUPPORT:
THE IDEAL SELF

A few days after the Spatowskys' cocktail party, Gloria sat at her desk, compiling the information from her interviews with the guests at the party: Sex? Estimated Age? Marital Status? Number of Children? Estimated Income? Occupation? Religion? Summary of Interviews. When she was through with the work, she packed the records into her bag, stood up and walked to the closet to take out her raincoat. When she caught sight of herself in the mirror, Gloria stopped, asking herself the same questions: Sex? Female. Estimated Age? Twenty-three. Marital Status? Single . . . (or, going steady). No children. Estimated income? Four thousand. Occupation? Graduate student. Religion? Episcopalian. Now for Gloria, as well, the questions on the form were answered. Is it really saying something about me, she wondered. What should it say, anyhow? Who am I?[1] Gloria moved closer to the mirror. Feeling annoyed, she grimaced, but then smiled: grabbing the sunglasses from her bag, tipping the linen hat forward, and turning up the collar of her raincoat, she thought to herself: is this the mysterious spy who came in from the cold? Then she removed the coat, hat, and glasses. Gloria took her lipstick and colored her lips heavily with red, looking obliquely at the mirror, as she undid two buttons of her blouse and lighted a cigarette: "Don't you want to come up for a drink?" she asked the mirror. Gloria laughed at herself. Then her eyes caught sight of the photograph placed on the console, of herself the day of her confirmation standing between her mother and father. "Am I all this? Am I the independent woman who won from her mother the right to her own hours, her own friends, and even her own apartment? Or am I the sweet girl who dissolves with pleasure in Randolph's arms when he is being nice to me? Or am I already what I am likely to become: an efficient junior executive at a desk in the Prudential building, trying to catch other people's mistakes and get a promotion? Yes, maybe, but couldn't I do better? Don't I have other talents yet unknown to me, talents that would permit me to become a writer, an artist, a politician?"

How will Gloria ever know for sure who she is or who she can be? How can she arrive at a clear perception of herself and of her potentials?

In the static and communal societies of the past, the primary groups fulfilled the function of telling individuals who they were and who they were expected to become. On the basis of either family origin or sex, individuals knew if they were going to be peasants, knights, seamstresses or princesses. But, as we said in the last chapter, today, the primary groups, in general, are not competent to define, direct, and encourage individuals in their search for identity. This does not mean that the family no longer has any function in the life of modern individuals. On the contrary. The anonymity and rationality of the outside world has made the family a deeply needed center of emotional nurturance. Consequently how well individuals fulfill their roles as husbands, wives, children, and parents still matters but only at the emotional level and within the sphere of the intimate.[2] These family roles, however, are not taken into account by society at large when judging the "value" of modern men, and more so every day of modern women. In the past, marriage and child rearing may have been considered as most worthy achievements, especially for women, whose ambitions culminated the day of their engagement.[3] But in an industrial and specialized society, family roles are just a minor item in the résumé and hardly count in defining modern individuals' social selves.[4] Due to the total separation between the home world and the work world, humans no longer achieve economic success on their family farms or in their family shops; but rather individuals achieve success in the outside specialized world of business, industry, or politics. Several members of the family may work outside. But each usually operates in a different sector of these outside worlds and the experience of one family member hardly helps the career development of the other members. Not only is the work sphere highly specialized but technologies change continuously, so that, even if children adopt their parents' occupations, the permanent change occurring in the work world makes the advice of the parents obsolete.[5] The family then has become incompetent to guide the performances of its members in the work sphere. There is still more: the primary ties, linking individuals to their families, neighborhoods, and churches, not only do not help individuals find themselves, but quite often hinder their attempts at moving ahead and upward. This may be due largely to the parents' fear that children will escape their control and reach a status much higher than their own. It is also due, in the case of women, to a traditional conception that parents may have formed of the women's role, which dictates that they should not seek a career but should rather marry and raise babies.[6] In both cases parents, while verbally encouraging their children to be success-ful, actually set barriers to the development of their children's careers. Therefore, the individuals who seek functions and identities in the outside world must look elsewhere for competent advice and sup-port. This applies not only to individuals' careers but also to the development of any role–identity people want to acquire in the out-side world of politics, business, sports or the arts.

In this chapter we would like to show how sociable conversa-tion not only remedies modern individuals' isolation, but also helps them in their uncertain attempts at defining themselves.

One could object that the occupational world, not social gatherings, is the primary setting in which individuals manifest them-selves and obtain recognition from others. One must recognize the importance of the occupational environment in the definition and the internalization of one's role–identity. But after having noted the essential function of occupational environment in an individual's experience, we will try to demonstrate that this environment alone inadequately fulfills the function of self-identification.

It is true that the occupational role is for many the most im-portant aspect of their identity. People are known to others as phy-sicians, psychologists, secretaries, truck drivers, or plumbers. Not only are individuals known to others through the occupations they hold, but they are most often led to think that they *are* the roles they play. People say I *am* a physician, a lawyer, a computer pro-grammer, and so on. In a recent gathering, Susan recounted the day she began as a typist for a law firm as if it had happened to some-body else, she knew herself to be a nature-loving mountain climber and a dynamic disco dancer: how strange it was to be closed-up in that small box listening to the recorded male voice talking of prices, percentages, and margins! A year later when introduced at a party, she matter-of-factly declared that she was a steno–typist at Sherman and Sterling. Far away were the woods, the mountains, and the water-falls. The same occurs to most people. They lose their senses of humor and imagination and become what they were only play-acting in the beginning.[7]

Unlike the roles acted on the stage, which are not real, peo-ple's roles in life are real and become part of themselves. Roles take on such a significance that even when individuals find themselves in situations which require acting a new role, they continue to act ac-cording to the dictates of their old roles. Roles contribute to the shaping of an individual's behavioral style; they modify vocabulary, they suggest the stories or the jokes to tell; roles are like windows through which people look at the world. And this is true not only of occupational roles, but also of the other specialized roles that indi-viduals play in society. These roles, too, become components of their personalities and if people were stripped of all of them—business executive, violin player, member of the Democratic party, Presby-terian, and so on—the remainder would be a shadow. An extreme example of this identity loss occurs in prison settings, as soon as a convicted prisoner puts on a jail uniform and proceeds to a solitary, barren cell.[8] Without the reinforcement of customary activities and companions, the identity is lost. Since we become the roles we play, those who want to know who we are must also know the roles we play. Much of the preliminary talk in conversations held in social gatherings is intended to discover others' role identities.

Some people do not hesitate to acknowledge their socially defined roles. They, possibly, like their roles because they feel at ease in playing them, perceiving a correspondence between their inner capabilities and the requisites of the roles. Quite often, too, they simply feel satisfied by having acquired a function in the world, a function recognized as useful, even if it is not especially prestigious. It makes life so much easier when people know what they should do, who they are, and how they can introduce themselves in a way which readily makes sense to others.

Another source of possible satisfaction with occupational roles is that—in the eyes of the holders—it permits a sufficient amount of liberty, initiative, or creativity. Most occupational roles somehow leave a variable margin of free interpretation. It is true that some of these roles are rather strictly defined; many manual workers' and clerks' roles exact a fixed and specific routine. According to Frederick W. Taylor, workers should not think but just rigorously follow the instructions they have received. However, most roles leave their holders at least a small degree of initiative. Most individuals are allowed to create a personal style. When shopping in the supermarket, I head for the line of my favorite cashier clerk, who is efficient, knows all the prices, and is capable of a couple of friendly remarks while weighing, registering, and packing my groceries. Some roles allow for and even demand a much greater amount of invention: the roles of lawyer, physician, college professor, journalist, and many others. These roles also impose some limits and suggest courses of action, but the expectation is that the holder of these roles will show initiative, intelligence, improvisation. This is even more true of composers, writers, poets and painters who, for this reason, may be proud of their roles.

Many individuals also identify with their occupational roles, because these roles confer on them high prestige. The positions of airline captain, bank director, or judge entitle their holders to widely held recognition. In other societies, nonoccupational achievements, like being an usher in the church, a Knight of Malta, or the mother of ten children, suffice to win much prestige. But our society is less impressed with these achievements than those in the occupational (economic or political) domain. Not all individuals of course are pleased with their occupational achievements. Many occupational roles carry little prestige, and, in a modern party, certain individuals are ill-at-ease when introduced as an electrician, a bank clerk or a secretary. They may perform their roles very well and to the total satisfaction of their employers, colleagues, or clients; they may even like the routine involved in their job, but they are disturbed by the little prestige they derive from performing these tasks. They may like to think that these are only preliminary steps in their careers and think of themselves as destined for more prestigious positions. They may also think that their real capabilities lie in another field. Our friend Anthony is a house painter; he is also a part-time playwright and he likes to think of himself as a playwright; he prefers to discuss what he has written, or is going to write, than types or brands of paint. Many famous artists have had to work at a bread-winning job in which their talent could not play any part. Famous composers were known as elementary-school music teachers, painters as low-ranked civil servants and poets as traveling salesmen.[9]

All these people were compelled to fulfill roles which they did not consider as true expressions of themselves, as many individuals do today. They have developed—and are continuously readjusting—an ideal view of themselves. It is this ideal self that they wish to present to their friends.

The idea that human beings are ambitious, that is, want to acquire more prestige and power, is not new. David McClelland has shown through the study of ancient authors that achievement has been encouraged by many societies of the past.[10] Individuals were not offered a variety of career choices, but, rather, were expected to be successful in the careers assigned to them by their birth and environment. David McClelland demonstrates that the achievement motive existed in preindustrial societies. Much of the evidence he presents, however, suggests that the achievement motive took the form of a better management of one's own business, as opposed to the planning of a career. Yes, humans were already planners, but they were planners of things, not planners of themselves.[11] Today, by contrast, individuals are invited to design for themselves a life plan.[12] In other words, not only must modern humans be achievers, but they must also decide what kinds of character they want to achieve. Robert E. Park gives to this model the name of mask: "In so far as this mask represents the conception we have formed of ourselves, the roles we are striving to live up to, this mask is our true self, the self we would like to be."[13]

A much better expression to designate this "self we would like to be" is that of "ideal self." The expression is now gaining currency among social psychologists.[14] The ideal self is a newly recognized component of the self. In the first chapter, following George Herbert Mead, we distinguished in the self two elements, the *I*, that is, the operating principle, and the *Me*, which is the evaluating principle. We now must add the *ideal self*, which is a model we set for our performances and which can be quite different from the judgment that we ourselves or others may form of our actual performances.

The term ideal self should not be confused with the *idealized self*, a feature of the self which favorably distorts our perceptions of our actions and role performances. Some people have a tendency to evaluate themselves more favorably than would an objective spectator. Others, by the same token, are hypercritical about how they actually operate. Neither view, however, is the ideal self; both views are what Carl Rogers would call the "perceived self."[15] By contrast, the ideal self is what people want to become. Some people develop an ideal self that cannot be achieved. These unrealistic expectations are a form of self-delusion which often manifests itself in the form of wild daydreamings. The middle-aged wife of the local high school principal imagines herself to be starring in the next Polanski film, and the three-times-defeated candidate to Littletown city council dreams of being elected president of the United States. Daydreaming, however, is not necessarily pathological. It can also provide release from frustration or a program of action. Among these two healthy forms of daydreaming, the first offers individuals a distraction, a substitute for actions, pleasures, or successes they cannot obtain. Daydreams of seeking revenge against a boss, or erotic fantasies about unattainable partners, can be useful ways of relieving internal pressures.[16] One can plausibly hypothesize that daydreaming as a substitute will be found more frequently in those who have no access to great or immediate success in life: lower-class individuals, young adolescents, or the elderly. The second form of healthy daydreaming could be called functional or programmatic daydreaming. In this type of daydreaming, the individuals imagine more or less realistic scenarios which they think could one day become part of their lives. Daydreaming as a plan of action is more likely to be found among would-be achievers, young men and women or the middle and upper-middle classes.[17]

In these last cases, individuals know that they have not yet reached the level they seek, and choose instead to focus upon their inner capabilities which they think represent them better than the temporary flaws which still mar their performances. Singers may think that they are not far from being a new Caruso or Callas; painters may suppose that the public will soon discover that they are the Matisse of our times; cooks may fancy that they are the new Brillat-Savarin; cops may think they are the avatar of Serpico; and taxi drivers may daydream about racing some day at Indianapolis.

Even if the construction of an ideal self is a very private operation, it is not done without the regular help of society. Actually society, or rather the various forms which the social environment has taken through the ages, has a permanent and deep influence in the shaping of the ideal self. For this construction, society provides both models and psychological support.

When individuals think about what they would like to become, they gather elements which are offered to them by observing others. These elements are taken from the various roles that these people fulfill. The building of an ideal self starts at a young age when individuals play at being what the adults around them already are in reality: father, mother, policeofficer, soldier, merchant, physician, and so on. During their time in school, the individuals progressively acquire the talents which enable them to perform rather than play-act some of these roles. A process of elimination and choice goes on as the individuals must choose among the various specialized alternatives offered to them. In spite of this specialization most individuals continue pursuing their ideal selves into the adult years and some never terminate this endless pursuit of an ever-changing ideal self. But even at a later age, the models they build for themselves are made of role identities that are borrowed from social experience.

Society, at the same time, provides support. In their tentative efforts at play-acting various roles, individuals keep their eyes fixed on their various life associates—teachers, peers, friends—and, implicitly or explicitly, look for their approval. If others deny or withdraw their support, individuals change their plans and tentatively devise for themselves new ideal selves, which will be revised regularly until sufficient encouragement and applause is found.

As a consequence, the effort at building an ideal-self is always a tribute paid to the values and norms of the group within which individuals operate. The values and norms may be those of the general society, as Erving Goffman suggests,[18] but they may also be the values of a specific social class, of a subculture, or of a counter-culture.

Whether people's ideal selves are a re-definition of one of the official roles they play in life, or of an altogether more creative nature, and different from the roles they already fulfill, any ideal self is built around one or several "roles," that is, around social functions as they are expected to be fulfilled in a given society. In other words, the self, idealized or not, cannot acquire a definition, an identity, without adopting an image which is supported by other members of society. The ideal self is always defined on the basis of some role to which the others can relate.[19] The butcher may prefer to be known as a (first-class) golf player, the bank clerk as a (talented) violinist or the computer programmer as a (champion) marathon runner. These new definitions, golf player, violinist, marathon runner, are also social roles which possess clear features in the eyes of the spectators. This means that the extent to which individuals distance themselves emotionally from their occupational roles does not release them into some nirvana state. People's dreams of achievement do not take them away from society. They always include the support, the encouragement, the applause of competent others.

Not only do achieving individuals define their ideal-selves in terms of socially meaningful roles; they also choose from among the many roles they play the particular role–identity which suits their current audience.[20] A great movie actress was once invited to grace a charity affair by presiding over a community luncheon. The leaders of the organization were thrilled and at the same time nervous at the idea of having to entertain a star. How should they handle the visit? What should they talk to her about? The actress had herself foreseen the difficulty and, instead of appearing at the luncheon in the sexy sumptuosity of her movies and TV displays, she chose simple clothes and arrived accompanied by a retired, forgotten singer, ex-president of the artists' union. This image of herself as a compassionate colleague permitted a very relaxed interaction with the community leaders. The same actress, the very next day, put on her "political uniform" when she joined in a rally in favor of an environmental cause.

This flexibility supposes, of course, that the ideal selves, which individuals devise for themselves, are constituted of various role identities and not of only one specialized role. This is usually the case in modern society. Our modern society is made of many compartmentalized and specialized areas, operating to a large extent independently of each other. People cannot be full members of any society without participating in its entirety. This means that in order to be members of the complex modern world, individuals must acquire a role—even if at times very limited—in each of the areas which together constitute this world. As a consequence each of us develops a political role identity, a cultural or recreational role identity and so on. The complexity of modern society is then reflected in the complexity of modern personalities. While this wardrobe of role identities can be full of variety or more modest, it is seldom reduced to one single component. For those who possess more complex personalities, it is a problem to impose some order upon this array of role identities. Which of these role identities should be given preeminence? This must be decided when the demands of the various roles compete for our attention or time. Most individuals establish—on the basis of their life partners' responses—some sort of a hierarchy within themselves and give salience to one or the other of their various roles.[21]

This is true of their performed roles but also of the role identities which constitute their ideal selves. In devising our self-images, we establish from among the various components of our identities some kind of rank order, taking into consideration both our potentials and other people's values.

Has everyone developed a clear ideal self? No. In all classes of society, one can find individuals who do not seem to look ahead and could not tell themselves or others who they would like to be.

We have already said that lower-class individuals find themselves trapped in a situation in which all avenues of achievement are closed to them. They do not see any possibility for advancement in their jobs and their lower education and poverty preclude the possibility of achieving in any creative way.[22] As a result, ideal self-development is stunted and these people are compelled to find support and recognition for their ascribed roles within their primary groups. While the lower classes cannot find a sense of self in personal achievements, the aristocrats have the option of defining themselves, not in terms of achievement, but rather in terms of their noble origin. Today, however, many aristocrats very consciously choose to enter the modern competitive rat race.

In this latter case, they find themselves in the same boat as the individuals of the middle classes, who are indeed invited to achieve and build for themselves a life plan. The invitation to achieve, however, is not always followed by success. The causes for failing in an enterprise, which is taken for granted by the middle classes, may be due to many independent causes. Some of these causes may be traced to particular life experiences, but the main problems derive from the very structure of the society which calls its members to compete and achieve.

Among those whose problems lie in their idiosyncratic experience, we find people who perceive within themselves a set of contrasting and even mutually contradicting role identities. Each of these role identities is clearly defined in their eyes and leads to good performances in the specialized theaters where they must be played. Take the case of James: As a surgeon he is self-controlled and meticulous in the operating room; he plays a kind of godfather's role toward his younger colleagues; he likes to frolic and speak nonsense when kissing and caressing the red-headed nurse. At home he is a father who is concerned about his children; he listens to their questions and answers them to the best of his ability and there is no better husband, always ready to help his wife, anticipating her smallest wishes. Politically he is a hawk, ready to throw an atom bomb on whoever irritates the American people. At Easter-time, he never forgets to confess his sins to a priest before receiving holy communion. Now, when James goes to a party, he does not know what side of himself to present. He has not decided which one of his contradictory roles he wants to emphasize. They lie jumbled inside him, in conflict, and somehow prevent each other from surging to the surface. During a flirtatious moment, James remembers his dear wife. After announcing that Iran should be bombed, he recalls his religion's commandment to love one's enemies. James, racked by inner tensions, never gives a frank, sound, straightforward performance.

Sandra's case is different. She has made a private decision about who she wants to be, and she succeeds in being herself by revolving in only very restricted circles. She then gives unrestrained performances of her ideal self, the liberated woman, free of moral and middle-class limitations, indulging in all kinds of hetero- and homosexual involvements. She takes drugs and dances the whole night. I was told that she had volunteered to pop totally naked out of a big cake box at a birthday party. However, this secretly cherished view of herself is kept only for a few friends and secret occasions. Her job puts her in touch with much more conventional people who also invite her to very conventional parties. There Sandra is lost. She feels unable to contribute. Her ideal self simply does not fit, and she has no substitute self ready for these occasions. She is aware that she cannot show who she thinks she really is. She is then overly ceremonious, formal, and restrained when expressing her opinions. All this, of course, seems very unnatural and contrived, and others feel it. She looks around, puzzled, bored, having only one wish: to leave as soon as possible and wait at home for the next opportunity to be herself again.

The problems encountered by most individuals who struggle to define their ideal selves, however, are much deeper than those just reviewed—deeper and more general. The development of a sense of identity, we said, is impossible without consistent support from others. This support, however, is not always available. As we also said above, in a static and communal society, individuals received clear and always consistent images of who they were and were expected to become. Even their ideal selves were ascribed to the individuals by a circle of relatives and neighbors, who constituted a constant and uniform *relevant other*. Today relatives and neighbors are no longer competent to help us define a meaningful identity in the outside specialized world. On the other hand, the competent individuals who could encourage and support us in our enterprise are not within our reach. At least they are not readily available. For the same reason they are unaware of our capabilities. In other words, those who know us are largely incompetent, and those who are competent do not know us. There is still more. Even if a certain number of individuals could acquire some knowledge of who we are and could become, they do not constitute a cohesive group within which discussion about us could lead to some kind of an agreement. Those who make up the "real" world, the worlds of business, of the arts, of science and so on, are a disconnected aggregate of individuals unacquainted with each other, who do not agree on values and goals and could only send back to us a contradictory set of expectations, regarding who we are or could be, like a fragmented image reflected by a broken mirror. This is what Peter Berger, Brigitte Berger, and Hansfried Kellner express in different words:

> If, on the other hand, the life plan is vague, there is likely to be anxiety of a different sort: the individual dimly knows that he *ought* to have some sort of plan, and he is made anxious and frustrated by the fact that he cannot really articulate what it is.[23]

And in this endeavor society does not help the individual, because it has become pluralized and compartmentalized:

> The pluralistic structures of modern society have made the life of more and more individuals migratory, ever-changing, mobile. In everyday life the modern individual continuously alternates between highly discrepant and often contradictory social contexts. In terms of his biography, the individual migrates through a succession of widely divergent social worlds. Not only are an increasing number of individuals in a modern society uprooted from their original milieu, but, in addition, no succeeding milieu succeeds in becoming truly "home" either.[24]

If the world is no longer home by itself and if individuals, however, need a home where they can develop and check their "life plans," it is likely that they will do everything in their power to rebuild artificially[25] some kind of a home even if it is an imperfect substitute for the lost "paradise."[26] The competent partners who are not readily available to individuals must be called, invited, provoked into offering them the support which in the past was automatically granted by the primary groups. And since nothing is offered for free in this individualistic and calculating[27] world, individuals must be ready to pay for the support they need from others. Given that these others are themselves in search of identity support, the repayment individuals are expected to make is the very same identity support that they are looking for themselves. Modern social gatherings have the function of offering to their participants artificially constructed microcosms in which they can meet each other and exchange identity support. Social gatherings are the marketplace of identity negotiation.

At this point let us observe that the artificial microcosms of social gatherings are mostly needed for encouraging the attempts people make at being something better than they already are, that is, for getting support for their ideal selves. By contrast people do not need a special theater or time for the sanctioning of their already acquired roles. Feedback occurring at their place of work or in their homes tells them everyday and every hour whether or not they are good clerks, accurate secretaries, efficient teachers, affectionate mothers or fathers. The actual performances of these roles are under constant scrutiny. At work, employees are under the watch of one or more supervisors, from whom they regularly receive verbal and non-verbal approval or disapproval. Employees usually know where they stand. Salary raises speak for themselves. Promotions are even more loudly orchestrated. In the playing of these socially defined roles, individuals cannot claim to be much different from what their actions show. Or if people pretend to be something they are not, the pretense cannot survive repeated failures. The pianist, auditioning for the symphony orchestra, may get away with a couple of missed notes at the beginning of the run-through, under the pretext that the warm-up time was not sufficient, but if the mistakes persist all through the concerto, the pianist will be denied a contract.

As a consequence, individuals are fairly well aware of their successes or failures in the actual performances of their occupational roles. But what is sanctioned in the office, the shop, or the classroom, is not the ideal self, not the self-in-the-making, but the actual self, the self in its effective and real accomplishments, including any flaws or mistakes that may be accidentally committed.[28]

What is needed, then, is a place where individuals are freed from the obligation of giving an actual demonstration of who they are—a place and time where and when they can present to others the tentative performances, not of what they have already succeeded in being, but of what they think they could become. Only a few sociologists and social psychologists have suggested a connection between modern "partying" and the need for a stage where individuals can play out their ideal selves. One of them, Anselm Strauss, writes in *Mirrors and Masks*:

> It is probable that some of the effect of experimental role-dramas is that drama allows and forces the person to play a range of roles he did not believe himself capable of playing or never conceives of playing; it brings him face to face with his potential as well as his actual self. Sociable parties, Robert Potter has suggested, by their very episodic and expressive nature, allow and further such explorations of roles.[29]

Social gatherings are, or at least could be, the stage where individuals can engage in experimentation with the still fragile self-images they try to devise. Social gatherings, however, take many different forms and may fulfill many different functions. What kinds of social gatherings are best suited for promoting identity building and identity negotiation is the question we have to answer next.

NOTES

1. "Who am I?" This question actually was used—it was the only one—in the Twenty Statement Test, designed by Manford H. Kuhn. See C. A. Hickman and M. H. Kuhn, *Individuals, Groups, and Economic Behavior* (New York: Rinehart and Winston, 1956).

2. As Paula Fass writes in her book, *The Damned and the Beautiful: American Youth in the 1920's* (Oxford: Oxford University Press, 1977) "The family [in the 1920s] became an agency of individual nurture and an environment for the development of intimate personal relationships. . . . Families were no longer hard, structural, economic atoms locked into the metal of society, but emotional clouds formed on the basis of love and unified through personality and emotional satisfaction" (p. 98).

3. While I was a student at the Institute for Political Science at the Sorbonne, I was once called by a seminar instructor to replace a female panelist who, three weeks before graduation, withdrew from the school "because [she had] become engaged."

4. Until recently a good marital status was a necessary condition for admission to many positions, especially public positions. A president could not be a divorced person, but now it has happened (Reagan); and, similarly, many individuals who in the past were and are still considered by a large proportion of the population to be sexually deviant, like homosexuals, are elected or designated to high public positions.

5. ". . . . [A]dults cannot afford to shape their children in their own image. Parents are often obsolescent in their skills, trained for jobs that are passing out of existence, and thus unable to transmit directly their accumulated knowledge. They come to be 'out of touch with the times' and unable to understand, much less inculcate, the standards of a social order that has changed since they were young." James Coleman, *The Adolescent Society* (Glencoe, Ill.: The Free Press, 1961), p. 2.

6. In a recent paper, one of my students described a clique of high-school classmates—all women—whose explicit goal in associating with each other was to help them prepare for a career and to resist the pressure of their peers, of their families, and of the town: "The group offers each of us moral support and push to fulfill our career goals, despite the home town atmosphere [which we suffer every vacation] of 'settle down and raise babies!' Consequently the group has become increasingly important as a means of socializing due to the alienation from our peers" (Candace Bell).

7. This Peter Berger wittily observes in the case of the newly commissioned officer. See Peter Berger, *Invitation to Sociology* (Garden City: Doubleday Anchor, 1963), pp. 96–97.

8. Peter Berger, op. cit., pp. 100–101.

9. Wallace Stevens (1879–1955) and William Carlos Williams (1883–1963) were respectively an insurance executive and a physician, but they are now mostly remembered as poets.

10. See David C. McClelland, *The Achieving Society* (Princeton, N.J.: D. Van Nostrand Co., 1961).

11. "In long-range life planning, the individual not only plans what he will do but also plans what he will be." Peter Berger, Brigitte Berger, and Hansfried Kellner, *The Homeless Mind* (New York: Vintage Books, Random House, 1973), p. 74.

12. Ibid., pp. 71–76.

13. Robert E. Park, "Human Nature and Collective Behavior," *American Journal of Sociology*, 1927, 32: 739.

14. Modern social psychologists, like George McCall and J. L. Simmons, perceive humans' identities not as simple sets of internalized social roles, but as sets of role–identities which are the various imaginative views that the individuals have of themselves. The organization of role–identities, as it exists at a given point in a person's life span, corresponds to what many theorists have called the ideal self. See George McCall and J. L. Simmons, *Identities and Interactions* (New York: The Free Press, rev. ed., 1978), pp. 73–74. The authors refer to Ruth C. Wylie, *The Self Concept: A Review of Methodological Considerations and Measuring Instruments*, rev. ed. (Lincoln: University of Nebraska Press, 1974). The idea was already in the mind of Charles Cooley:

If we never tried to seem a little better than we are, how could we improve or "train ourselves from the outside inward?" And the same impulse to show the world a better or idealized aspect of ourselves finds an organized expression in the various professions and classes each of which has to some extent a cant or pose, which its members assume unconsciously, for the most part (Charles H. Cooley, *Human Nature and the Social Order* [New York: Scribner's, 1922], pp. 352-353).

One should resist a superficial association between what is called here the ideal-self and what Freud calls the ego ideal. Both are social products; but the parallel cannot go further. Freud's ego ideal is contained within the structure which he terms "superego". The superego is in a negative relationship to the libidinal instincts. The superego is repressive of the libido. Freud, however, does not see in repression the only way to deal with the demands of the id. There is also sublimation: "It is true that the ego ideal requires such sublimation, but it cannot enforce it; sublimation remains a special process which may be prompted by the ideal but the execution of which is entirely independent of such incitement. . . . As we have learned, the formation of the ideal increases the demands of the ego, and is the most powerful factor favouring repression; sublimation is a way out, a way by which the claims of the ego can be met without involving repression" (*Collected Papers*, London: The Hogarth Press, 1953, Vol. 4, p. 52). What we call here the ideal self is not the ego-ideal or the superego or the conscience, it is the result of a sublimation process, by which the ego finds a way of expressing itself through accepted social channels. The formation of a sublimated ego can be encouraged by the superego reflecting itself the demands of society. The Protestant ethic, which became simply the work ethic, has facilitated the fusion of the superego and of the sublimated self at least in one area, that of productive activities, while the superego went on controlling the consuming impulses of the individual. Today, however, the repressive aspect of the work ethic has been almost entirely pushed aside, and what remains is society's encouragement of the ego to develop its possibilities to the utmost. The work ethic has been replaced by a success ethic. The ideal self is also different from what Karen Horney calls the idealized self, which is a neurotic substitute for the real self. See Karen Horney, *Neurosis and Human Growth* (New York: W. W. Norton and Co., 1950).

15. See Carl R. Rogers, *Client-centered Therapy* (Boston: Houghton Mifflin Co., 1951).

16. The wishes from daydreaming are, according to Freud, "either ambitious wishes serving to exalt the person creating them or they are erotic" (*Sigmund Freud*, "The Poet and Daydreaming," in *Collected Papers*, op. cit., Vol. 4, p. 176).

17. "It is possible," writes Jerome L. Singer, in his book *Daydreaming* (New York: Random House, 1966) "that membership in an upwardly mobile social group might produce a greater tendency to daydreaming. Just as a football player looks for an opening between the shifting mass of men, the person seeking advancement in a social status seeks out avenues of fulfillment. . . . For a social group that has attained a relatively stable or secure status, the future may be less intriguing or demanding of imaginary exploration" (pp. 64-65).

18. Erving Goffman writes:

Thus when an individual presents himself before others, his performance will tend to incorporate and exemplify the officially accredited values of the society, more so, in fact than does his behavior as a whole (*The Presentation of Self in Everyday Life* [New York: Doubleday, 1959], p. 35).

19. "Although the more or less autistic elaborations that form part of the content of one's imaginative view of self in a given social position are often somewhat bizarre, perhaps fantastic, it is important to note that role–identities are not at all purely idiosyncratic standards and expectations that would be held toward *any* occupant of that status. That is, among the contents of any role–identity are included those vague and abstract expectations we have discussed as social role. It is through these conventional contents of one's role–identities, acquired in the socialization process, that one is irrevocably a member of his culture. Personal elaborations of these conventional contents are exceedingly important, yet they represent, in most cases, variations on culturally established themes" (George J. McCall and J. L. Simmons, op. cit., p. 68).

20. See G. J. McCall and J. L. Simmons, op. cit., pp. 85–91, where the authors using the concept of "situational self" explain how individuals present to others in every specific situation those role–identities which, depending upon the circumstances, make sense to them.

21. See G. J. McCall and J. L. Simmons, op. cit., pp. 73–79, where the authors develop the concept of "prominence" to describe the organization and the hierarchization individuals establish among their various identities.

22. Of course, some of them could imagine themselves as revolutionary fighters for the radical transformation of society. For this dream to become a life plan, however, the social conditions for the staging of a revolution must exist and this is not always the case, as is evidenced by the failure of American revolutionary movements. Loren Baritz, in his book, *The American Left* (New York: Basic Books, 1971), shows that radicalism never succeeded in finding a wide popular basis in the United States.

23. Berger et al., op. cit., p. 73.

24. Ibid., p. 184.

25. Georg Simmel, writing on sociability, recognizes the artificial character of sociable interaction. But in his eyes, "artificiality" is not necessarily a negative characterization. It can be the mark of humans' purposeful and artistic creations. See *The Sociology of Georg Simmel*, Kurt H. Wolff, trans. (Glencoe, Ill.: The Free Press, 1950), pp. 48–49.

26. "By losing his fixed place in a closed world man loses the answer to the meaning of his life; the result is that doubt has befallen him concerning himself and the aim of life. . . . Not having the wealth or the power which the Renaissance capitalist had, and also having lost the sense of unity with men and the universe, he is overwhelmed with a sense of his individual nothingness and helplessness. Paradise is lost for good, the individual stands alone and faces the world" (Erich Fromm, *Escape from Freedom* [New York: Rinehart and Co., 1941], pp. 62–63).

27. "Modern mind has become more and more calculating. The calculative exactness of practical life which the money economy has brought about corresponds to the ideal of natural science: to transform the world into an arithmetic problem, to fix every part of the world by mathematical formulas" (Georg Simmel, "The Metropolis and Mental Life," in *The Sociology of Georg Simmel*, op. cit., p. 412).

28. G. J. McCall and J. L. Simmons observe that situational conditions may prevent an individual from displaying his or her "ideal self." "Other factors, closely linked to the person's short-run life situation, very often cause less prominent role–identities to become temporarily quite salient in the person's actions" (op. cit., p. 84).

29. Anselm Strauss, *Mirrors and Masks* (Glencoe, Ill.: The Free Press, 1959), p. 97. The connection between the ideal-self and the party is suggested by Hans Gerth and C. Wright Mills, in *Character and Social Structure: The Psychology of Social Institutions* (New York: Harcourt, Brace & World, Inc., 1953), p. 12: "An adolescent girl enacts a different role when she is at a party composed of members of her own clique than when she is at her family breakfast table. Moreover the *luxury of a certain image of self* implied in the party role is not often possible in her family circle . . ." (italics mine).

3
SOCIABILITY, FESTIVITY, AND SOCIETY

As is the case in all human institutions, the form and structure adopted by social gatherings are strongly related to their social functions. In this chapter, after having analyzed the essence of sociability, we will study how the forms of social gatherings have been modified in response to the needs created by a specialized, compartmentalized, and competitive society.

What are the basic features characterizing all types of sociability by contrast with other human interactions, particularly by contrast with purposive, rational, or goal-oriented interactions?

"Sociability," wrote Georg Simmel, "is the play form of human association."[1] The word *play* has two meanings. First, in play, people do not engage in goal-oriented activities, but they act only as if they were pursuing goals. The accent is on performing well, not on achieving a given result. Likewise, in a social gathering, the participants do not try to attain external goals similar to those achieved during the fulfillment of daily roles, but rather they perform their identities, which are composed of a variety and combination of these roles. Since this play is done after work has been completed, it contains an aspect of free exercise, joy, and festivity.

The word *play* also means a theatrical representation. The participants of a social gathering offer a representation of society. Their gathering represents and symbolizes the social bond, that is, the unity of society. There is a difference, however, between theatrical plays and social gatherings. The difference lies in the fact that in a social gathering, audience and actors are the same people. This gives to social gatherings a formal, almost ceremonial aspect, as if participants were engaged in some kind of a tribal ritual.

The first of these features—the festive, nontask-oriented character of social gatherings—is common to all social gatherings, past and present. The second feature—the representational aspect of sociability—is also a constant, but since the society which is represented or symbolized has varied considerably throughout history, it is not surprising that the changing reality of society is reflected in the form of the gatherings themselves and has given birth to a variety of gatherings. In the final part of the chapter we will study two types of social gatherings: the family gathering and what we will call the modern gathering.

Georg Simmel says that in social gatherings we play the game of "pure" society.[2] This means that sociability excludes all the goal-oriented activities such as economic transaction, political negotiation, or sexual intercourse. Sociability retains something from all these activities, but not their contents, only their "social form." It is obvious that individuals do not perform tasks in social gatherings. People gather not to fabricate anything, or to create a new corporation, or to sell goods or services; they gather for the pleasure of conversing with each other in a "disinterested" and festive way. In a social gathering the other guests are not considered as useful, but as pleasant in themselves. In our modern gatherings, sociability may not be dionysian, but it can still be poetic. The message becomes a communication of the soul, a respectful homage to beauty and to the sensibilities of others. In the same way sociability, in a social gathering, has a useless and playful character which tells others that we do not seek their goods, their money, their services, but themselves.

We resent those who use social gatherings for more pedestrian and artless commercial exchanges. Of course, no one thinks of bringing goods for sale to a party, and we know it is not the place for buying goods. At most, we can get a good tip at a party on what is for sale where. But often guests are more tempted to get advice from professionals. The professionals themselves do not come to a gathering with the intention of distributing free what they usually sell for good dollars. They are an easy prey, however, to other guests interested in getting either a free consultation or maybe simply in escaping an ill-defined situation by moving to the more solid ground of the expert–client relationship.

I remember a party in Washington where a locally famous

physician was the object of competition on the part of the female guests. Conversation was moving deep into the secrets of heart transplants and other medical curiosities. One of the guests, a vibrant and passionate woman, pretending to be ignorant of these scientific mysteries, thought it clever to lighten the conversation by asking the star physician what she should do about some inner pain she was feeling somewhere between her ribs. Another doctor (or, in a similar situation, a lawyer, stockbroker, or other professional) would have suggested to the woman: "call my office tomorrow morning." But the hero of the story had a less prosaic definition of the situation. "All right, Madam," he gallantly answered with a twinkle in his eye, "here is a sofa. Now strip to the waist and I shall examine you." Unfortunately for the prospective voyeurs, the woman understood her mistake and retreated from her definition of the situation.[3]

The fact that sociability excludes purposeful, task-oriented interaction, gives it an after-work, leisurely, and often festive character. The burden of work is forgotten. Social gatherings are feasts, that is, moments set apart for rejoicing. This does not mean that social gatherings are places and times of total freedom, as if no rules governed their course of events. On the contrary, social gatherings seldom offer total relaxation. The participants are freed of their occupational duties, but they must conform to other specific expectations. Social gatherings, we said, are representational rituals and like all rituals are governed by formal expectations. In other words, in all social gatherings one may find an element of formality.

Formality refers to the expectation that people—the hosts and their guests in this case—will follow some specific rules different from those applicable to their usual social behavior, that is, rules which these people have not wholly internalized. In this sense, the concept of formality, as we use it here, extends to many behavioral rules which are not currently considered to be formal in daily conversation or in books of etiquette. Formality as we understand it, may require people to wear a tuxedo or a long dress at a dinner party. It may also demand designer jeans and a Lacoste shirt at a lunch in the country, a bathing suit on the beach, and even nakedness in a nudist colony. In each case, the participants are supposed to respect the type of formality proper for the occasion which, of course, is not limited to peculiarities of dress. Not only is it provocative to walk fully clothed on a nudist beach, but there are tacit rules on how to sit, how to touch (or rather, not touch) others; there are rules regarding whom and when and at what angle one may photograph, and so on.[4] Formality means that the participants must conform to the specific norms of the situation.

The formality which characterizes social gatherings is of a special nature. It is ritualistic and festive formality. This implies, as we indicated above, interruption of work. It implies more: an element of solemnity and an almost ceremonious behavior. Participants are invited, like actors on the stage, to put on "costumes" that is, nonpractical clothes which are usually more expensive than those worn for daily routines; a special room also is chosen to serve as a stage—the drawing room (the room to which the party withdraws after dinner); the "stage" also can be a special, nontask-oriented rearrangement of the living-room. What reminds us of work, like typewriters, sewing machines, and tools are put into closets. The meeting place is not only cleaned and rearranged for conversation but is often adorned with flowers. The best china, crystal, and polished silver are set on the dining or cocktail table. At a seated dinner one or several centerpieces in silver or china may delight the eyes of the commensals. The food is different, usually better, often a little exotic or special. Fine bottles of wine are opened.

Festive association is not always easy. It requires effort and inventiveness. In the eyes of many individuals, it is not a spontaneous activity and may appear artificial. Georg Simmel has acknowledged that social encounters are "artificial," but he does not think this to be at all negative.[5] On the contrary. In artificiality there is art, and art is a superior human creation. Art shows our capabilities at their height. Sociability calls upon our artistic creativity, and festivity creates the proper mood which prompts us to perform in the best possible manner. Festivity elicits from us adventurous moves and conversations. We feel encouraged to approach people we were always afraid of engaging in conversation. We are reminded of exciting stories or episodes in our travels. Our replies are more witty. In a festive gathering, laughter can be heard exploding constantly in this or that duo, trio, or small group. Sometimes it is the whole gathering that is intently listening to a fascinating account or reeling with laughter at a very good joke.

Festive formality is not reserved for the elaborate receptions of the wealthy. Years ago I was a guest of a family who lived in a small Italian village. One day a neighbor arrived at my hosts' house to help prepare for a party, and then reappeared two hours later. The contrast in appearance was startling. At first appearance she was wearing heavy shoes with wooden soles, thick stockings, a solid cotton dress with a leather belt. Her hair was in curlers. After rolling up her sleeves, she put on an apron and busied herself with the task of preparing delicacies. She moved around efficiently as if at home, opening cupboards, closets, and drawers, taking whatever initiative was needed to reach the common goal. While working, she had interspersed advice on how to prepare or serve cookies or pies with gossip about the village girls and the young men. When everything was ready, she left for home in order to "get ready for the party."

When she came back, she wore a necklace, fine leather pumps, nylon stockings, and a light red dress with matching belt which showed from beneath a linen jacket. Her face was lightly made up, her hair as though she had just come from the hairdresser. She entered with deliberate steps and a slightly shy hesitation. Her back was straight. She mimed kissing the hostess (to preserve each other's make-up), and—although knowing very well where her coat would eventually be brought—waited until her friend's daughter took it and carried it to the bedroom. She stood clasping her fine handbag from which she extracted a small, intricately embroidered handkerchief for an unnecessary brushing of her nose. She waited to be seated until she was asked. It would not have occurred to her to go help herself from the buffet before the hostess had invited her to do so. She participated in the general conversation about the new factory expected to come to the village and the consequences for its economy. This was a high-level conversation, indeed, followed by comments on the new choirmaster and the beautiful singing in church the previous Sunday.

This story shows how social gatherings differ from other types of human association and require from the participants a very specific kind of behavior which, in comparison with the daily routine, seems very formal. The problem for the guest is even more complex because, for several reasons, social gatherings contain varying degrees of formality, which in turn require guests to assume specific attitudes and behaviors.

Given this variability in the degree of formality, and given that the guests must prepare themselves to fit each gathering, they need to be told in advance what will be the degree or the kind of formality of the gathering. This will enable them to decide whether they wish to attend, that is, whether they think they can accept the definition of the situation and adapt to it in terms of psychological or physical presentation. In other words, guests want to be sure that their definition of the situation matches that of their hosts. Guests must know whether the gathering will be a *fiesta* in the open, a garden party, a small informal gathering in a coffee shop or a bar, a cocktail party, or a costumed Halloween party. Men must know whether the invitation is for a black-tie dinner, at which they must wear a tuxedo; or for a buffet dinner or cocktail party, at which they may wear a pin-striped or a glen plaid suit; or some office party, for which a club jacket, grey flannel trousers, and a red tie of simple design will do; or even a garden party which will suggest cotton slacks, sport jacket, and a scarf. To dress inappropriately can bring discomfort to both guest and host. Guests are usually well aware of the different dress codes. We remember one guest who became the cynosure of all eyes because she did not know these codes: Dark and tall, this slim young woman attended a large cocktail party wearing a form-fitting, red, sleeveless and backless long dress, with a deep-plunging décolleté, and a side-slit up her thigh. This outfit—perhaps slightly modified—might have fit a very festive dinner party but it was out of place at a cocktail party.[6] Evidence of it was that practically no other woman wanted to talk to her—and no married gentleman dared. She was instead surrounded by bachelors, who were secretaries at various foreign embassies.

Sometimes a too brief definition of the gathering, "formal" or "informal," does not convey a clear message. As the following example demonstrates, the word *informal* does not always have the same meaning. In the summer of 1973, my friends Richard and Elisabeth accepted an invitation to dinner from a young woman, while they were on a trip through Italy. They knew her as very "in," belonging to the jet set of young Roman society. Beforehand they had inquired about the degree of formality. When they got the "informal" answer, they thought they had correctly assessed their hosts' expectations. Richard put on a beige summer suit and a tie, while Elisabeth wore a Cacharel skirt and blouse. When the door opened they realized their mistake: the women wore tight-fitting, low-slung jeans and silk or cotton tops adorned with dozens of gold chains. The men also wore jeans of various colors and T-shirts. Most were barefoot. In Richard and Elisabeth's vocabulary, "radical-chic" would have better described the situation than "informal" which, strangely enough, means to them a rather high-level of formality. Richard rushed to the hostess's bedroom, took off his tie, rolled up his sleeves and knotted around his neck a scarf borrowed from a coat hanger. It was far from being the real thing but it showed his good will.

The formal character of social gatherings stems from their representational character. They offer more than tasks to be performed well; they must symbolize society. The third constant feature of social gatherings is their reference to the larger group or society which they represent or of which they symbolize the unity. Since, however, society has radically changed over the last centuries, the form of social gatherings has also changed in order to adapt to the new form of society. To simplify, in a traditional and communal society, social gatherings mostly celebrated existing social bonds, while in a modern post-industrial society, they symbolize the creation of new ones.

The opposition between the two types of societies, of course, is not radical. Modern society still encompasses areas of communal solidarity. But if we contrast today's society and, let us say, the medieval world, it clearly appears that modern society, despite a remaining substructure of communities, is characterized by an enormous edifice of specialized and compartmentalized sectors.

Inasmuch as a society was and still is bound together by ties of a primary and emotional nature—the ties of tribes, clans, families, or nations—the social gatherings are called to revive sentiments of belonging which may have been weakened by everyday routine or selfishness. The group finds in the effervescence of the gathering the cohesion necessary to enforce in its members norms or attitudes which may require a sacrifice of their immediate interests. Participants, in turn, find in the celebration some kind of salvation. They come to sense the strength of the group and feel protected by it. All individuals secretly desire to be immersed in a larger unity, to be part of a totality. Tribal or national gatherings give individuals the feeling that their existences, which otherwise would be powerless and meaningless, have acquired full human dimension and value. This need for a community has manifested itself in many ways. Particularly in the past, events such as a king's birth or the harvest were celebrated with national feasting. To manifest the importance of these events the group indulged in some kind of nonroutine and nonproductive excesses.[7] Its members spent time, energy, and invention in making special food and drinks, in putting on expensive and impractical costumes, and in performing useless activities like singing and dancing. All this was done to awaken the group to the significance of what was celebrated. Those who might have been tempted to sleep were aroused by the sound of trumpets or the beating of the drums, by bells ringing or the explosion of fireworks, by the stampede of the dancers or the popping of champagne corks. Thus, the group was made to remember what has been and continues to be of prime importance in its past or present life.[8] The private and petty interests of its members were drowned under the torrent of public rejoicing.

Public festivities were much more common in preindustrial societies. There are many explanations for their past frequency. Societies—cities, provinces of the past—were smaller and could be more easily assembled. People were also more emotionally attached to their communities. According to Durkheim, because each family unit produced all the goods necessary for its survival, the community was not bound by economic ties. Therefore there was great danger that the group would dissolve through selfishness or feuds. There was also fear that the group would lack the unity necessary to fight off the enemy. As a result, total cohesion of the group, or "sticking together" was a necessity. The participation in local and national celebrations was a way of showing one's loyalty to the group and a way to guarantee the other members' loyalty. These celebrations were highly emotional, since they had their origin in the primordial fear of society's dissolution and fear of the individual's isolation and death.

Today these emotional public celebrations have not disappeared but they are less emotional and less frequent. Individuals—through the division of labor—are linked to each other by innumerable economic, political, and other functional links. People are compelled to remain within society and the various group members do not fear the dissolution of society. It is true that individuals have been freed from the bonds which link them to family or neighborhood. But while individuals have acquired much more freedom in defining their places in society at large, they cannot refuse to participate. They must find a function within one of the specialized sectors which constitute society. They are also given the chance to have their say in the political process and are not compelled to submit emotionally and actually to the irrational decisions of traditional authorities. Individuals are not given the right to withdraw from society, but they are allowed to select their mode of participation.

The new modes of participation in public life are membership in political parties, social defense groups, civic organizations and unions and, of course, the assumption of an occupational function.

Modern humans have been socialized to be rational members of society, not passive, emotional, marching, singing patriots. Therefore, many today frown upon the emotions aroused by public festivities which can so easily be used by group leaders for the ideological and political control of the citizens. Democracy, by stressing individuals' active, intelligent, and articulate participation in public decisions, has replaced the festive and emotional endorsement of princes and monarchs with political discussions and debates. When public festivity is found today, it often takes the character of folklore, it is a distraction, a temporary halt in people's rational pursuits. In other cases, it is limited to a sector of the population or has become entirely private. It is found in large sporting events which gather many categories of people, but only the exceptional matches can command a national dimension. The same must be said of popular music festivals which usually cater to a specific age group. Festivity also has become more private. It is found in private gatherings which are organized either at the occasion of the old public feasts or around some private event that must be celebrated: a birth, a wedding, an anniversary, a house-warming, a birthday, and so on. One may regret the phasing out of public festivity; it was a rewarding manifestation and revival of tribal or national unity. But public festivity was better geared towards eliciting violent and nonrational emotions than towards promoting sociability, that is, interpersonal exchange and understanding.

While private festivity rarely elicits a high degree of effervescence, such as wild shouts and ecstatic dances, its tamer atmosphere fosters conversation. Private festivity always existed. Family gatherings, like christening or confirmation parties, weddings or birthday parties, were called to celebrate an event in the life of a family member and at the same time to reinforce the family bonds. The upper classes also had their parties, dinner parties, tea parties, garden parties, and dances of all sorts. They, too, were occasions to celebrate the existing ties between the members of the "society." In agrarian civilizations, the so-called "society" or ruling class constituted a very small percentage of any given community and it was no problem to gather the whole society into the mansion of one of its members. Sometimes a stranger was introduced and by the same token made a member of the local "aristocratic" family. These upper-class gatherings had one similarity with the modern gathering: their reference was the "world" in its local totality. But they also differed from the modern gathering. They were not so much representing the world, as do the modern gatherings, but actually gathering it. What was represented was the unity of a world often torn apart by rivalries, envy, and political feuds.

What makes modern sociability different from traditional festivity—family gatherings or upper-classes parties—is that they do not aim at reviving feelings of belonging, but rather focus on building interpersonal exchanges. They do not celebrate the unity of an existing society, but act to reunite the members of a society which has become a vast, anonymous, differentiated juxtaposition of sectors without any deep sense of unity. The mutual and organic need individuals have of each other may provide them with a sense of being functionally interdependent, but at the same time they lack the sense of being part of an integrated community. Modern individuals face a disorganized succession of encounters with partners who do not know them well and who send conflicting messages about who they think these individuals are. If individuals are to be given coherent social identities, it can only be done by a coherent group. We discussed in Chapter 2 why the family and the neighborhood can no longer fulfill this function; they no longer constitute the real society where the economic, political, educational games are played. On the other hand, since society, as such, escapes effective reintegration, individuals must content themselves with some representation of society, that is, with microcosms which provide convincing images of the larger evanescent society. Social gatherings are those events where society is represented, or better, where people play at representing society. This means that while emotional communion has retreated to give place to interpersonal interaction and identity negotiation, it has not disappeared entirely. It is still needed—even if at lower decibels—to persuade the participants in the gatherings and themselves that they somehow constitute a microcosm representative of the unattainable "society." To be taken seriously, a social gathering today must appear to individuals as somehow being "the world."[9] This means that a social gathering cannot be a simple assemblage or juxtaposition of individuals. It must be perceived by each participant as constituting a totality of people in communion.

Since the "world" outside is no longer a community, the communion found in modern gatherings is not the consequence of preexisting ties, but the result of the very organization of the gathering, particularly of the festivity of the setting and the choice of the participants. This "artificial" unity of the gathering will be recognized by some external signs, especially by the level of animation of the conversations. A friend of mine tells me that when he goes to a party, before ringing the bell of his hosts, he pauses at the door. If he hears a concert of high-pitched voices, he knows immediately that the party is going to be a good one. The high-pitch of the voices indicates the excitement of the participants at being with each other, that is, of constituting some kind of microcosm or representation of the whole world. The excitement of a modern party is very different from the effervescence of the public festivities of communal societies. The excitement is not an end in itself, it is the necessary condition for the identity negotiations between the participants to take place. It makes them worthwhile; it makes recognition and support that each participant collects from others appear to be granted not by disconnected, incompetent and worthless individuals, but by "the world," which the gathering so aptly represents. Modern social gatherings are no longer celebrations of existing links, but they are "representations," or rituals of association in which the elements of communion facilitate the exchange of recognition among the participants. Communion is not only the condition of good conversational exchange, it is also a result of it. If the proper people have been invited, that is, if those invited are individuals who are excited about meeting each other, because in their eyes these various participants constitute a good representation of "society," their contentment will manifest itself in common excitement. Of course, what constitutes "the world," *le grand monde*, society, *Gesellschaft*[10] is relative to the individuals invited to the party. It does not contain the same people if held in Peekskill as it does in Dubuque or in San Francisco. Even a lower-middle-class party can, for its members, represent "the world," that is, that part of the world which the participants judge competent in understanding them and in giving them support in their search for identity.

Although sociable conversation and the modern parties which it characterizes have eclipsed traditional communal celebrations, they have not eliminated them. Independent of the public festivities which may still exist here or there, it is still possible today to find social gatherings organized for the celebration of existing communal bonds. Even if modern men and women do not really count on their primary ties to define their ideal selves, they have not completely eliminated past loyalties from their lives. They still largely define themselves according to their family, neighborhood, or church memberships. In addition, the school, the army, the past places of occupation are also included in individuals' self-definitions. Each of these institutions may organize social gatherings to celebrate the past, sometimes still living, loyalties. These gatherings in a broader sense, too, could be called "family gatherings." In these gatherings the main goal is not really conversation, in the sense of identity negotiation, it is a celebration of the past communal bonds. As long as these still exist and are meaningful to the participants, the gathering can be a success and all guests feel happy at having reinforced links they deem essential or very useful to their mutual welfare. But when these bonds have become tenuous, or even never really existed, the efforts at an emotional communion are resented by the participants. This is often the case of office parties in which a well-intentioned boss tries to persuade himself and his employees that they all constitute a happy family. Family reunions are usually more authentic, particularly for the very young and the very old. The first have not yet sailed away from the family harbor and the latter have come back to it. But in the eyes of the young adults and the adult members of the family, the gathering may look very narrow in scope and incapable of representing what has become for them the theater of their life plan. In no way does the family gathering seem a representation of the outside world or a means to get access to it. This is particularly the case for the upwardly mobile individuals of the lower-middle class. By contrast, in better established upper-middle-class families, a family reunion that joins relatives who are professionals, politicians, and business executives may be a much more plausible representation of the "real world." In those cases the celebration of the primary family ties may also constitute a very good theater for exchange of identity support in social conversation.

Communal sociability still exists in today's world under the form of family gatherings. But for modern human beings, that is for the achieving individuals in search of identity, communal sociability and emotion will not fulfill their psychological needs. Conversational sociability through which people can perform their ideal selves is a must. Once the primary ties have been severed, there is no return to their enticements, no return to the primordial symbiosis between self and community.[11] This does not mean that individuals are prevented from maintaining that fundamental communion with nature and mankind. This communion remains as a background to all human endeavors and an invitation to reconstitute the human unity. But this will not be achieved by reversing history. It will be achieved by moving ahead and rebuilding consciously and rationally a unified world of freely cooperating individuals.[12] The program is challenging but the final result may look so desperately out of reach. Instead of a rebuilt universe, humans are perpetually confronted with the disconnected, competitive, and calculating world of modern business. The reconstruction may seem so utopian that people are tempted to give up and opt for either of two choices: collaborate and enter the competitive race without any attempt at redirecting it, or withdraw from the competition and "escape from freedom."[13] The analyses in this book will often concern themselves with people having made the first of these two choices. As for those who choose the second, Erich Fromm sees two possible ways of retreating from freedom: political mechanisms of escape, that is, fascism, or neurotic escape.

Fascism provides an immediate, submissive, and unreflected way for individuals to belong to a group; it is a masochistic way of overcoming the growing gap between individuals and the community from which they have arisen; it is a retreat from the construction of rational and democratic society. As we just mentioned, fascism—and even more so Nazism—has been successful in organizing festivals of communion in which individuals gave up any kind of rational and personal contribution; they could only sacrifice themselves to the irrational guidance of a supposedly illuminated *Duce* or *Führer*. Humanity has bitterly learned the cost of such a surrender.

Other ways of escaping freedom are the neurotic escapes; they are processes of deindividuation. In these cases individuals, incapable of integrating themselves into a network of meaningful relationships, or unwilling to do so, give up becoming someone and through various artificial devices, regress into a nirvana state of primitive sensations. Alcohol, drugs, meaningless sounds, images, or lights may be used by individuals to deindividualize themselves and desert the fight for self-definition, and achievement.

Neurotic escapees have always existed. There were individual cases, the stubborn bums of skid row, the quays of Paris, the Bowery. Some poets joined them for a while. However, in the late sixties the phenomenon took on a social dimension. The counterculture denounced the pursuit of self-identity and defined the world of competition as selfish, irrational and materialistic.[14] Its followers rejected this world in favor of the brotherly and sisterly love of immediate communions. This choice meant not only giving up a career in the capitalist market, but everything associated with it, including the form of sociability typical of the modern competitive world: sociable conversation.[15] By contrast, the adepts of Consciousness III, as Charles Reich designates them, try to abolish the frontiers of the self. Turning their backs on rational discourse and the clash of theories or opinions, they retreat into the communion of similar sensations, they listen to the pure rhythm of rock music, they smoke marijuana or take acid, they lose themselves in the contemplation of psychedelic lights, hold hands and make love indiscriminately.

The sensuous gatherings of that counterculture have not totally disappeared. But these gatherings are seldom presented today as an alternative to careerism and personal achievement, nor are they seen as a substitute for conversational exchange. The rituals of immediacy are often found today preceding or continuing the more rational exchanges of modern sociability. In a kind of "half-way covenant," the generation which experienced the counterculture phenomenon surrendered the utopian withdrawal from the game and consented to deal with freedom. However, its members continue to express, through rituals of communal sensation, the message that the conquest for an identity in the world is useless if that achievement is not directed towards a reconstruction of the broken unity. In spite of their continued search for unity, these individuals have also rediscovered that love is no substitute for competence and hard work.

If the essential message of brotherly and sisterly love is kept in mind by the participants of social gatherings, it is likely that their conversation will not be limited to the exchange of identity support. This essential function will give way to the search for common values and the rebuilding of culture—at least after the basic credentials have been exchanged and trust has been established among the partners. This last condition is a sine qua non.

This means that even those who plan to dedicate their existence to the transformation of society's institutions, like all humans in the modern world, need to assess their potentials through interacting with others in social gatherings. Of course, they also use sociable conversation to convey their messages to others.

Not all gatherings offer the same chance of success for identity discovery and identity support. The participants will not be able to play their parts if the proper climate has not been created. Identity negotiation requires from the modern gathering that the guests have been correctly selected. They must represent "the world," they must possess some status homogeneity, they must constitute a balanced mix of previously acquainted and previously unacquainted individuals. Identity negotiation also requires a climate of freedom which permits each guest to engage the other guests at the party.

The choice of the participants depends essentially on the type of gathering. In the case of the family gathering, every member of the family is invited. This is true also of the gatherings which congregate school alumni and alumnae, veterans from a regiment, members of the local chapter of an association, or the colleagues in the office. This was also the case in the traditional upper-class larger gatherings to which all the members of the local aristocracy were invited. By contrast small dinner parties were and are limited to a few of the potential guests. Similarly selectiveness is the mark of modern middle-class parties, cocktail parties, buffet-dinners, and even larger receptions, which, given the size of the middle and upper-middle classes, could not pretend to congregate everyone. Not only could modern parties not do it, but their very character demands that they be selective.

A climate of excitement as well as the sense of festive formality could not be achieved if the modern gathering were not perceived as selective. As we said, modern social gatherings are representations of society in the two meanings of the word: first, they represent society because, since the whole society cannot be gathered in one place, the gathering contains only a sample of it. This supposes that the invited guests are judged as good representatives of "the world." People are then flattered and excited at the idea that they have been selected out of so many other possible candidates. This impression of selectiveness could not be elicited if the gathering were open to anyone who wanted to come, or if, given the size of the world, that is, of the local community, the gathering were so large that it conveyed the feeling that everyone in that community were present. Such gatherings resemble more the gatherings of the past which were not geared to incite daring performances from the participants, but rather aimed to establish a sense of belonging to the community.

Large numbers is not the only obstacle to the staging of an exciting societal play. The number of people must be related to the size of the room in which the gathering takes place. A well-filled room conveys the sense that everyone who was invited judged the gathering worthwhile attending, and this increases the feeling among the guests that they are participating in an important event. It increases their excitement, which in turn will manifest itself in animated high-pitched conversations and enhance performances. The same number of people, scattered in a large hall, would create the impression that very few people wanted to participate.

The impression of selectiveness is important not only to boost the morale of the participants, but also to facilitate their access to the other guests. Classical books of etiquette[16] tell us that even if not introduced to each other, all the guests who are gathered "in the house of a gentleman" are mutually accessible. They have been chosen by the hosts, people whose taste and judgment they trust. This selection then creates among the guests a sense of mutual ease which encourages them to approach each other confidently: the other guests will be a good match for them because they certainly belong to the same world. This alleged selection by the hosts is true only in part or rather only on those occasions when all the signs point to the idea that the other guests have been really chosen by the host. It may be that the gathering is in no way selective, either because the hosts wanted to repay their obligations to all whom they were in some way indebted; or perhaps they must host some official function which makes them the victims rather than the masters of a guest list. In a gathering perceived as very unselective, individuals do not feel totally entitled to approach unknown others. If, on the contrary, the guests perceive the party as being very selective, they will develop the conviction that they are among the chosen few who have been called to celebrate the occasion with the hosts. This fellowship brings the guests together and one does not hesitate to approach each individual.

No sense of selectiveness would be conveyed if the participants did not also have the feeling that the selected guests are good representatives of society, whatever this last word evokes for them. This alleged representational quality manifests itself in two ways: first, the gathering must contain representatives of the various walks of life which, for the invited guests, constitute the real world. If the guests come to a gathering with the more or less conscious desire to check themselves against the world, they must be convinced that the world is there in its variety if not in its totality. Second, the partners they meet must also possess a status which makes them valid, competent partners, as we shall conclude in Chapter 6. This means that they hope to find people, if not of a higher status, at least of a status comparable to their own. This in turn condemns any social gathering to be somehow homogeneous in terms of those determinants of status in a particular society. In our society status is mostly defined by education, income, and occupation. Homogeneity of status, however, does not mean similarity. Similarity of occupation may help start the interaction because of the common interests. It may also make it very dull. In exchange for the easiness of the interaction one must suffer the absence of challenge, of new discovery, and of provocation. The shop talk which easily develops among colleagues contradicts the very essence of a party as a representation of the world and as a stage for the performance not of one's daily roles but those of one's ideal self. In the same way, similarity of gender is not conducive to much excitement. In a society where sex roles are still quite different, the presence of representatives of both sexes may bring balance and richness of ideas and opinions. Moreover, sexual gratification, even if sublimated in the play form of flirtation, is part of most gatherings, at least in the case of heterosexual gatherings. Similarity, however, seems necessary in the area of social status. Social status almost always is associated with the class position, marked by specific manners, style, and taste. Everyone's social world is made up of people sharing the same life-style and values and this is true at whatever level of social stratification system one belongs. Seldom will a gathering with people of diverse social classes be successful. We mentioned already the difficulty for poorer people to "reciprocate" invitations from wealthier individuals. But even during the gathering itself people of different milieux will rarely have easy interactions, devoid of condescension and resentment. I remember a gathering in the house of a friend in Europe. Within a short period of time a segregation had occurred: a group of young (and rather poor) aristocrats met in one corner of the drawing room and were discussing genealogies, while the elegant bourgeois, executives and lawyers occupied the rest of the space and were talking of politics and movies. The barrier of language and interests which separated the two groups was even more profound than one of status. An effort at bringing them together would have been totally unnatural, a contrived enterprise bound to fail. In the United States class boundaries are not so clearly marked, but differences in income and cultural expectations still make it difficult for most laborers to have an interesting conversation with, say, a music critic. For example, the longshoreman's problems with his bosses and his union do not match the music critic's disputes with editors or a performer. The longshoreman's interest in the heavyweight championship may leave the music critic indifferent, while the comparison of the conducting styles of Pierre Boulez and Zubin Mehta sounds to the longshoreman like Martian philosophy. They do not have any common ground. As will be evident again and again in this book, the staging of oneself has no meaning if the other person(s) cannot understand the words and the syntax.

At a gathering—especially a large one—if people of different status are found, it is likely that they will contribute subgroupings. This is often seen at wedding parties at which the bride and the bridegroom are of different backgrounds. Each family at the party constitutes a separate gathering. Sometimes a third group develops, made up of a few individuals of both families who have discovered between themselves some affinity. Quite often the true reason for such splitting can be traced not to family links but to social class differences which make the interactions across family lines very difficult. A trained observer will easily find evidence for it in the ways the two parties are dressed, gesticulate, and express themselves.

If a gathering is very heterogeneous, it is not likely that it will at any time engage in a general conversation. This splitting of most gatherings into smaller groups facilitates our analysis. We shall indeed dedicate a chapter to the problems involved with general conversation, but all the remaining chapters will consider the most frequent cases of the small interacting groups: dyads, triads, foursomes, fivesomes—either when they constitute the gathering itself or when they are found within a larger party.

A last criterion in the choice of the participants is their degree of mutual acquaintance. To aptly represent the wider society in the eyes of the participants, a modern gathering must offer partly acquainted and partly unacquainted guests.[17] Partygoers feel reassured when they meet someone they know. The fact that some of the partygoers' regular acquaintances have been selected as good representatives of "the world," means that they themselves are not oddballs, but rather men and women of the world as well. On the other hand, guests know that their circles of friends and acquaintances do not constitute the whole world. Then in their desire to meet a wide representation of the world, partygoers expect also to find in the party many unknown individuals.

Modern gatherings are not only characterized by the type of guests who are invited, but also by a new structure of the gathering itself. This brings us back to our previous discussion of the varying degree of formality. Family gatherings are usually informal affairs, while the traditional dinner parties, dances, and garden parties of the upper classes were located at the more formal end of the continuum: introductions were quite solemnly performed, the topics of conversation were of a high level, a general conversation was often conducted by the host and the dress code was strict. Modern gatherings are more relaxed. They are called to permit interaction among the guests, and this presupposes that they can move around freely and engage in conversation whomever they wish. As we said, the game is mostly conversation, more precisely identity negotiation within conversational exchanges. This could not happen if the hosts had organized their gathering as a strictly written play, in which all the moves and activities of the guests would be planned: a seated dinner followed by a musical entertainment, itself followed by quadrilles or charades.

The guests want some freedom of movement within the gathering so that they can address those whom they think would be rewarding companions. This explains why typical modern gatherings are buffet dinners and cocktail parties, where people can circulate and change partners. Even seated dinner parties are usually preceded or followed by a period of freewheeling exchanges.

The guests also prefer a less formal atmosphere in terms of dress, speech, manners and so on. They do not want the gathering to look like a perfectly ceremonious ritual. They want a margin of freedom, permission to tell a risqué joke; they may want to act foolishly, to cross barriers of conduct; they want to flirt and amuse themselves. In other words, they demand a relaxation of the usual social controls. This relaxation in turn will help them to relax their own inner controls. This is why social gatherings in which freedom and relative informality are stressed usually contain a large number of relatively unacquainted people. The reason for this is that social control is lessened when the group is large and made up of relatively unacquainted people. This may seem surprising. People may feel more at ease, even freer in a small group of persons they know well. True. But their feelings of freedom and ease do not come from an absence of social control; rather, the climate of freedom originates in a clear understanding of mutual expectations. However strict these expectations may be, they are well known and no one has any problem determining how to behave. If two married couples, Robert and Jane, and Susan and Steve, eat together in a highway diner, Robert may know that Steve will not object to his kissing or even jokingly pinching Susan, while he knows extremely well that any mention of Steve's homosexual experiences in the navy will set off an explosion. Steve, on the other hand, may know that Robert does not object to jokes about his having been in jail a couple of times for smuggling cigarettes, but does not permit any familiarity with his wife. In this small group, social control is strict, deviance is immediately sanctioned, but since the rules of the game are well known, everyone can feel free to operate within their boundaries. In larger gatherings and when one does not know the other guests, the mapping of the situation is less clear. One may feel awkward not knowing what to say or do. On the other hand, since this situation is "very clearly unclear," one is allowed a certain boldness of speech and actions. If one makes a mistake it will be perceived by only a few, and the breaking of the crowd into smaller groups prevents the mistakes from being broadcast around or whispered about. They will fall on the silencing cushion of anonymity.

The greater flexibility found in modern gatherings does not mean, however, that these gatherings can be totally informal. Some people think that the more informal the party the more freedom they will have in showing their ideal selves. It is not true. Too much formality may be unbearable, but informality is not conducive to very exciting events. Too much informality makes the gathering feel so much like "business as usual" that the guests are not challenged to make any real effort to perform at their best level. By contrast with the generation of the sixties, young people today have rediscovered the artistry of the formal, or, at least, of what they call the semi-formal parties.

Actually many modern gatherings are announced as being "semi-formal." This designation conveys to the guests a duality of messages: the invitation to be dressed elegantly but also to use imagination in the selection of their clothes, the invitation to be ready for artistic performances of oneself but also to select freely one's companions and be relaxed when speaking with them. The modern gathering is then a blend of formality and flexibility, of elegance and creativity, of courtesy and audacity. It is more formal than the family gathering or the office party, but less ceremonious than the traditional upper-class parties.

The various features which characterize social gatherings—their nontask-oriented nature, their more or less formal quality, and their congruence with the type of society in which they occur—permit them to be proper settings for the performances of the participants. They do not determine the contents and the details of the guests' expected behavior. They define the limits, the boundaries or the rules of the games, not the game itself, which in a modern gathering remains the attempt to impress others with the presentation of one's ideal self and the readiness to reward others by supporting their own performances. Now that the stage has been properly set, the performances remain to be presented by the guests. The study of these performances will be the subject of the next chapter.

NOTES

1. Georg Simmel, *The Sociology of Georg Simmel*, Kurt H. Wolff trans. (Glencoe, Ill.: The Free Press, 1950), p. 45. Social gatherings are one among the play-like activities. There are also sacred celebrations, athletic competitions, games of all sorts, sports, and so on. These, too, belong to the large category of feasts, of plays, of nonwork activities. But what is said in general about festivity and play can be said in particular of social gatherings. Compare what we said in this paragraph with this passage from J. Huizinga's *Homo Ludens*:

[Play] . . . is never imposed by physical necessity or moral duty. It is never a task. It is done at leisure, during "free time". . . Here, then, we have the first main characteristic of play: that it is free, is in fact freedom. A second characteristic is closely connected with this, namely that play is not "ordinary" or "real" life. It is rather a stepping out of "real" life into a temporary sphere of activity with a disposition all of its own (J. Huizinga, *Homo Ludens* [New York: Roy Publishers, 1950], p. 8).

2. Ibid., p. 43. By contrast, task-oriented interactions are those "in which individuals grow together into units that satisfy their interests . . ." (p. 41) like "erotic instincts, objective interests, religious impulses, and purposes of defense or attack . . ." (p. 40).

3. William I. Thomas (see, for instance *The Unadjusted Girl* [Boston: Little, Brown 1923], pp. 61–63) coined the well-known expression the "definition of the situation," meaning that individuals in social interactions act according to the way they interpret the situation. If their interpretations correspond to those of their partners, the interaction will run smoothly. The more socially typified is a situation, the more it is likely to be similarly defined by all the participants in the interaction.

4. See Martin S. Weinberg, "Sexual Modesty, Social Meaning and the Nudist Camp," *Social Problems*, Vol. 12, no. 3 (Winter 1965), pp. 314–318.

5. Georg Simmel, op. cit., pp. 48–49.

6. Being very conscious of the possible dangers, one of the women we had invited to a cocktail party telephoned us at the last minute to say that she had given up attending our party. Until then she had thought she could combine

in one evening both our cocktail and a later Halloween costume party. But upon looking at herself in her Halloween costume, she had decided it would not present a favorable image of herself in our more sedate party: "People will think I am crazy [she meant frivolous] if I come dressed as I am: that is . . . as a harem princess, with my arms, shoulders and belly naked." We tried to persuade her that everybody would enjoy looking at her—and it was sincere since the woman is very attractive—but who knows, her fears perhaps were justified and even the good excuse of plans to attend a later Halloween party would not have stopped the gossip.

7. On the "excessive" and "chaotic" character of festivity see Roger Caillois, *Man and the Sacred*, Meyer Barash, trans. (Glencoe, Ill.: The Free Press, 1959).

8. This shows that festivity—and festive sociability—is not a departure from history; on the contrary, there would be no history if humans were not able to transcend their daily activities and point to those which are more important and must be brought to the consciousness of the whole group.

9. "Sociability is a *symbol* of life as life emerges in the flux or a facile and happy play; yet it also is a symbol of *life*." Georg Simmel, op. cit., p. 55.

10. The translator of Georg Simmel observes that *Gesellschaft* "is both 'society' and 'party' (in the sense of 'social or sociable gathering')." (Ibid., p. 44).

11. "Paradise is lost for good . . ." writes Erich Fromm, in *Escape from Freedom* (New York: Rinehart & Co., 1941), p. 63.

12. "By one course he (man) can progress to 'positive freedom'; he can relate himself spontaneously to the world in love and work, in the genuine expression of his emotional, sensuous and intellectual capacities; he can thus become one again with man, nature and himself without giving up the independence and the integrity of his individual self." (Ibid., p. 140.)

13. "The other course open to him is to fall back, to give up his freedom, and to try to overcome his aloneness by eliminating the gap that has arisen between the individual self and the world." (Ibid.)

14. A first adumbration of the counter-culture's musical expression can be found in the discovery and adoption of jazz by a large segment of the middle classes in the 1920s. Jazz in its freer rhythm, its nostalgic melodies, played at least at the onset by nonprofessionals, was an art form born on the outskirts of the affluent competitive society. It was a way of already opposing the immediateness of sensations and soul to the efficiency and the productivity of the industrial world. Jazz, however, was soon co-opted by business and became a sophisticated art form, with its professionals, its trade-marks and its schools.

15. A very negative description of sociable conversation can be found in Charles Reich's *The Greening of America*. Reich, who is an enthusiastic supporter of the counterculture, ignores the elements of "miterleben" which can be found in all sociable gatherings:

> Consider a social event among professional people—a dinner, cocktail party, garden party, or just a lunch among friends. Everything that takes place occurs within incredibly narrow limits. The events are almost completely structured around conversation. No one pays any sensual

attention to the food, the mind altering experience of the drink, or to the weather or to the non-verbal side of personality; the people do not listen to music together, or lie on the grass and look at the sky together or share food, or sit silently and exchange vibrations. They do not talk about philosophy or subjective experience. They do not strive for genuine relationships but keep their conversation at the level of sociability, one upmanship, and banter, all of which leave the individual himself uncommitted, and not vulnerable. Above all there is no exchange of brotherhood and love . . . the party is a dull affair (*The Greening of America* [New York: Bantam Books, 1970], p. 163).

Oscar Lewis, by contrast, compares cocktail parties to the exchanges that could be found in folk–rural societies, which certainly would have been considered by Charles Reich as more authentic: "In some villages, peasants can live out their lives without any deep knowledge or understanding of the people whom they 'know' in face-to-face relationships. By contrast, in modern cities, there may be more give and take about one's private, intimate life at a single 'sophisticated' cocktail party than would occur in years in a peasant village." Oscar Lewis' further observations on the "Folk–urban Continuum and Urbanization with special Reference to Mexico City," in John Walton and Donald Carns, *Cities in Change* (Boston: Allyn and Bacon, 2d ed., 1973), p. 63.

16. See Erving Goffman, *Behavior in Public Places* (New York: The Free Press, 1963), p. 135. Goffman quotes from *The Laws of Etiquette*, by a "Gentleman" (Philadelphia: Carey, Lee, and Blanchard, 1836):

If you meet any one whom you have never heard of before at the table of a gentleman, or in the drawing-room of a lady, you may converse with him with entire propriety. The form of "introduction" is nothing more than a statement by a mutual friend that two gentlemen are by rank and manners fit acquaintances for one another. All this may be presumed from the fact, that both meet at a respectable house. This is the theory of the matter. Custom, however, requires that you should take the earliest opportunity afterwards to be regularly presented to such an one (sic) (p. 101).

17. The only exceptions to this rule can be found in parties which do not really fit the definition of the "modern gatherings," like gatherings of a society's aristocrats (the old nobility or the modern power elite) who know the whole aristocratic family and cannot think that anybody in a gathering they attend could be unknown to them. The same could be true of the diplomatic colony that haunts the reception rooms of a capital city.

4
STAGING ONE'S IDEAL SELF

Joyce looked at her boyfriend John, who stood stiffly outside their host's front door. She could hear the chatter of unfamiliar voices. Joyce grabbed her lipstick and mirror from inside her purse and began going over and over her already perfect lips.

"Aren't you going to ring the bell? My hands are busy," she mumbled. John slowly withdrew his hands from his pockets and pressed the doorbell. Both straightened up expectantly. A burst of laughter exploded from within.

"It sounds like a good party, don't you think?" Joyce said, putting her lipstick away.

"As parties go, I guess, it sounds OK," John replied, looking downward.

"Oh, John, relax! Nobody's going to bite you. Why are you always so nervous?"

"No more nervous than you, my dear," he said, as the door opened.

Now the stage is set for the guests to meet the host and the other guests. Trepidation often seizes them when they are faced with the task of playing their ideal selves in front of strangers. This is particularly the case of those who have not formed any ideal image of themselves. For them, modern social gatherings take on an awesome aspect. They enter their hosts' living room gripped by stage fright, asking themselves why the devil they came. They would prefer to be cooking at their stoves, dictating letters to their secretaries, or supervising the shoe department.

For guests who have developed any ideal selves at all, the situation is not much more comfortable, even if the type of gathering is most conducive to self-presentation. While guests may be thankful to the hosts for offering them the opportunity of presenting the ideal selves to which they aspire, this gratitude does not eliminate the anxiety that accompanies any risky adventure. Individuals know that, in attempting to present their ideal selves, success is not automatically granted. No longer does the community tell people unequivocally who they are or will become. Therefore, in order to find themselves, individuals must make tentative performances for which they may receive applause as well as smirks of condescension or polite silence. Only after the fact will people know, through the reaction of others, whether they were convincing or not, whether they should go on in the same direction or change tracks. Modern individuals try their various role–identities, ultimately choosing the ones which they play best and for which they are most often rewarded. The tentative and consequently imperfect nature of these performances condemn individuals to try again and again.[1]

Another reason for the endless trials is the variety of values and norms found in the various partners to whom individuals present themselves in a "modern social gathering." Some of them may feel or think on wave lengths different from those of the performer. Individuals may also doubt the competence or the sincerity of those who grant them support. All this means that the identities for which individuals are trying to get support are continuously in need of new legitimation. This then explains why in a modern gathering guests are continuously shifting partners. After having been encouraged by an apparently too benevolent interlocutor, guests may try to get confirmation for their performances from a more severe judge. Or, on the contrary, after people have been snubbed by a recalcitrant partner, they may be looking for a more rewarding companion. This explains not only the shifting of partners but also the unending desire to attend new social gatherings in the hope of finding better (or at least continued) support for one's fragile ideal self.

We shall study later—in Chapter 8—how the reciprocal nature of sociable performances manifests itself in conversation. Here we analyze how all participants in the gathering try to define their parts in the play and stage it with success.

We can compare the part of the guests in a social gathering to that of performers in the sixteenth to eighteenth century commedia dell'arte tradition. However, those performers' parts were much easier to play, because even if they had to improvise the details of the script, the roles themselves were clearly defined: the childlike and amorous Arlecchino, Columbine the soubrette, or Pantalone the rich but miserly merchant. In a social gathering the performance is much more problematic, because the role itself must be chosen by the performer, who must "play" it in the same sense that children play, by choosing a certain role and by trying to stage a convincing performance.[2] Social gatherings are testing grounds for role–identities. Performances are then a way, not only of showing what individuals think they are, but also a way for people to discover their possibilities, and their limits. The rule of the game in modern social gatherings is trial and error, a difficult process which may create anxiety in the participants. The difficulty is compounded by the imprecise character of the situation: individuals do not know their audience, and consequently do not know whether they will be able to stage a convincing performance. Given this situation, participants in a social gathering are confronted with three interrelated problems: first, they must present to the other guests an aspect of themselves—a role–identity—to which they can relate; second, they must perform this role–identity in a way that matches the audience's conception of what this role is; and third, they must possess the expressive tools—words and appearances—which will convey to the audience the image they intend.

The first problem could be called the problem of the situational self.[3] Arriving guests must present one or several role–identities which are compatible with their prospective audience's areas of expertise. Unfortunately, often the arriving guests do not know who their audience will be. Theoretically, they represent a good sample of society, but this is pure theory. The world of today is so differentiated that people cannot hope that each social gathering will attain such a level of universal representation. Quite often we hesitantly search for proper partners and do not find them. A person who is a computer programmer, a football fan, a stamp collector, or a born-again fundamentalist is in trouble when introduced to an audience where no one has any interest in computers, football, stamps, or religion. When we meet guests at a party we really cannot be sure that we shall be able to establish any rapport with them. Each time we meet a new partner, we are faced again with the problem of discovering areas of mutual competence and interest.

We shall discuss later—in Chapter 8—how we proceed to uncover and discover these mutual areas of interest. What must be stressed here is that guests are seldom "at peace" during a party, but rather they hover in a state of limbo, wondering if they possess the role–identities necessary for conversing with the other guests.

Not only must the guests choose from among their role–identities one which will be of interest to their audience, but they must also adapt their play to the audience's perception of the roles they have chosen to perform. This second problem is even more difficult to solve than the first one, because it supposes that the performers know how their partners' minds are structured, how they see the world, what their values and ideologies are. Symbolic interactionists have insisted upon this rather elementary truth already propounded by medieval philosophers: whatever message is received by our partners in conversation is interpreted by them according to their minds' structure.[4] In a party, before guests can perform successfully one of their tentative roles, they must discover how their audience defines them. For instance, a man must know how his audience perceives a great violinist, a good journalist, or a good business executive, in order to successfully convey the impression that he is that great violinist, that good journalist, or that good business executive. Regular readers of *Time* magazine, who want to convince others that they are foreign policy experts may easily succeed with people who spend their whole leisure time watching sports on television, but, while conversing with more informed guests, they must present other credentials besides the reading of *Time*, if they want to fulfill their definition of an expert. And stockbrokers who win applause when they tell an audience of how they helped bankers increase their income by 15 percent in each of the last four years, may prefer to tell how they are specializing in helping lower-middle-class families to protect their savings from inflation when they converse with politically committed leftists. The nouveau riche man who wants to be known as a paragon of elegance will get approving glances from a group of successful traveling salesmen when he puts on his flashy blue polyester tuxedo, his flowery embroidered shirt, his red tie, and his five-colored patchwork shoes, but he may suspect that he must dress more soberly when invited to an upper-middle-class dinner.

Some people excel at speaking the language of the various audiences they encounter. A music critic we know can discuss the fine points of atonal composition with a professor from the Manhattan

School of Music, but he can also converse with an opera fanatic on the respective merits of Luciano Pavarotti's and Placido Domingo's voices, and he can successfully question a group of high school students on what constitute the exact differences between ordinary rock and punk rock. He always plays the same role—that of musical critic—but he performs the role in a way that is meaningful to each of his different audiences.

Few people, however, have the ability to relate to a great variety of audiences. They can present themselves successfully to only one category of people, for instance their colleagues, their classmates, their relatives, or their small neighborhood cliques. They always play the same tune to the same audience. This may be due to their limited knowledge of the world beyond their own small circle. They prudently remain on the ground they know. They may also have a rather good perception of how they should perform in order to be recognized by this or that partner, but feel unable to meet their expectations.

The limitations they perceive in themselves constitute the third and not the least of the problems met by would-be performers in a social gathering: do they possess the talents needed to stage an efficient performance? These talents are quite different from those needed for the actual fulfillment of daily tasks and roles. There, competence, knowledge, and perhaps physical ability are needed. But in a social gathering the "tools of the trade" are of an expressive, not a technical nature. The best banker in the world, the most astute politician, the very successful engineer, do not necessarily know how to express themselves. Sociability requires the use of expressive tools which they may not possess; these tools are: appearance, body language, and words which, given the specific audience, will convey who the performers are or want to be, without having to give an actual technical demonstration. Many feel inhibited by physical or intellectual limitations in their attempts at expressing themselves. Also, they may feel that they do not possess the flexibility necessary to alter their speech habits, their body postures, and their symbolic clothes and accessories. The limitations may be due to financial constraints, lack of education or a narrowness of life experience which mars the performers' abilities to successfully perform for more than one audience. This inflexibility may be found at every level of the social class system, it may affect any of the means through which we present ourselves to others in a social gathering.

Among our expressive tools, the most flexible is the content of our speech. While our clothes and accessories can hardly be changed during a party, they can be chosen beforehand to suit each gathering, supposing at least that our wardrobe is diversified enough. We can also modify our body postures, our gestures, and our manners, but these changes require some learning and practice. The same can be said of our pronunciation and accent. The very shape of our bodies—which says a lot about who we are—is the least flexible of our expressive tools. We cannot change our shape, at least not without considerable advance notice and exertion.

Modern gatherings consist essentially of conversation. The main element of our performance is what we say, the stories we tell, the memories of past experiences, the plays or shows we have attended, the people, the places, the countries we know, the books or articles we read, the music or paintings we like, the funny sides of our work, the dramatic events in the lives of known or unknown people. We express ourselves through statements, evaluations, approvals, criticisms, questions, and answers. Not only is our speech the most important element of our party performances, it is also the most flexible one. Theoretically, it can be modified any time, considering the partner with whom we converse. This theoretical flexibility, however, is limited by the history of each individual. Human beings' language is determined by their experience within the many sectors which constitute the social universe. Each of our role–identities connects us with a subworld of activities, people, instruments, techniques, standards, and values. These in turn are designated by trade names or words that anyone familiar with that subworld knows. There are the subworlds of automobiles, of baseball, of cosmetics, of law, of religion, of films, of fashion, or of foreign politics—itself divided into so many geographical areas. Every conversation that goes beyond the weather is carried within one of these subworlds. And when individuals pass from television to golf, it is like putting a new cassette into a player. If we hope to interact with a film buff, we will pull out of our memory our own film subworld made of the specific movies we saw, of directors, filming techniques, actors, film critics, and so on. If, then, our partner suggests shifting to golf, we will choose another "cassette" on which are recorded descriptions of various golf courses, golf champions' records, brands of clubs, comparisons of various tees, greens, fairways, sand traps, and mounds. This supposes, of course, that we do possess the right cassettes. Well-rounded personalities, that is, men and women of the world, possess in their heads large collections of such cassettes, which permit them to converse with a wide variety of individuals at a party. And it is great fun for them to jump elegantly from one universe into another. Of course no one has attained a total flexibility; no one possesses the full collection of cassettes corresponding to all possible subworlds. This would require an encyclopedic mind like that of the fifteenth century's Pico della Mirandola whose was a most famous and perhaps last example. On the other hand, few are as unfortunate as my friend Susie who told me of a disastrous date that took place during the winter of 1957 in Chicago. She had been invited to dinner and a movie by a young man named Bob. But during the dinner they could not find any common topic of conversation. Bob could only speak of automobiles, physics, baseball, and girls. Susie was only interested in sixteenth-century music, fashion, tennis, and boys. They sat silently in the restaurant for a full hour, anxiously waiting until it was time to go to the movie theater to see *God Created Woman.* This is an extreme case. Most of us, however, when we attend a party are more or less anxiously wondering what common interests and expertise we possess to meet others' subworlds.

The fact that various social classes have developed subworlds of verbal and behavioral symbols is not necessarily a handicap for those who aspire to a higher status, if they succeed in learning to make an appropriate use of those symbols. At a social gathering individuals are expected to do their best and no one objects if people skillfully, without overdoing it, use speech patterns, behavior, or dress that belongs to the class best represented by the gathering.

In every conversation we mention names of people, places, and things that are the signs of our roles and status in society. And this is perfectly normal. Much of this is done almost unconsciously and naturally in the course of a conversation. As these references pile up, they give others an increasingly clear impression of the subworlds in which we operate. The simple mention of a specific name, place, or object may, at times, suffice, if they are known only to a very select number of people. They act as passwords. The very fact of uttering them locates one within the select circle. This select circle, by the way, is not necessarily upper-class. It can be any ingroup which has developed its own symbols. It can be the in-group of baseball, or rock singers, or stamp collectors, or a social class. I remember how in the early 1950s, at the time of the cold war, the European working class was passionately divided about endorsing or not endorsing the Stockholm Peace Appeal. To some it was a symbol of real love for peace and to others it was sheer Soviet propaganda. But whether they approved or not, no one in the working class ignored it. At a business bargaining session, the famous Appeal was mentioned by one of the union leaders, to which a representative of the corporation replied: "Sorry, what did you say? What is this 'Stockholm Appeal'?" The union members looked at each other in thorough amazement, as though saying, "How is it possible not to know the Stockholm Appeal?"

Many individuals, who do not possess any real expertise in their partners' subworlds, still do not hesitate to converse with them on the basis of prestigious key words, such as names of actors they've never seen act, titles of books they have not read, famous resorts and hotels they have never visited, popular politicians whose precise activities and policies they do not know, fashion designers from whom they do not buy, and so on. To show their expertise, they drop the name at what they think is the appropriate moment. They praise politicians because of their good looks, declare an actress fantastic because she is sexy, extol a film because the critic Vincent Canby likes it, applaud a dress because it is expensive or comes from the right designer. They sprinkle their conversation with adjectives like splendid, fantastic, superb, and so on, without ever being able to explain or analyze what makes the play, the film, the actor, the dress, or the politician so admirable. The game, however, is futile and counter-productive. It is also risky because the dropping of a name may, in fact, reveal that the speaker just pretends and does not have a precise knowledge of the place or of the person. Anyone can pick up names from television commercials or news. The game can be dangerous or devastating if individuals' partners in the conversation are better informed than they on the whereabouts of the people mentioned or on the details of the symbolic places, shows, books, whatever. If, for example, a speaker attributes to Fellini the film *A Clockwork Orange* or if they refer to San Francisco as "that beautiful city in South America," not only is the desired effect not produced, but the speaker completely loses face. Name dropping characterizes what could be called a fake performance. By contrast, a real performance, even if it does not reveal perfect expertise, shows some familiarity with the subject, an interest which goes to the very root of it, an effort at reaching for the merit of things, whether they be politics, dressmaking, or films, and not, as in fake performances, making a purely extrinsic evaluation on the basis of fashion and fads. Name dropping, instead of permitting the performers to demonstrate their ideal selves, on the contrary destroy the images which they are trying to present.[5]

Less flexible than speech content, but still capable of much adaptation to the circumstances, are the clothes individuals wear when they go to a social gathering. Of course, unlike our vocabulary, we cannot change clothes during a party. We are stuck with them and with the message they convey to our host and the other guests. Many of us have experienced the lasting embarrassment of being too formally or too informally dressed, given the nature of the party. However, if we had been told in advance what the party would be like, we might have tried to adapt to the expectations. This presupposes not only that we have expectations, but also that we possess the appropriate clothes. Lack of money, however, may not be the sole explanation for not having them. If one excludes very limited snobbish circles in which it is expected that the members buy the latest very expensive designer clothes, most groups are contented with someone wearing affordable clothes. The problem, then, is less financial ability than knowledge of what the various types of clothes disclose of one's identity, given the group's expectations.

People often base their first impressions on the clothes worn by a new acquaintance. And first impressions themselves are responsible for putting a human interaction on the right or the wrong track. A first impression suggests the topic of conversation, and determines the questions that one guest will direct to another. In turn, target individuals will answer according to information gleaned from those first questions—in an area they did not choose but that they may involuntarily have suggested through their presentations—and their responses will tend to reinforce the first impressions.[6] In this sense the first impressions are self-perpetuating, and it is in the interest of individuals to control them, by seeing to it that others intuitively and immediately perceive them as they want to be perceived.[7] If the interaction has advanced on the proper course from the beginning, individuals will have gained time and plausibility in staging the role–identities they have chosen to present. Unless they want to confuse their partners or play some kind of practical joke, guests will make sure that their presentations in general and their clothes in particular convey to new acquaintances an impression in keeping with the role–

identities they have chosen. Seldom do clothes immediately reveal a role–identity. But they often reveal the social class to which individuals belong and since role–identities and social status are associated, clothes either confirm or deny a specific role identity.

The variability of clothing style according to social class permits an experienced eye to assess at first sight the social class of an individual. In Peter Benchley's *Jaws*, the Brodys (the Amity police chief and his wife) have organized a dinner party in honor of Matthew Hooper, the young shark specialist of upper-class origins.

> At 7:05 the door bell rang and Brody answered it. He was wearing a blue madras shirt, blue uniform slacks, and black cordovans. He felt crisp and clean. Spiffy, Ellen had said. But when he opened the door for Hooper he felt, if not rumpled, at least outclassed. Hooper wore bell-bottom blue-jeans, Weejun loafers with no socks, and a red Lacoste shirt with an alligator on the breast. It was the uniform of the young and rich in Amity.[8]

In certain instances the clothes directly reveal the role–identity of an individual. Certain occupational roles require their holders to wear a uniform. This was more often true in the past, when army or navy officers, ministers and bishops, or priests and nuns were required by their superiors as well as the public to wear a uniform, even at social functions where it was clear they were not supposed to perform their official duties. Some other roles are indicated by less readily visible signs, such as political buttons or club insignia. In all of these cases the role holders are easily identified. It brings clarity to the expectations others may have towards them but puts severe restraints on the individuals who might at times prefer to offer another image of themselves. The bishop becomes an easy prey to those who want to discuss the last Vatican decision. He might have preferred to discuss his stamp collection. The army officer must sustain a difficult conversation on the army's role in Korea or Indochina, when coins or baroque music are his real passions. Nowadays, most of these role holders leave their uniforms at home before joining a social gathering. They are freer to redefine their roles, even if their anonymity may create some problems, as was the case when a pretty but "anonymous" nun baffled observers by resisting an elegant bachelor's repeated invitation to dance to a slow, romantic ballad with him.

There are cases where the absence of the expected clothes deprives individuals of social credibility. Saint-Exupéry in *Le petit prince* tells the story of a Turkish astronomer who was not initially accorded the credit due him for his discovery of an asteroid because he lacked the proper clothes. When he presented his findings in a paper at a world convention before World War I, no one paid attention to his words. Dressed in a traditional Turkish costume, he could not convince his Western audience that he was a reliable scientist. But after the war and after all the Turkish men were compelled by Kemal Ataturk to wear European-style clothes, our astronomer read his paper again, this time impeccably dressed in striped suit, white shirt, and black and white tie. It was greeted with great applause and little Asteroid B 612 was at last given recognition.[9]

Similarly, if when visiting our spouses's boss we want to underscore our role as a serious member of the community, we will avoid clothes which directly contradict that script, such as a provocative dress or pair of pants. Similar remarks could be made of the judge, the police officer, the minister, the president of overseas services, the secretary of the Movement for the Ordination of Women, and so on. Since persons of responsibility represent important values in society, they shy away from clothes which may be interpreted as frivolous and sexually alluring or, worse, associated with criminal behavior. Judges cannot dress like hippies or wear leather jackets and bicycle chains around their necks. Ministers would have difficulty getting approval if they appeared wearing a pink cravat and five gold rings, looking like pimps. Similarly, the president of the corporation will not usually be seen at a dinner party in a canary yellow three-piece suit with a green and red tie.[10]

Let us remember, however, that everything depends on what individuals want to convey. They might want to tell new acquaintances at a social gathering that their official roles really do not reveal their inner capabilities. In this case individuals distance themselves from their roles: "Role distance," writes Peter Blau, "is an attempt to show that the demands of a role are beneath one's capabilities."[11] The holders of the role will then very intentionally display themselves in clothes which are at variance with what others expect of their socially imposed roles. The famous district attorney will dress in an Italian tailored suit and wear a carnation in his lapel. This will perfectly fit his conversation—if you hear it—about *The Last Tango in Paris* or a newer film of that ilk.

More difficult to change than our clothes, and consequently less apt at conveying to others the image we hope to present are our body postures and gestures. People accustomed to slumping in their armchairs will probably not sit erect while eating at their bosses' tables, nor will they persuade their bosses that they could become good public relations representatives for their companies. A certain abandoned or ungainly way of walking is more typical of lower- or lower-middle-class men. How could they in a social gathering aspire to a status that their gestures deny? Seldom would upper-class adults—at least in the presence of others—rest their feet on a table or, in a movie theater, on the back of the seat in front of them. They sit straight on their chair or armchair, with their legs crossed or in a parallel position. By remaining noticeably stiffer or more formal than everyone else, upper-class guests often hope to be distinguished from their more "ordinary" counterparts. Similarly, a young woman who has seriously studied ballet will have developed a form of carriage which will distinguish her from the other women at the office party. She just does not seem to be "one of the girls." Many political candidates never succeed because their refined manners place them among the rich and privileged people: How can the poorer classes be convinced they would take their interests to heart? It is not that the candidate does not try. I know of a political candidate who always took off his tie when visiting with his proletarian "friends." But this could not erase the elegance of his posture and gesticulation which associated him—in the eyes of the audience—with the upper echelons of society.

Our pronunciation and accent are even more difficult to correct and adapt to the situation. Our speech reveals our regional origin; more often, it betrays our social class. This means that in the presentation of ourselves, we won't be able to claim an identity associated with a class too different from the one revealed by our accent or pronunciation, particularly if our partners can be considered competent judges. A cockney shopkeeper may want to be introduced as an upper-class businessowner; this act may be *bought* by other cockney-speaking individuals, but will be unconvincing to the alumni of Oxford or Cambridge. These individuals, in turn, will not easily convince their companions in a railroad dining car that they are just workers like themselves. Native Spaniards, who, from their first years, have used the lisping pronunciation of the letters c and z, will have a hard time convincing their Mexican friends that they feel just as they do about Mexican culture and independence. A heavy accent must be corrected if one wants to convince an audience that one is an up-and-coming speech coach for the American Academy of Dramatic Arts. The play *Pygmalion* and the musical version, *My Fair Lady*, depict some of the hardships encountered when one struggles to modify speech patterns.

Speech patterns which have become a kind of second nature are also very hard to modify and adapt to our different audiences. The problem is that they may reveal a social origin which is not compatible with the role–identity we would like to portray. In France, for instance, while lower-class people are very direct and may use the equivalent of the American "Hi!" ("*salut!*"), middle-class individuals have adopted and employ an array of expressions from the old bourgeoisie which are strictly rejected today in upper- or upper-middle-class circles. We may mention among others; "*Enchanté*" (Delighted), "*Au plaisir*" (Hope to have the pleasure of seeing you again), "*A votre santé*" (To your health), and so on. The rejection of these and other expressions by the upper classes is so strict that the use of one of them once may exclude an individual from being invited, dated, or married.

In general, Americans do not detect differences in manners of speech as sharply as do Europeans. However, an abundant use of four-letter words and ungrammatical expressions such as "I ain't," and sentences such as "Him and mom went to the movies," or "It don't make no difference to me," will be interpreted as signs of lower-class status by a middle-class listener.

The least flexible and adaptable of our expressive tools is the body itself, and more precisely its shape. To a large extent the body is genetically determined and only drastic measures can modify this heritage; other aspects are the result of our past exercise, our activities, our occupations, our diet, and so on. Once these have shaped the body, the results cannot be changed easily. Our bodies have become a rather inflexible expression of what we are. Our bodies speak. The problem is: Do our bodies say what we wish them to say, in particular to the other people we meet at a gathering? There are two aspects to the question: first, does the body appear to be under the discipline of the mind, or, on the contrary, does the body seem to dominate the mind, and secondly, if the body's control is not complete, perhaps as a result of past activities, what does it tell the audience?

People cannot live as human beings and perform daily chores without having some control over their bodies. Lean figures, agility and rapidity of movement, healthy-looking skin and hair will convince the audience that the individuals' minds are really in charge of their bodies. And the more individuals can rely on their bodies as faithful and flexible instruments, the more roles they can hold and the better they can perform them. Self-control and internal security are a must for staging any role–identity but artistic roles especially require even greater mastery of the mind over resistance of the body.

Past occupations have marked our bodies and left in them signs which are obstacles to communicating identities too different from those associated with the occupations. These signs may help guests to persuade new acquaintances of their identities if they want to insist upon the said occupation, but the signs will belie all effort if these individuals want to identify with a different role or status. Strong bodies reveal individuals dedicated to physical exercise. The coarseness or the elegance of the body structure will suggest whether the vigorous quality comes from heavy manual work or from athletic pastimes. Except in the professional athlete, a strong but elegant figure, accompanied by a healthy tan, will reveal not only preoccupation with good appearance, but also availability of time and resources demanded for elite sports. Opposite is the impression received from the heavy-set man accustomed to carrying merchandise. Mary McCarthy again in "The Genial Host" observes the inconsistent picture presented by the stocky merchant Pflaumen in his elegant clothes. He had made an enormous effort to learn good manners, but he had not succeeded in dissimulating his plebeian body structure.[12] This suggests that the shapes of our bodies is determined relatively early in life and that correction at a later age, while not impossible, is not easy, and consequently limits the possibility of deviating considerably from former role–identities in the building of one's new identity.

A final element (and not the least) in the presentation is the companion with whom individuals make their entry at a social gathering. The people we publicly associate with are a very vivid expression of who we are. Our association can be extremely flexible if we are totally unattached, but for those who are linked to a partner by marriage or a similarly solid bond, little can be done: Their companion becomes part of their performance. Would-be diplomats, politicians, ambitious young executives, all are very conscious that the choice of their spouses plays a great role in persuading others of how successful they are or are going to become. Their entrance at a party holding the hand of an attractive spouse speaks more about their self-images than anything they could say. Of course, if their partners are in no way appealing and the audience very critical, the opposite message will be conveyed.

For those who are unattached, there may be several reasons for not going alone to a party. In some cases, the gathering is so large and anonymous that there will probably not be many people one knows and with whom one would be able to converse. In these cases, people feel uncomfortable entering a room full of strangers, so they often bring along a friend. The excitement of a large gathering may function as a backdrop for two friends or a couple who entertain each other and exchange impressions. Others feel awkward at being seen entering a room full of guests alone: Perhaps they do not want others to believe that they are alone in life and could not find a friend to accompany them. To arrive at a party accompanied by a "good" companion enhances the image that the arriving guest communicates. On the contrary, if people are not totally enthusiastic about the presentations made by their spouse, lover, or friend, they may be tempted to dissociate themselves from their companion. They may try to conceal their tie to the undesirable individual. But, apart from the tension that this betrayal may create between the two spouses, lovers, or friends, it may lead other guests to commit a *faux pas* and get embarrassed, if, for instance, they start openly courting an "undeclared" lover or spouse. This shows that little can be done to avoid the consequences of one's personal bonds of friendship or marriage. They too belong to the rather inflexible signal system by which we tell others who we are.

The previous reflections in this chapter suggest that the expressive instruments we possess set limits to the range of role–identities which we can hope to present in a social gathering and to the range of audiences which we can favorably impress. Even if in our "inner-forum" we have succeeded in persuading ourselves that we possess great talent and potential yet unknown to our audiences, nevertheless our resources may be inadequate for staging a persuasive performance. An awareness of our limitations may convince us we should not try to engage certain audiences whose expectations are beyond our capacities to fulfill. Our vocabularies, clothes, manners, physical appearance, may fail to meet the standards of a given group and so we feel shut out. Experience has taught us that our education, income level, and past experiences make us incompatible with people who are too much above or too much below our social class. This awareness is at times distressing, when, after entering a social gathering, we suddenly realize that we do not fit in, or when, after attempting a conversation with a guest, we realize that we possess few common interests and experiences. The feeling may be pain or embarrassment. However, we can take consolation in the thought that no one can really pretend to please everyone.

There is actually something much more unfortunate than the awareness of not fitting in properly. It is an unawareness of our audience's standards and a consequent blindness to what our performances mean to the others.[13] Sometimes we mistakenly believe we acted magnificently or at least appropriately because no one tells us of the negative impression we created. A regional accent, for instance, may win sympathy from those coming from the same area, but may sound extremely provincial to those from another area or from a more cosmopolitan setting. Performers may be totally unaware of the impact of their accents. Other individuals may be very conscious and proud of their choice of words but unaware that they may be interpreted as a sign of pomposity, vanity, or ignorance by another audience. The same is true of manners. Many people have painfully learned what they think are good manners, not knowing that these "good manners" are very relative to the social subworld in which they move. When invited, they confidently carry with them their good manners and are persuaded that they act according to the most exquisite etiquette. In reality they may demonstrate that they are outsiders. Norbert Elias, in his entertaining book *The Civilizing Process*, refers to a conversation between a certain Abbé Cosson and the poet Delille. The poet narrates how he challenged the conduct of the over-excited but well-intentioned Abbé at an elegant dinner party at Versailles:

> A short while ago Abbé Cosson, Professor of Belles Lettres at the Collège Mazarin, told me about a dinner he had attended a few days previously with some *court people* . . . at Versailles.
>
> "I'll wager," I told him, "that you perpetrated a hundred incongruities."
>
> "What do you mean?" Abbé Cosson asked quickly, greatly perturbed. "I believe I did everything in the same way as everyone else."
>
> "What presumption! I'll bet you did nothing in the same way as anyone else. But I'll limit myself to the dinner. First, what did you do with your serviette [napkin] when you sat down?"
>
> "With my serviette? I did the same as everyone else. I unfolded it, spread it out, and fixed it by a corner to my buttonhole."

"Well, my dear fellow, you are the only one who did that. One does not spread out one's serviette, one keeps it on one's knees. And how did you eat your soup?"

"Like everyone else, I think. I took my spoon in one hand and my fork in the other. . . . "

"Your fork? Good heavens! No one uses his fork to eat soup. . . . But tell me how you ate your bread."

"Certainly, like everyone else: I cut it neatly with my knife."

"Oh dear, you break bread, you do not cut it. . . . Let's go on. The coffee—how did you drink it?"

"Like everyone, to be sure. It was boiling hot, so I poured it little by little from my cup into my saucer."

"Well, you certainly did not drink it like anyone else. Everyone drinks coffee from the cup, never from the saucer. . . ."[14]

Similarly during a Christmas party we attended several years ago, the general manager of a major industry wanted to demonstrate to his employees and their families that he was a good-natured, friendly boss. In trying to be "one of the crew," he stepped outside of his bounds and indulged in obscenities, which conveyed to his employees that he was an outsider, after all. His employees may not have spoken the King's English, and they may have occasionally used some profane words, but rarely if ever would they do so at a fancy party.

In a similar way many people are unaware that their demeanor, clothes, and accessories convey to their listeners an impression totally different from what they had intended. The 65-year-old woman dresses as a teen-age girl and thinks she makes a wonderful impression on every man at the party. They do not tell her what they think of her, of course. I once met a very old man who had had a face-lift, had dyed his hair, and dressed like a dandy. When he left, I heard someone commenting: "Why don't people let themselves age naturally?"

What is slightly frightening is that one single serious flaw may be the ruin of an otherwise effective performance. The staging of one's ideal self must demonstrate real familiarity with the intended role as it is perceived and expected by the audience, in order to be convincing. If we make a significant mistake—and one is enough—it shows that the pretended role is not really part of ourselves and we are accused of playing at something that we really are not.[15] How can one believe Anthony is a real wine expert if he mentions Tokay as a wine from Argentina? How can Susan claim to be an international bridge player if the name of Ely Culbertson does not mean anything to her? How can a violinist be taken seriously and never have heard of Paganini? And who is this pretended gourmet who cannot distinguish between beef Stroganoff and a goulash soup? How can one pretend to be an expert on American painting and then confuse the work of Thomas Doughty with that of Thomas Cole?

Here, again, the mistakes to avoid are relative to the "audience." The self-declared music critic may confuse two composers, say Tchaikowsky and Shostakovitch, in front of a musically ignorant partner. The very utterance of these difficult names will win the title of music expert, unless the critic is in a group of musically sophisticated people, where the confusion will constitute irrevocable failure.

While only one negative trait may destroy a performance, several of the positive traits that constitute a role–identity must be exhibited, if one wants to be convincing. The display of merely one impressive quality could be taken as some kind of fortuitous event or good luck. Painters may allude to the fact that their paintings get sold before they are even dry. But one hesitates to attribute to them the identity of great painter before one also knows that they exhibited last year in the major galleries in New York, London, and Paris. Executives who say they are being sent by their firm to the World Congress of Young Executives in Bali will be even more convincing if they add that they will also chair a special commission on "How to Elicit the Spirit of Enterprise in Developing Nations." Jet-setters offer to show their partners the latest dance step they saw at the fashionable night club, but they will have more credibility if they can mention whom they have seen there recently, and if their attire corresponds to the listener's expectation of a jet-setter.

These examples reaffirm a basic principle: In an attempt to impress others, performers risk failure if they stage performances that are too distant from their actual life experiences. This compels individuals to stage role–identities with which they are really familiar and to perform for audiences of which they know the language and the norms. It is true that in the presentation of themselves at a social gathering, people are encouraged to use imagination, inventiveness, and to make an effort to impress others. But their inventions and choices must remain within the limits of reality. Except for some very rare occasions when the common understanding is that we can lie about who we are and conceal it entirely, as during masquerades and carnival parties, people cannot totally dissociate from their marital status, occupation, age, place of origin, and so on. Margins of deviance are allowed regarding our precise hierarchical position or age, but here, too, discretion will prevent us from assuming a status with which we have really no familiarity. To do otherwise would lead to unavoidable pitfalls, which would ruin the carefully contrived performance.

Given the difficulties encountered in making a convincing presentation of one's ideal self, the reader may be tempted to think that most performances in a social gathering are condemned to fail. The obstacles are overwhelming: We must offer others a variety of role–identities, possess a wide flexibility of expression in order to meet the expectations of all kinds of audiences, and we often wonder what these expectations could be. Given all the difficulties, would it not be better to give up and retreat from playing a role? Why not relinquish any personal claims and simply sit back modestly, at most playing the part of the gracious listener? The answer is: It will be less of a strain, perhaps, but will not bring much reward either to the modest individuals nor to their companions. Those who have chosen modesty end up either receiving no recognition whatsoever from others, or else collecting support for aspects of themselves which they consider insignificant or unworthy. A case in point is a mathematics professor I know who considers himself, and possibly is, a good violinist, but must, again and again, answer questions about the best methods of teaching math in grade school. Maurice was a chemical scientist but his real interest was in literature and music. I have often heard him politely answer questions about chemical processes which did not interest him. He was extremely modest and most people were unaware of the fact that under a pseudonym he was writing the music criticism column in the local daily. Modesty has another drawback. Modest people are considered to be less desirable companions at social gatherings because most others look for support from prestigious people. "So and so told me I was very elegant," or very witty, or extremely interesting, and so on. All these reinforcements would not have been noticed if so and so were not someone whose judgment is sought, that is, if so and so had not convinced others that his or her judgments were important. Conversely, as Peter Blau observes, an effort to impress others signifies to them that their approval is deemed important. It is said that when Cocteau met Diaghilev for the first time, he said to him: "Astonish me!" Similarly the young man who tries his best to impress his date by mentioning important people and places shows that he cares about the image she forms of him.

Conversely modesty may also be offensive to the other guests, for modesty tells them indirectly that they are not worth the performers' efforts. Strangely enough, then, modesty can be interpreted as a sign of arrogance.[16]

Modest and shy guests are also irritating to the hosts. "People who take a wait-and-see attitude I could kill; they spoil it for everyone," said Kate Medina, a Doubleday editor. "A wonderful guest is one who doesn't sit on the edge watching. A wonderful guest is someone who charms, who communicates—who, in short, really wants to be there. A wonderful guest notices the effort the hosts have put into it, and for the next few hours, anyway, makes a commitment to really *be* there, to give something special of himself, to really *tell* you about his day."[17]

Modesty is useful only if a high reputation has preceded it or if a first performance has succeeded in creating such an impression on others that they may be tempted to shy away from the interaction, especially if they consider themselves unattractive, dull, or unimportant. J. A. St. John in his "Preliminary Discourse" to Lady Mary Montagu's *Letters from the Levant* relates a reply by a certain Miss Furnese, a young heiress who was a contemporary of Lady Mary's daughter: "I will honestly own, your praises of Miss Wortley make me sure I shall dislike her. You tell me she is lively and clever, now I know I am very dull; so, of course, she will despise me and turn me into ridicule, and I am resolved to keep out of her way."[18] Lady Mary is said to have concluded her remarks to her daughter: "If ever, then, you feel yourself flattered by the reputation of superiority, remember that to be the object of suspicion, jealousy, and a secret dislike, is the sure price you must pay for it."[19] She could have added that a good way for people to compensate for the high idea that others may have formed of them is to demonstrate by some act of modesty that they are indeed similar in status to their partners. A successful executive we know, when interacting with a plumber laughed at a blunder he made when trying to fix something in his house. Similarly we heard that a very serious and respected university president with whom no one dared to talk at a college mixer came down from his pedestal and danced with a student to the strains of Saturday Night Fever. Likewise, we read somewhere the story of a

VIP who, having related his recent lunch at the White House, re-established himself at a more modest level by telling his audience that he spilled his soup on the first lady's dress.[20] As a rule, modesty is useful as a corrective device. But it supposes that people have got something to correct: the inflated opinion that others may hold of them, an opinion which is not always justified and may require adjustment. More often, however, we are faced with the opposite problem: how to impress others with our ideal and true selves and how to do so in a way which corresponds to the audience's expectations?

Individuals' performances do not operate in a vacuum nor are they staged in front of a passive audience. Performances at a social gathering are co-performances, that is, they are part of a larger act, where the other participants of the gathering also want to play their parts. No single performance can be successful, that is, be accepted by others, unless the performers offer to their partners the same chance of successfully performing themselves. Civility is the condition necessary for someone's performances to be welcome.

NOTES

1. "There is almost always some discrepancy between the detailed content of the role–identity and the role support gained from our performance; our overt role–performances are almost never brought off perfectly, and audiences are typically demanding. Accordingly role–identities are seldom altogether legitimate. There is always some tension between the fostered reality of one's identity and the discrepant impressions garnered from the external world." (G. J. McCall and J. L. Simmons, *Identities and Interactions* [New York: The Free Press, Rev. Ed., 1978], pp. 71-72).

2. This chapter possesses much affinity with a special variety of interactionist theory, that of Erving Goffman's dramaturgical theory. See the Introduction of this book, note 5.

3. The concept that we are made of multiple selves and that we enact a different self—a situational self—in each social context is common to both the school of symbolic interactionism as formulated by George Herbert Mead (see note 4 below) and that of exchange theory (see Introduction, note 3). See Peter Singelman, "Exchange as Symbolic Interactionism: Convergences between Two Theoretical Perspectives," *American Sociological Review* 37 (August 1972), pp. 414-424. On the "situational self" see G. J. McCall and J. L. Simmons, op. cit., pp. 85-86.

4. "Quidquid recipitur ad mentem recipientis recipitur." Since we cannot expect others to respond to our actions in a satisfying way unless we act according to their own symbolic system of interpretation, we need to know this sym-

bolic system in order to act in a productive way. This knowledge is incorporated in what Mead calls the "Me." The theory which develops this idea is called symbolic interactionism. Its origin can be traced to the works of George Herbert Mead, especially to his book *Mind, Self and Society* (Chicago: University of Chicago Press, 1934). On symbolic interactionism, see the Introduction of this book, note 4. In *Mind, Self and Society*, Mead writes:

> In so far as a man takes the attitudes of one individual in the group, he must take it in its relationship to the action of the other members of the group; and if he is fully to adjust himself, he would have to take the attitudes of all involved in the process. The degree, of course, to which he can do that is restrained by his capacity, but still in all intelligent processes we are able sufficiently to take the roles of those involved in the activity to make our own action intelligent. The degree to which the life of the whole community can get into the self conscious life of the separate individuals varies enormously (p. 256).

5. In the eyes of Simmel, play—and sociability is play—is not an activity unrelated to reality of life. Conversation in a social gathering is not a superficial game without a link with the conversants' experiences and knowledge. ". . . Actual forces," writes Simmel, "needs, impulses of life produce the forms of our behavior that are suitable for play . . . in both art and play, forms that were originally developed by the realities of life have created spheres that preserve their autonomy in the face of these realities. It is from their origin, which keeps them permeated with life, that they draw their delight and strength." Georg Simmel, *The Sociology of Georg Simmel*, Kurt H. Wolff trans. (Glencoe, Ill.: The Free Press, 1950), pp. 42–43.

6. "Another reason why impressions may be self-fulfilling is that the expectations they arouse in others influence the individual's conduct. In this case, an external standard for evaluating accomplishments exists, but the expectations an individual has created in others either serve as incentives for living up to them or have a dampering effect on his performance. The poor impression the self-conscious and awkward person makes leads others to expect to be bored in his company, and their apparent lack of interest causes him discomfort and makes his conversation less stimulating than it otherwise would be" (Peter Blau, *Exchange and Power in Social Life* [New York: John Wiley & Sons, 1964], p. 73).

7. It is well known that the way we dress not only determines the image we give of ourselves to the other guests, but also colors our own perception of ourselves. In the *Party Dress*, Joseph Hergesheimer well describes this change in self-perception. He analyzes Nina's reactions in front of her mirror while trying on her new party dress which just arrived from the Parisian dressmaker, Ishtarre:

> It was at once true and unimportant to say that it was the most becoming dress she had ever worn. Ishtarre had not merely made her look her best; he had made her seem different. . . . Her face was affected, changed, as well—it seemed to Nina that her chin was sharper, her throat

firmer, than they had been only the shortest while before. The flecks of green and brown at the irises of her grey eyes were brought out. Her white face was more pointed, more vivid, than she remembered it. . . . She had looked into a mirror; and after more than forty years, found there a stranger in place of herself. . . . She sat down. If that is what a dress will do to you, Nina said to herself, it is all wrong. It isn't fair. It's immoral. . . . It wasn't simply that her appearance, her face and figure, were changed; her mind, her attitude toward the whole world were different . . . (Joseph Hergesheimer, *The Party Dress* [New York: Alfred A. Knopf, 1930], pp. 8–11).

8. Peter Benchley, *Jaws* (New York: Bantam Books, 1974), pp. 129–130.

9. Antoine de Saint-Exupéry, *The Little Prince*, trans. Katherine Woods (New York: Reynal and Hitchcock, 1943), pp. 16–17. In an article written for the New York *Times* (March 5, 1979, Sec. B, p. 9), Ron Alexander summarizes the advice given by Mr. Rich Hinden, the president of Britches of Georgetown, a group of Washington-based men's stores, to students interested in career change, on how they should dress for an interview:

. . . the basic interview suit should be navy blue or dark gray wool, either solid or pin striped, with lapel widths between 2 3/4 and 3 5/8 inches. The suit, he continued, should have natural shoulders and a softly shaped waist, be a two-button single-breasted model "worn buttoned. But as you sit down, unbutton it." Shirts should be white ("nothing has more integrity"), made of cotton ("polyester is for the common guy") with a straight collar—not a button-down—between 2 and 3 1/4 inches ("anything longer is at least two years old"). The necktie must "always be all-silk" and have burgundy and white in it to pick up the shirt. Mr. Hinden suggested that jewelry be kept to a minimum. Cuff links "are a symbol of insecurity." "What about wristwatches?" a man in a short-sleeved shirt asked.—"Wear a white-faced watch with Roman numerals. And a leather strap. Stretch metal bands are out except on a Rolex."—"What about wearing a hairpiece?"—"Believe me" answered Mr. Hinden, "nothing will say you're insecure like a hairpiece."

10. See Edward T. Hall, *The Silent Language* (New York: Doubleday, 1959), pp. 120–121.

11. Peter Blau, op. cit., p. 40.

12. McCarthy, "The Genial Host," *The Company She Keeps* (New York: Simon and Schuster, 1942), p. 141.

13. Edward T. Hall points to the fact that through socialization we learn many ways of behaving, like walking, driving, writing, speaking, which become second nature and are unconscious. He mentions as an example the tone of voice of upper-class English people. By opposition, technical behavior is highly conscious. He quotes Harry Stack Sullivan, who thought "that there are signifi-

cant portions of the personality that exist out of one's awareness but which are there for everyone else to see." Edward T. Hall, op. cit., p. 84. Similarly Erving Goffman in his *Presentation of Self in Everyday Life* (New York: Doubleday, 1959, p. 2) distinguishes in our presentation between the performances we give (the conscious ones) and those we "give off" (the unconscious ones).

14. A. Franklin, *La vie privée d'autrefois, les repas* (Paris: 1889), p. 283, quoted by Norbert Elias, *The Civilizing Process* (New York: Urizen Books, 1978), pp. 98–99.

15. This suggests that the different details of individuals' presentations should be congruent. It is true in particular of the various pieces of clothing we wear. Congruence in dress consists in combining various elements which the audience expects to see together, like white tie and tails, or corduroy pants and sweater, with possible leather boots and a woolen scarf. One would laugh at a man wearing jogging shorts with a club jacket and a silk tie. Congruence depends partially upon the logic of clothing: Warm pieces of clothing are worn together because they are intended to protect against the cold. The same is true of summer wear. But they depend also upon cultural or subcultural, that is, conventional customs. To show congruence in one's clothes is as much a sign of technical intelligence. On congruence, see Edward T. Hall, op. cit., pp. 159–163.

16. Peter Blau (op. cit., p. 58) quotes Aristotle who, in his *Nicomachean Ethics* (London: Heinemann, 1926, p. 245) wrote: ". . . and sometimes such mock humility seems to be really boastfulness, like the dress of the Spartans, for extreme negligence in dress, as well as excessive attention to it, has a touch of ostentation."

17. Jane Geniesse, "The Perfect Guest," New York *Times*, November 23, 1978, Sec. C, p. 8.

18. Lady Mary Montagu, *Letters from the Levant during the Embassy to Constantinople* (New York: Arno Press, 1971), p. lxii.

19. Ibid.

20. Other examples are given by Peter Blau, op. cit., p. 48.

5
THE PACT OF CIVILITY

The need for recognition is present in every human being from early childhood. First this need is satisfied by the family and later by other primary groups. We have said in previous chapters that in a competitive and compartmentalized world, the primary ties no longer provide most individuals with valid identity support. One key source of support is found in social gatherings which permit identity negotiation in conversation.

However, partygoers in search of recognition and support quickly learn that they are not automatically granted it. Just as they seek rewards, so do all the other guests. Thus, in order for sociable conversation to be gratifying, participants must grant others exactly what they seek themselves. The rule of the game is reciprocity.[1] According to Georg Simmel the same axiom which is responsible for the foundation of law in the nation, governs sociability at a party:

> If we apply this (Kant's) principle to the sociability drive, . . . we might say that each individual ought to have as much satisfaction of this drive as is compatible with its satisfaction on the part of all others. We then formulated the principle of sociability as the axiom that each individual should offer the maximum of sociable value (of joy, relief, liveliness, etc.) that is compatible with the maximum of values he himself receives.[2]

One consequence of this principle is that individuals must impose limits to their drives, in order to be able to grant to their companions in the party a fair counterpart of the rewards they get from them. This capacity of civil self-restraint is called *tact* by Simmel:

Perhaps its [tact's] most essential task is to draw the limits, which result from the claims of others, of the individual's impulses, ego-stresses, and intellectual desires.[3]

Unfortunately tactful behavior is not always found at a party. Much sociable interaction, instead of being a rewarding exchange of identity support, becomes a "zero-sum game,"[4] through which individuals derive their pleasure by defeating their partners. In other cases, participants are confronted with minor forms of aggression expressed by others in postures, gestures, poor control of their instincts, or a contemptuous ignorance of the expected manners. In this chapter we will review these various infractions of the rules of civil reciprocity, starting with the most direct acts of hostility and continuing with more indirect and unconscious forms of aggression. The analysis will apply both to guests who want to avoid unintentionally offending others, as well as to the victims who are often not conscious of having been mishandled and are therefore unable to pinpoint the source of their discomfort.

Before embarking on this review of uncivil ways of behaving, let us briefly answer the question: Why would someone prefer incivility to tact and courtesy?

There are probably several answers to the question. First, the reason may be situational. Individuals may find themselves in a situation where the others have been very slow at rewarding them for their performances and they fear that they will not be acknowledged at all. They then flood the others with words, boasting about imaginary acquaintances or exploits; or they humiliate their partners by openly disdaining their achievements or by simply not listening to them. The uncivil behavior can also have a deeper psychological origin. Some people may have experienced a faulty socialization, the result being an inability to dispel aggression in acceptable ways. To some extent, we all suffer from a faulty socialization. Parents teach us that we may not demonstrate anger in the ways that would come naturally but are unacceptable in society, like hitting, killing, and so on. Along the way we are taught to suppress anger completely, never learning how to verbally and constructively direct it against our parents. So we come to adulthood with a well of stored-up anger towards these primary figures. In work and physical activities some of our anger is sublimated in acceptable ways, but so often we cannot completely vent our feelings, for instance, those feelings we may have not only against our parents but our spouses, bosses, or colleagues. The anger gets stored away. When we attend a gathering, we may use our interactions with unknown people, who have no power upon us, to inflict on them some of our stored-up aggression. Often our anger is directed towards others who remind us unconsciously of those figures (parents) for whom our resentment has never been adequately dispelled. This unconscious release of aggression can take the form of inappropriate laughter, inept jokes, sarcasm, and in general, incivility.[5]

A third explanation of uncivil behavior at a modern social gathering can be traced to the particular climate of insecurity in today's individualistic society. There, individuals find themselves alone and compelled to fight for their rights. Charles Derber writes:

> As Fromm has suggested, people in an individualistic society experience feelings ranging from vague apprehension to acute panic about their economic and social isolation and their capacity to cope without community support. This insecurity intensifies preoccupation with oneself and has a major bearing on face-to-face behavior. It heightens one's own needs for attention and reduces the ability to give it, as one becomes riveted on one's own needs and fears.[6]

It is Charles Derber's thesis that modern humans in their pursuit of attention reach levels of intemperance and narcissism that make them very poor partners in sociable conversation. We shall come later to Derber's analyses of the ways through which, in conversation, individuals persist in steering their partners back to their chosen course of conversation. Here, in a more general way, we will review how individuals show their incivility, starting, as we said, with the most obvious and conscious acts of aggression.

While it is rare, occasionally guests may experience a mild form of physical attack; they might be drawn into a conversation with an abrupt tug, or prevented from breaking away by a firm arm grip. More common than the aggressiveness of the hands is the aggressiveness of the eyes. Staring at the other guests is usually resented by them. Staring, of course, is different from looking. When we speak to others we must look at them. Our eyes are directed at the eyes of our partner; this exchange of glances is part of the communication process. The small movements of our pupils, of our eyelids, of our eyebrows accompany and provide nuance to our speech. This is not staring, but communicating. Staring, on the contrary, consists of looking at others without making an exchange, observing them as if they were inanimate objects. In a slave market, the prospective buyer did not communicate with the slaves, but simply stared at the prospects to assess their value for whatever his purpose may have been. The buyer would talk—either to the owner or to his companions—*about* the slaves. He would not talk *to* them. Similarly, in a gathering, people object when others stare at them. At best they would accept being glanced over rapidly by someone who is conversing with them or manifests such an intention, but they would expect the inspection to be followed by, or even better, to become part of, an intelligent conversation between two equal human beings. I still remember the way an Italian graduate student at the University of Chicago greeted his female guests at the door of his apartment. He would rapidly look at them and then greet them by thanking them for having put on such a nice skirt, or pair of shoes, or a necklace. This was not staring: he was complimenting them and showing appreciation for the effort made in his honor. In turn, the guests were very flattered that their intentions had been noticed.

To be stared at is embarrassing to us because it may also mean that there is something wrong with us, or our presentation, perhaps with our clothes (Is my shirt inside-out? Is my zipper undone? Do I have paint on my forehead? Am I wearing unmatched shoes?); or with what we have done or said (Am I using the wrong fork? Did I spill coffee on my tie? Did I say something wrong? Do I appear to be drunk?). Because a stare is embarrassing, one can use it to punish someone who has done something offensive. I still remember how an Austrian skier, having spotted a foreigner who had succeeded in sneaking his way to the head of the line for the ski lift, skied next to him and for a long minute stared at him without a word. The crowd around them was laughing and the gate-crasher blushed. Who had been the more uncivil of the two? Make your own bets. The case involved two strangers and the punishing individual could be considered to be the voice (rather the eye) of the public. But in a social gathering, it would be the responsibility not of any individual, but of the host, to re-establish any breach in the rules of civility. To arrogate this role to oneself would be another clear breach of civility, which would be an attack not only against the culprit, but also against the host.

This restraining of one's judiciary tendencies leads us to a more general rule of civility which enjoins people to ignore whatever blunders, mistakes, or errors the others may have committed during the gathering. Some of the so-called "errors" are, in fact, nature's mistakes, like warts or pimples. Everyone has been told since childhood not to pay any attention to these and other handicaps with which people may be afflicted. While people know the rule, it is not always easy to follow. In these instances, our eyes seem diabolically magnetized to the unhappy flaws. And the more we stare at another place or try to maintain eye contact with the afflicted individual, the more it becomes evident to the latter that we are noticing what we try so hard not to see. To cite an example somewhat different in spirit, I had a similar experience when, at the age of fourteen, I was attending a cousin's wedding party. I was seated before a young woman who, like the other maids of honor, was wearing a low-necked dress. I had never seen a woman's breast, except in statues or paintings. The more I tried to look elsewhere, the more my eyes returned to the woman's décolleté. I was desperately embarrassed and felt a blush rising from beneath my collar; the woman, noticing my lack of composure and blushing herself, tried to come to the rescue by pulling up her dress to better cover the *corpus delicti*. One can forgive a fourteen-year-old boy. Adults would not be so easily absolved. They are supposed to practice "civil inattention."[7] It is impossible to list all the occasions where this principle should be applied. The list would have to detail all the possibilities of human blunder, which are infinite. We are not supposed to see the wrong clothes nor the wrong accessories. Similarly, we are not supposed to become aware that a man's suspenders have become unreliable nor that a woman's stockings have escaped the garter. A fortiori, one is not supposed to pay any attention to the movements and operations necessary in both cases to restore the proper order. According to Arthur M. Schlesinger, who cites an anonymous nineteenth-century "Laws of Etiquette" book, "if the lady at your side should raise an unmanageable portion to her mouth, you should cease all conversation with her and look steadfastly into the opposite direction."[8] Similarly, if someone spills wine on the tablecloth, breaks a cup, or drops food on his clothes, it should be ignored. More trying, but as necessary to civility, is to remain impassive as one's partner splutters upon one's clothes or face. No one with a minimum of courtesy will notice if, in one corner of the drawing-room, two lovers or spouses quarrel, and one will pass rapidly by two individuals who, in the darkness of a hallway, exchange an extramarital kiss. It is also very difficult to abstain from laughing if a foreigner makes very funny mistakes when speaking our language. I was told that when the late Cardinal Cento left Brussels where he was the apostolic nuncio, he said in his farewell speech to the diplomatic corps: "When I look at my behind [he meant my *past*] I see it divided into two almost equal parts. . . ." Nobody flinched. This is remarkable courtesy, indeed.

Another way of offending others is to openly snub them. A guest who dislikes another guest at a party may succeed in avoiding this person, but if the occasion places the two in each other's way, a greeting is in order and an exchange of a few words must follow. Whatever the interests or feelings that estrange them, they should be able to demonstrate that they are "bigger" than their antagonisms, and that beyond the opposition, there are two human beings capable of intelligent and courteous exchange. And it would be very aggravating for the hosts to witness conflicts between their guests and to become involved in their disagreements. Civility, then, requires that both parties avoid areas of conflict and engage in a benign discussion of some common interests. Erving Goffman found an extreme case, mentioned in Emily Post, where only the multiplication tables could be accepted as "common ground" between two guests:

> At dinner, once, Mrs. Toplofty, finding herself next to a man she quite openly despised, said to him with apparent placidity, "I shall not talk to you—because I don't care to. But for the sake of my hostess I shall say my multiplication table. Twice one are two, twice two are four—" and she continued on through the tables, making him alternate them with her. As soon as she could, she turned again to her other companion.[9]

Mrs. Toplofty had found a way of not offending her hosts, as well as the other guests who would have resented being exposed to an argument or an overt snub. However, she did not succeed in showing much civility to her neighbor. Her words were almost as offensive as sheer silence.

Civility does not require agreement. It demands that if we think we must disagree, our disagreement be directed towards the opinions or the ideas expressed and not the speakers themselves, in the same way that soccer players are supposed to kick the ball, and not the other players. If we want to be civil, we make it evident that we distinguish between what other people say—it can be a temporary or lightly held opinion—and their person. Speakers must be given a chance to review, modify, diversify their assertions. We shall discuss these matters in a future chapter. What counts here is the basic rule that disagreeing need not be offensive.

People who are "aware" have learned to refrain from openly insulting others. It is more difficult for them to avoid ridiculing or embarrassing their interlocutors. Few resist the temptation to impress others with their wit by making a good joke at the expense of someone else. We read in Jane Austen's *Emma* that Frank Churchill suggested on behalf of Emma that everyone in the party contribute something entertaining, "either one thing very clever, be it prose or verse, original or repeated; or two things moderately clever; or three things very dull indeed; and she [Emma] engages to laugh heartily at them all." Miss Bates then naively volunteered: "I shall be sure to say three dull things as soon as ever I open my mouth, shan't I?" To which Emma could not resist replying: "Ah! Ma'am, but there may be a difficulty. Pardon me, but you will be limited as to the number—only three at once."[10] This witty remark brought later to Emma a severe reprimand from Mr. Knightley: "How could you be so unfeeling to Miss Bates? How could you be so insolent in your wit to a woman of her character, age, and situation?"[11]

There are borderline cases. Some influential people may think it their duty to oppose conduct which they feel is inappropriate. To do this they may resort to light jokes which can be resented by their victims. I heard that the papal nuncio in Paris, Cardinal Angelo Roncalli, who later became the great reformist pope, was once seated at an official dinner at the Elysées next to an ambassadress who was wearing a very revealing evening dress. The chief of protocol had encouraged the woman to accept a shawl from Madame de Gaulle, since she was going to be seated next to such a high religious dignitary. The woman had brushed aside the suggestion: "The Nuncio—I know him well—is a man of the world and I am sure he will not object." The dinner unfolded nicely and the ambassadress was feeling triumphant over the chief of protocol who had instilled needless fear in her. After dessert was served, the cardinal called a waiter and asked him for an apple. The cardinal cut it in two pieces and offered one to his scantily clad neighbor, adding with a smile: "Madam, eat from this apple. It will open your eyes. It was only after she ate the apple that our mother Eve discovered she was naked." At this point the ambassadress vehemently wished she had accepted Madame de Gaulle's shawl.

Debunking others is another temptation that some people cannot resist. Sometimes one of your friends boasts about some success he or she had in climbing an imaginary mountain. You may prefer to leave your friend to dream and refrain from interrupting: "Come on, you liar, everyone knows you never left Long Island." Civility suggests it is best to wait until one is alone with the friend to laugh together about his or her ability to fool others; this solution asserts the strength of the friendship while at the same time shows that one is not fooled by the braggart's stories.

Tact also prevents the introduction of topics which will be embarrassing to the people present. A French proverb says: *"On ne parle pas de corde dans la maison d'un pendu."*[12] One avoids mentioning the miseries of being handicapped in front of a crippled individual, nor does one speak of the pathetic pretenses of old singers while talking to one who is approaching the turning point. Homosexuality is not mentioned in a group where one suspects the presence of a homosexual. It is tactless to mention that one's best friend just died of lung cancer in the house of someone who recently underwent surgery for the same disease.

People can be offensive not only by directly attacking individuals but also by attacking their beliefs, their values, their customs, and their manners. In other words, human beings deeply identify with certain beliefs, values, and customs, and an attack upon them is interpreted as an attack against the person identifying with them. The same is true of political opinions. In a large group it is likely that many beliefs and opinions are represented. It makes the discussion of any political, religious or philosophical subjects very difficult without offending one or the other of the guests. Should the difficulty, however, lead to an exclusion of these fundamental subjects? The difficulty may be overcome only with great tact, by exploring the ground slowly and by avoiding any strong statements of assertion or condemnation too abruptly before one has had time and opportunity to get a clearer sense of the various tendencies and attitudes in the group.

Last but not least, individuals should avoid aggressiveness against their partner's "teams." Everyone belongs to many social categories through the various positions and roles they have in life. Since people identify with each of them, they interpret any ridicule or attack against these categories as a personal affront. The extent to which we feel offended depends upon the depth of our own identification with the categories, or teams. A divorced Texan physician, who is a cigar-smoking Democrat, a Methodist, and an amateur fisherman will resent attacks or jokes directed at Americans, Southerners, Texans, physicians, divorced people, Democrats, cigar-smokers, Christians, Methodists, amateur fishermen, and so on. The same is true of nonnatives, who might resent an American reference to foreign nations as "those countries over there." It seems that we are particularly sensitive to attacks or ridicule against our "ascribed" teams, that is, against those categories we belong to involuntarily. These categories are part of our person, whether we want it or not: if one is a Black, or an Arab, or an Italian, it is for life. We are somehow less strongly identified with our occupations or religions especially in a country where both occupation and religion result from a free choice and theoretically could be changed. These traits do not stick to our persons as strongly as do our family names or our provincial origins. This is, however, only a matter of degree. One day in a social club in New York, I was introduced to a banker as a professor of sociology. His reaction was: "What? Sociology? Oh, that s***!" This immediately terminated my interaction with the "gentleman."

Does this mean that all ethnic, religious, and occupational jokes are excluded from conversation in social gatherings? No. But these jokes—and, a fortiori, more forceful onslaughts—can be made only in small circles where one is sure no representative of the team is present. They could also be uttered in the presence of members of the team but only by those who consider themselves as belonging to it. To belong to the team does not always suffice. In order to be acceptable, a joke or criticism must come from an *unequivocal* member of the team. Jews can crack Jewish jokes. However, if they are only partly Jewish, very liberal, nonpracticing, they would not get away with making jokes about Orthodox Jews. The same is true of nominal Catholics, newly naturalized citizens, and so on. In a similar vein, nonteam members have learned politely to refrain from bursting into laughter when they listen to a joke made by a team member in the presence of other members of the team.

Jokes or criticisms made by members in good standing of the team are pleasant because they signify a sense of humor which enhances most social exchanges. Even though individuals listen uneasily to derogatory remarks made about an absent category of people (one imagines, then, how one's team also is dealt with when none of its members are present), we are fully amused when any of the members of our own teams mock our team's own habits or ways.

Sometimes when individuals are not themselves members of the team, they nevertheless try to persuade their audience that they are intimately connected with one of the team members or with the team itself, thinking that this entitles them to make criticisms and jokes against the team. I remember at a party someone telling a small group of guests: "One of my friends is a captain in the Airforce; do you know the joke he told me about the difference between crocodiles and colonels?"—"Well, I would like to know," answered another guest. " I am myself an officer in the Airforce and am curious about that funny difference. . . ." It was evident that the "officer in the Airforce" was not too happy about a team joke being told to and repeated by a stranger, even if the stranger had declared himself a friend of the family.

The offensive behavior reviewed so far could be called *direct* forms of incivility. Direct attacks, however, are not the only ways to offend others at a party. There are also indirect ways. These include sending nonverbal signals by which we show to others indifference or hostility, behaving as if others were not present, freely expressing one's impulses, which are expected to be restrained; or bluntly imposing one's individuality without any consideration for others' legitimate expectations, or deliberately ignoring the expected behavior. All this does not seem to be directly hostile, but it is interpreted by others as a more or less subtle way of being told: "I want to do my thing, and don't really care if you are here!"

There are nonverbal ways for people to show to others that they are not interested in them. Through one's facial expressions and the way one holds one's head or body, erect or stooped, one indicates how one feels about being with others: annoyed, bored, interested, pleased, or excited. When sitting with someone else, a parallel, rather than head-on, position is a sign of coldness. Occasionally turning our head in the other's direction does not compensate for the cold treatment. Yawning, looking to the ceiling or through the windows, an absent-minded manner, accompanied by perfunctory "yeahs," "of course," "you don't say," and so on, are further marks of disinterest. Even more aggravating is the habit of some people who, while talking to someone, scan the audience for better partners, or stare at the door, waiting for the entrance of Prince Charming or of "Number 10."[13]

These are mild examples of an often unconscious, yet very offensive, form of behavior, which could be named the *nonperson treatment*. It consists of acting and speaking as if someone who is nearby were not present. The nonperson treatment occurs most frequently in the conversational trio; therefore we will study it later in the book.

There are more indirect ways of telling others that we choose to ignore their presence. They consist of unrestrained manifestations of one's bodily needs and impulses. Every society has established some limits on the expression of these physical needs. Universally, bodily functions are aggressive when they are unrestricted manifestations of one's brutal animalism. In controlling these functions we tell others that their presence is respected. The point here is not the contents of the rules, which have varied considerably through the ages, but the significance of these restrictions. While in sixteenth-century Europe individuals were expected to take food from their plates with only three fingers instead of the full hand, today in America we are expected to use a fork or a spoon but are also permitted, in certain cases, to hold food like an ear of corn with the fingers. In capturing the essence of civility, what counts more than the specific rules, which vary according to period and society, is the idea that when individuals observe the restrictive rules of their given era and culture, they are acknowledging their respect for their neighbors.

While there is not space here to speak endlessly about specific rules of civility, there are three main ways in which people from every society are invited to discipline their bodily needs and impulses: postponement, ritualization, and sublimation.

Certain activities are considered to be so animalistic that individuals are supposed to refrain from engaging in them when with company. For example, people are not supposed to scratch intimate parts of their bodies and they should reserve their grooming for the bathroom, that is, one should not comb hair or apply make-up in front of other guests. To look at one's reflection in a mirror may seem quite inoffensive; however, it indicates so great a concentration on oneself that others feel ignored and offended. Burping is avoided in most societies and we are not expected to put our feet on the table while sprawling on the sofa. All this is considered selfish, loud, animalistic, and, in a word, antisocial.

Other activities are not excluded but regulated and can be engaged in on the condition that one follows the proper ritual. Eating and drinking are activities which are biological necessities but at the same time capable of spiritual meaning.[14] Eating together can become an exercise of friendship and communion, but only when these functions are controlled by ritualization can they become deindividualized and really social. The basic rules are universal and aim at restraining the quantity of food consumed, the speed in eating it. The technique for getting it, the noise made chewing it, the disposal of remains (like bones, fat, pits, and so on), and the gesticulation appropriate to conveying food to the mouth are all governed by individual and tacit rules. These rules address the way we hold our fork and spoon or glass, the way we break our bread, what we do with our napkin, whether or not we cut certain foods with a knife or a fork, whether we may pick up a bone with our fingers or not, how we eat our soup, whether we peel fruit or not, hold it with a fork, or with our hands. Special dishes have suggested specific rules, like spaghetti, artichokes, and asparagus. Other dishes (like fish or mangoes) must be eaten with specific tools. And one knows that the little scented water bowl which is brought with the fruit or after spare ribs is not for drinking.

The rituals invented for embellishing or toning down other body activities are not so elaborate, but they exist. Sneezing and coughing are muffled with one's hand or a handkerchief. Blowing one's nose is accomplished with the least possible noise and without paying it undue attention. The general law applies here as before. The ritual aims to deanimalize the activity, that is, to make it inconspicuous.

A third way society channels human bodily impulses is through sublimation. This is particularly true of sexual impulses. For reasons which vary with time and culture, sexual intercourse is not allowed in public. However, societies have devised some sublimated means of giving sexual impulses some partial satisfaction. The Middle Ages permitted troubadours to sing publicly their love for the noblewoman. Dances of all kinds, from the most ritualistic group dances to the intimate duos have permitted a muted but very eloquent expression of one's feelings. Courting and social flirting are common during parties without as much as a kiss having been exchanged. Here, again, restraint is a mark of respect for others, especially for those one admires and those one desires amorously.

The last remark demands some explanation. Many people interpret the taboos imposed by society on the public display of sexual activity as the result of some condemnation from the dark ages. It may be that some of the details of these taboos could be traced to specific religious or philosophical traditions, but many of these prohibitions originated in the necessity of protecting individuals and particularly women from the sexual aggressiveness of men. The Italian law, for instance, prohibits public exchange of love kisses. This is at times interpreted—even by magistrates—as an attempt at protecting "public decency." But the origin of the prohibition points elsewhere. It was intended to protect a woman from a man who might attempt to compel her into marriage by compromising her publicly. Either because a woman was, at that time, expected to come to marriage in a state of total purity—and a single kiss would stain it—or because a woman was supposed to be unable to resist the appeal of a passionate kiss; if she was made an accomplice by a kiss, no one other than the aggressor would ever consider marrying her after her reputation had been so tarnished.

Such rules and prohibitions were based on a condition of sex roles and expectations which is gradually changing, at least in the upper classes. In lower classes, it is still common to find the conviction that women are possessions of their men and that any attractive appearance of the women to others will automatically lead to marital infidelity, given that "women are women and men are men." In other words, there is neither faith in the capacity of the women to make up their own minds nor confidence in the capacity of men to discipline themselves once they are sexually aroused. This may explain also why in lower-class gatherings husband and wife are often seated next to each other. As the Sicilian proverb goes, "To trust is all right, but to distrust is better."

In a previous chapter, we attempted to show how individuals' presentations of themselves reveal who they are. The presentations may also manifest how the individuals feel about others. People may offer an appearance that tells their audience that they do or do not much care for their presence, and this too is a form of aggression.

Each society has formed an idea of how a desirable body should look. Society expects that its members will try to control their bodies so that they approximate the ideal aesthetic shape. Excluding certain past eras when Rubenesque women were considered more attractive, most modern cultures favor the slim man or woman, whose every limb and muscle, freed from unnecessary fat, quickly responds to the command of the mind. Such a controlled and "necessary" body tells others that the individual who possesses it is conscious of his or her presence and has exerted some effort to maintain the body in such a way as to fulfill others' expectations. Their bodies then have become "social" bodies, fit for public consumption, or at least for visual consumption.

The opposite impression is conveyed by the unfashionable figure of heavy bodies. Of course, to be fat may be the consequence of an illness which cannot be helped. But in these cases, fat individuals manifest their concern for other people's presence in other ways— through posture, dress, accessories, and so on. Otherwise, the fat body is a confession of carelessness and gluttony, betraying an obsession with the satisfaction of its own appetite, unconcerned with what the external image will communicate to others. Similarly messy hairdos, smudged make-up, untrimmed or uncleaned nails, and a total absence of ornamentation are an indication that the individual did not put much effort into getting ready for the gathering. On the contrary, evident care of our external appearance is a sign of respect for others. Those who are afflicted with physical deformities usually try to draw attention away from their most anomalous aspects. On the other hand, if we are overweight, we will be intent on deemphasizing the apparent earthiness and lack of discipline of our bodies by wearing inventive and artistic clothes. A friend of ours, once, told us of a gathering in which all the guests were stunned by an obese woman who suddenly entered. Her assured and easy walk and her sumptuous dress proclaimed to everyone the power of the mind over body, and the problem of her obesity was instantly overlooked.

By attempting to shape our bodies according to the aesthetic expectations of others, or when we cover them with inventive clothing, we actually "socialize," that is, universalize, our bodies. We can apply to these transformations what Simmel says more specifically of adornment:

> In an aesthetic form, adornment creates a highly specific synthesis of the great convergent and divergent forces of the individual and society, namely, the elevation of existing for others through the emphasis and extension of the ego. This aesthetic form itself stands above the contrasts between individual human strivings. They find in adornment not only the possibility of undisturbed simultaneous existence, but the possibility of a reciprocal organization that, as anticipation and pledge of their deeper metaphysical unity, transcends the disharmony of their appearance.[15]

In simpler words, every signal we give others, through our behavior and external appearance, that we respect their expectations
is a way of substituting harmony and peace for the aggression of idiosyncratic differences and divergences. The principle applies to the
shape of the body as well as to any other aspect of self-presentation.

Simmel defines elegance as the "being-for-others" of our
presentation. And this being-for-others is expressed through a partial
deindividualization of the body, through the adoption of clothes and
accessories that hide the specific idiosyncrasy of the body and have a
more impersonal, social, universal appeal. This is shown by wearing
"metallic ornaments"[16] or "new clothes," which "have not yet ad-
justed to the modification of the individual body." The same could
be said of ironed clothes, which appear new and deindividualized. By
contrast, Simmel sees in the absence of elegance, a brutal assertion of
one's individuality shown by "older clothes which have been worn
and are pulled and pinched by the peculiar movements of its wearer":

> thus completely revealing his particularity . . . A long-worn piece of
> clothing almost grows to the body; it has an intimacy that militates
> against the very nature of elegance, which is something for the "others,"
> a social notion deriving its value from general respect.[17]

Does Simmel favor the total elimination of individual features
in the way we dress? It is not likely, because he is fascinated by the
way clothing styles translate, rather than suppress, individual traits
into a universal language. But Simmel stresses the necessity of trans-
forming the individual's body features: 'Style is always something
general. It brings the contents of personal life and activity into a
form shared by many and accessible to many"[18] and:

> the essence of stylization is precisely this dilution of individual poign-
> ancy. This generalization beyond the uniqueness of the personality—
> which, nevertheless, in its capacity of base or circle of radiation, carries
> or absorbs the individuality as if in a broadly flowing river. For this rea-
> son, adornment has always instinctively been shaped in a relatively
> severe style.[19]

Simmel wrote from the perspective of a philosophy which
stresses reason, universality, or, in a word, classicism. One is reminded
at this point of the very classical declaration of Pascal in the seven-

teenth century. "The Me is hateful." Other periods, on the contrary, have stressed the individual pole of the individual–social continuum. Late eighteenth century writers and philosophers stressed a
more romantic conception of the self. The "me" claimed its right to
expose itself in poetry, painting, music. The romantic movement
extended also to clothing, helped destroy the highly ornamental
styles inherited from the baroque ages and left the individual with
more freedom of presentation. However, social intercourse needs
recognized means of expression and soon the revolution of yesterday turned into the fashions of today. Romanticism was followed
by a new age of classical and impersonal expression. It was not the
return to the elaborate formalities of the court, but an assertion of
the no nonsense order of the bourgeoisie. It was expressed by neo-
classicism in architecture, painting and poetry, by the Biedermeier
and the Louis Philippe styles of furniture, by the Victorian life-style.
From these times until recently, men's fashion became so restrained
and sad as to exclude fantasy of forms and colorful fabrics. This does
not mean, however, that the "me" was forever condemned to silence.
Various artistic movements, like Impressionism and Expressionism in
painting, symbolism in poetry and music, and, especially in America,
the jazz adventure of the twenties, tried to shake the formal tranquillity of the bourgeois order. But these movements seem to have
been more concomitant with the bourgeois formality than destruc-
tive of it. They were some kind of compensation to indulge in, while
visiting exhibitions on Sundays or dancing on a Saturday night.
Middle-class formalism continued to dominate the social scene, at
least until the appearance of what has been called the "me generation"; the counter-cultural revolution of the late sixties succeeded
in converting to self-expression large numbers of young people, if
not the whole society. This proclamation of the dignity of the "me"
has found its clearest expression in the presentation of a body which
utterly refuses to be hidden under formal adornments and arrangements. The hair was left uncut, washing was reduced to a minimum,
clothes which adhered to the body were preferred. This new style
which so radically contrasted with what Simmel called elegance, and
was rejected with disgust by the middle classes, has been enthusiastically described by Charles Reich, in his *Greening of America*:

> . . . The clothes [of the new generation] are earthy and sensual. They
> express affinity with nature . . . The clothes express freedom. Expen-

sive clothes enforce social constraints . . . The new clothes give the wearer freedom to do anything he wants . . . [The new clothes] are not as uniform as people think . . . they are extremely expressive of the human body and each body is different and unique . . . The pants of a suit give no hint of a man's legs, and when they wrinkle along body lines they are quickly taken to the dry cleaners to be pressed back into straight lines. Jeans express the shape of the legs, heavy or thin, straight or bowed. As jeans get more wrinkled, they adapt even more to the particular legs that are wearing them. . . . [20]

In the middle-class parties such an outfit was hardly seen, except when worn by a representative of the counter-culture, invited to give some distraction to the bored bourgeoisie.

The rebellion of "Consciousness III" as Reich calls it, was not entirely successful, however, in part because every revolution unconsciously evolves into a new style, which many, if not everyone, adopts. One could say that the revolution was already on its way out when adults and even the elderly could be seen wearing jeans and long hair. Second, not only were the new styles adopted by many, but they were transformed into fashionable elegance. Long hair did not disappear but became nicely "styled." Jeans became designers' jeans. Blouses reappeared, and T-shirts could be found in elegant shops with original designs and insignia. Sociability has always required recognized forms of self-presentation and when the old ones are denounced as expressionless, new ones arise out of the destruction of the old ones. They, in turn, allow individuals to present themselves in ways which are meaningful to others; they permit a return to elegance. As Simmel says, refusal or adornment, that is, the refusal of submitting to others' expectations in terms of clothes and other aspects of one's presentation, today as in the past, is taken as a sign of haughty pride, that is, of incivility:

> . . . pride, whose self-consciousness really rests only upon itself ordinarily disdains "adornment" in every sense of the word.[21]

The rules of civility reviewed so far could be explained as universal social expectations, even if they always take on a specific content: They are the direct expressions of respect for others. But there are customs to which it would be difficult to find some kind of universal justification. They are pure conventions. However, we are also expected to abide by them: "When in Rome, do as the Romans do." It would be offensive to manifest contempt for these expectations of our partners.

Each society has its own specific conventions. These rules are all the more idiosyncratic in that societies are without mutual contact. The same is true of various provinces or classes within the same society. Once when drinking wine with a farmer in Savoy, I wondered why he constantly filled up my glass, as soon as I had sipped from it. After a while I observed: "If you go on filling up my glass, I will never be able to finish drinking it." The farmer then explained to me that among farmers in the area, it was a duty for the hosts to offer their guests a full glass of wine and to keep it full at all times, but as a counterpart, the guests were supposed to leave their glasses untouched until they were ready to go. At that moment the guests would stand up, pick up their glasses, drink them in one gulp and take their leave. In other social circles, the hosts would not pour any wine into a glass which is not quite empty. The first custom may be intended to show the hosts' generosity and the guests' restraint to avoid imposing on the hosts. This custom is more likely to be found among poor people who may be short of supplies, while the second custom, found among richer people, may be meant to respect the guests' right to sobriety, supply being no problem for the host and consequently no preoccupation for the guest.

If the differences can be found among the various social classes of one single country, they will exist all the more between different countries. Many Westerners have experienced the Orientals' exquisite politeness. To the latters' eyes, many Western customs are simply barbarian. It seems that at a much earlier time and to a much greater extent than in the West, Orientals learned to control their impulses and to present others with a very socialized self. Their extreme preoccupation with not imposing themselves on others may look to Westerners like a disguise of their thoughts. In reality, the disguise exists only in the Westerners' minds, given their incapacity to understand subtle differences of yeses, nos, and silences. When I was a student at the University of Paris, I had organized a two-week ski vacation in the Alps. When the list of the group was almost complete, someone suggested also inviting Mr. Li, a Chinese student. I invited him but he answered, "No, thanks." I learned many months later that he had been very much disappointed not to have been accepted in the group. To another Chinese his "no" would certainly have meant yes. But I was not trained to distinguish among the various meanings of no. And as far as saying yes, it would never have occurred to Mr. Li, who believed "one must respect the rules of civility." This may appear strange, but have we never heard the story which emanates from our sexist cultural tradition about the difference between a diplomat and a lady? The story goes: If a diplomat says "yes," he means "perhaps," if he says "perhaps," he means "no" and if he says "no," he is no diplomat. Now the lady: If she says "no" she means "perhaps," if she says "perhaps," she means "yes" and if she says "yes," she is no lady. Other differences between the civility of the West and that of the East, of the North and of the South are less a matter of refinement than a question of contingent social creations. Is it per se more polite to converse with someone with one's hat on one's head, or holding it in one's hand? Or is it more civil to take off one's supposedly dirty shoes before entering a house or to conceal one's supposedly not so attractive socks or feet? Is it more refined to leave some food on one's plate in order to show the hosts that they have fully satisfied one's appetite, or to eat it all to show that one liked the cooking? Is it more courteous to shake each other's hand at the risk of exchanging microbes and viruses or to bow gently, or bow while joining the hands? Is nose rubbing more extraordinary than the Hispanic *abrazo*? When abroad, it should be taken for granted that the customs will differ from one's own and one should make every effort to get to know the essential differences. At home one should be civilly inattentive to the mistakes of foreigners who go on following their customs, imagining they are universal. It is their way of being polite. Their intention is more important than the way it is manifested.

The specific rules of civility are also relative to the time; they have evolved considerably in the West since the Roman Republic. One can still see today in Ostia public toilettes, where Roman citizens could satisfy essential body functions and engage in conversation at the same time. Bathing naked together in public, for both women and men, was apparently normal in the late Middle Ages and Calvin had great difficulty in convincing the owners of the public baths to open them to only one sex at a time. Urinating in public was normal at least for men at the court of Louis XIV and special servants moved around carrying utensils appropriate to the satisfaction of this need. This does not mean that there were no restrictions. On the contrary. Erasmus in the sixteenth century in his *De civilitate morum puerilium* prescribes a hundred rules that must be observed. These rules were different from our present ones; they were also less restrictive.[22]

It is the thesis of Norbert Elias that the rules of civility that are intended to control human behavior are much stricter today than they were three centuries ago. This may seem strange to the reader, accustomed to thinking that this century has become more permissive. Elias admits that on specific points there may be an ebb and flow of severity. We agree with him, however, that the apparent relaxing of dress codes, for instance, should not be interpreted as a decrease of sexual strictness. On the contrary. When clothes become more sexy, or permit more visual access to others' bodies, it does not mean that promiscuity is encouraged. It means that individuals who show more of their bodies—for instance, on a beach or at a social gathering—are less afraid than in the past that others will be incapable of curbing their possible sexual attraction. One expects that people have acquired more internal controls.[23]

This evolution from external controls toward more self-control in the area of sexual relations is only one example of a much more general movement which corresponds to the ripening of the concept if not of the reality of civility.

This last assertion, however, seems to need some qualification. How can we see progress toward civility in our times when the world around us seems to become every day more insecure?[24] The answer is that there are some islands of security and high-level civility that individuals succeed in building together where they feel safe. However, outside of these relatively safe havens, the outside, unorganized urban world now looks more like a jungle. The streets, the subways, the hallways of apartment buildings are not safe, and far less, civil. And even social gatherings, when regrouping ambitious narcissistic individuals, are not always the peaceful and rewarding stage where one can exchange with others identity support. They look more like a market of ruthless and competitive bidders.

The feeling of uncertainty that we experience regarding the civility of others in general and more specifically of the other guests in a social gathering explains, in part, the prudence with which we approach them and the care we take in choosing appropriate, that is rewarding, partners. This choice is particularly difficult in a modern gathering, where many of the other guests are unknown to us. This will be the topic of the next chapter.

NOTES

1. Simmel has, in his own words, already insisted on both the need for recognition and the willingness to please others in turn: "Man's desire to please his social environment contains two contradictory tendencies . . . on the one hand it contains kindness, a desire of the individual to give the other joy, but on the other hand there is the wish for this joy and these favors to flow back to him, in the form of recognition and esteem, so that they be attributed to his personality as values." Simmel applies this theory to body adornment, but it could be said of all the elements of one's sociable performance. See Georg Simmel, *The Sociology of Georg Simmel*, Kurt H. Wolff trans. (Glencoe, Ill.: The Free Press, 1950), p. 339.

2. Ibid., p. 47.

3. Ibid., p. 45.

4. A zero-sum game is an interaction in which the gains of one person automatically become the loss of the other. A classical application of this game is that of the "mixed motive" Prisoner's Dilemma, in which "the participant is presented with a choice between only two alternatives: he can decide to share the outcomes equally with the other person or he can try to maximize his own gains at the expense of others." John K. Chadwick-Jones, *Social Exchange Theory, Its Structure and Influence in Social Psychology* (New York: Academic Press, 1976), p. 73. For more details, see his whole Chapter Four, "The Development of the Model," pp. 66–93.

5. See Sigmund Freud, *New Introductory Lectures on Psychoanalysis* (New York: W. W. Norton & Co., 1965), p. 98.

6. Charles Derber, *The Pursuit of Attention: Power and Individualism in Everyday Life* (Boston: G. K. Hall, 1979), p. 89.

7. See the interesting pages of Erving Goffman on "Civil Inattention," in *Behavior in Public Places* (New York: The Free Press, 1963), pp. 83–88.

8. Arthur M. Schlesinger, *Learning How to Behave* (New York: Macmillan, 1946), p. 23.

9. Emily Post, *Etiquette* (New York: Funk and Wagnalls, 1937), p. 273.

10. Jane Austen, *Emma* (London: Macmillan, 1927), p. 334.

11. Ibid., p. 338.

12. "One does not allude to ropes in a house where someone has hanged himself."

13. *10* is the title of a film by Blake Edwards depicting a middle-aged man in search of the perfectly beautiful woman. He rates the women he meets on a scale of one to ten. One day at last he sees one to whom, he thinks, he can grant the number "10."

14. Georg Simmel, op. cit., p. 33.

15. Ibid., p. 344.

16. Ibid., p. 341.

17. Ibid.

18. Ibid., p. 342.

19. Ibid. Erving Goffman in *Behavior in Public Places* (op. cit., p. 26) quotes an anonymous book of etiquette, *The Canons of Good Breeding* (Philadelphia: Lee and Blanchard, 1839):

> A negligent guise shows a man to be satisfied with his own resources, engrossed with his own notions and schemes, indifferent to the opinion of others, and not looking abroad for entertainment: to such a man no one feels encouraged to make any advances. A finished dress indicates a man of the world, one who looks for and habitually finds, pleasure in society and conversation, and who is at all times ready to mingle in intercourse with those he meets with; it is a kind of general offer of acquaintance, and provides a willingness to be spoken to.

20. Charles Reich, *The Greening of America* (New York: Bantam Books, 1970), pp. 252–253.

21. Georg Simmel, op. cit., p. 342.

22. "In the sixteenth century, Monteil tells us, in France as everywhere else, the common people blow their noses without a handkerchief, but among the bourgeoisie it is accepted practice to use the sleeve. As for the rich, they carry a handkerchief in their pockets; therefore, to say that a man has wealth, one says that he does not blow his nose on his sleeve." To this Erasmus reacted in asserting that only the use of a handkerchief can be allowed. He is not so severe about "retaining wind": "If it can be purged without a noise that is best. But it is better that it be emitted with a noise than that it be held back." He, then, repeats an old Greek suggestion to cover the sound with a cough. To "retain a wind" was supposed to be harmful to one's health. See Norbert Elias, *The Civilizing Process* (New York: Urizen Books, 1978), pp. 145 and 130. Elias refers to: Desiderius Erasmus, *De civilitate morum puerilium* (On the civility of children's behavior), Rotterdam, 1530.

23. See Norbert Elias, op. cit., passim. It may be also that the target individuals are perceived as free and independent persons, capable of deciding whom they want to accept as husbands, wives, fiancés, friends, or lovers. This is particularly true of women. Due to their newly acquired educational, occupational and financial independence, women are in a position to refuse the advances of men who don't interest them. Consequently their sexually attractive presentation cannot be interpreted as a sign of universal availability. Being more confident about their other sources of social power, women can present themselves attractively for the pleasure of their audience and with the consciousness that they, themselves, will select among possible candidates those they will allow in their company. On the other hand the women who are publicly tied to a partner, do not find it dangerous to dress in a revealing and attractive way. Their only avowed purpose is to please the other guests in a gathering and interactions with them will at best reach the level of inconsequential flirtations.

24. Thomas Hobbes, in his *Leviathan* (1651) was correct in stating where a total absence of authority would lead. But he was wrong in assuming that this danger could be upset only by absolutism.

6
THE CHOICE OF PARTNERS

If partygoers are to derive satisfaction from a social gathering, they must receive identity support from guests whom they admire. Identity confirmation is only meaningful when offered by people whom they consider competent to judge them. Not everyone is a good match for everyone else.

Two separate elements are contained in the problem. First, when individuals accept an invitation to what we have called a modern gathering, they assume that the party will offer them a sample of "good" partners, that is, a representation of the world as they understand or imagine it. The assumption is usually based upon previous experiences and the knowledge we have of the hosts and of their circle of acquaintances. The more individuals are competitive, ambitious, and even pushy, the more discriminating they will be in accepting an invitation. If they suspect that the other guests will not be good matches, they may find a pretext for not attending.

Even if the guest list is a good sample of the "world," not everyone in it is an equally good partner for the arriving guests. Therefore, guests must choose from among the various potential companions those who will better reward them. As George T. McCall and J. L. Simmons write,

> All kinds of people serve as audiences to one's performances and perhaps accord role support in varying degrees, but their reactions are not given equal weight, just as in the theater itself, the reactions of professional drama critics are taken more seriously than those of casual tour-

ists visiting Broadway. Some audiences are recognized as having special competences and credentials.[1]

The problem, then, for someone who arrives at a modern social gathering is, especially when it contains many unknown participants, to choose the right partners. In this chapter, we will analyze the steps and the "mechanisms" involved in these choices. First, we shall examine how the setting and the type of gathering more or less controls whether someone will converse with fascinating Pamela, handsome George, or boring Fred. In many cases guests have a wide margin of freedom in choosing their partners. Whom they elect depends first upon whom they find attractive. The law governing attractiveness is a little more complex than one may think. In fact, attractiveness, physical or otherwise, has many drawbacks, because people often avoid rather than seek out the most attractive guests. How someone rationally and consciously balances the possible costs and rewards associated with choosing this or that partner will be the concluding topic of this chapter.

Not all social gatherings offer the same amount of freedom of partner choice. The setting that offers the least freedom is the dinner with prearranged seating. Many people resent being told where to sit, without realizing that in most cases prearranged seating is to their advantage. True, guests may think that they could have received a more pleasant lot if they had been free to choose. But what is the guarantee that the brilliant journalist Elisabeth or the fascinating car racer Johnny, would have picked them as their companion? When seats are assigned, one cannot blame oneself for having to converse with boring Fred or arrogant Cynthia. Nor can we complain when we are compelled to sit next to a sexy or interesting partner who would not ordinarily have chosen us. Pleasant seating arrangements may occur either out of sheer luck or because the hosts guessed their guests' secret preferences. In quite a different situation, while traveling on an airplane, I was once seated by the airline next to Rosi Mittermaier, the German ski champion. If I had been free to choose, I would no doubt have picked a different seat. I hate to look like a sports fan in pursuit of autographs. But the compulsory seating permitted me to get her autograph for my skier nephew. Another time, as I was boarding a plane and patiently pushing my way into the aisle behind a long line of slowly moving, puzzled passengers, I spotted far down the aisle an amazingly attractive young woman busy folding her overcoat and placing it in the rack overhead. In a free seating situation, I would probably have managed to sit not too far away for the pleasure of seeing her, but I would have refrained from imposing upon her the possibly unwanted presence of a middle-aged intellectual. Well, I had not the leisure to pursue further my reflections on what I would have done or not done in a free situation; as I neared the row of seats where she had already settled, it became clear that I would be her neighbor by the grace of Icelandic Airlines. Before taking my seat, I very openly looked at my ticket, and when I had made it clear that I had no other choice, I eventually sat down. After one hour of flight, we started a very interesting conversation on various topics of social psychology in which my companion had just been granted a Ph.D.

Even when the compulsory seating arrangement assigns to guests what at first appears to be a poorer lot, they may end up discovering that Fred, their not very attractive neighbor, is a fascinating individual who has a great variety of interests in common with them and is better capable than any other guest of evaluating the performance staged for them. When seated next to someone for the whole length of a dinner, one is compelled to explore various conversational avenues until one proves rewarding. It is a well-known story that many people eventually marry someone whom they did not find especially attractive at first but with whom they had to converse out of some sort of necessity. The necessity can be a stalled car or confinement to a mountain resort by heavy snow-fall. It could also be—why not?—the compulsory seating at a dinner party.

The worst situation I can imagine is a seated dinner with no seat assignments. Everyone bears the responsibility of finding a seat and ends up sitting next to a boring colleague with no one else to blame for it. If seats had been assigned by the hosts, they would likely have tried to match their guests with compatible neighbors. Random choices or previous acquaintances are rarely an improvement. And the unhappy interaction must last for the duration of an elaborate dinner! One may object: "Yes, but you may also happen to sit next to Sally who always tells amusing stories or Tony who is not as glum as Howard." Of course, but enjoyment is not guaranteed. Individuals may choose to eat next to people they know or next to the guests they most admire but then the negative consequences of having chosen beautiful Jackie will have their full impact: One must then bear the responsibility of one's choice and since the interaction will last a whole dinner party, it will look as if one has monopolized the most attractive guest.

More conducive to good companion selection is the situation created by a buffet–dinner, because one does not have to remain seated at the same place for the whole dinner: at any time one has the excuse of getting up to go and fetch more food from the buffet. One may then have the luck of finding an empty seat and a new set of neighbors. This will happen especially if there is a lot of movement in the party. This movement can, in turn, be arranged by the hosts. Instead of bringing all the food at once, they sometimes bring it to the buffet in installments giving a motive for everyone to stand up several times during the party. I know hosts who at this point suggest a rearrangement of the seating by discreetly making new introductions or murmuring to someone that Susie or Andrew would very much enjoy his or her company.[2]

In all the occasions analyzed so far, guests are seated. From the point of view of physical comfort, it is certainly quite advantageous. And in a very informal context, as is found in family reunions or get-togethers of close friends, it is probably the best solution. Knowing everybody, one can avoid the most incompatible proximities, and if there is compulsory seating, the hosts will have foreseen how to avoid possible problems. On the other hand, in case of free seating, the informality of the reunion permits the guests to move around when they feel it is desirable. Free seating presents the greatest drawbacks when one does not know the other guests, knows few of them, or knows them very superficially. This is where the danger is the greatest of getting stuck next to boring Fred or shy, unresponsive Adele.

For this reason, when hosts want to invite a large, disparate, and unacquainted crowd of guests, they often choose the formula of the cocktail party or its variation, the cocktail–buffet dinner party. In the cocktail party the guests are standing and feel much freer. It is not much of an effort for guests to make a few steps in one direction or the other and thus find themselves within radar-distance of Jackie, Susie, or George. Several of the guests will not even hesitate to exchange a few words with Fred because they know they will be able to escape him rather easily. Enid Nemy interviewed a few habitués of New York cocktail parties for the New York *Times* and relates:

"You don't get trapped if you stand" said Dick Daniels, associate executive director of the New York Association for the Blind. "You make a half turn to the left or a half turn to the right and you can move away easily." Another stander is Jason Grant, an actor–director who is working on a play called "In Three Easy Lessons." "When you create a character on stage, and he sits down, he is, in a sense, establishing territory and saying, 'I am going to stay here,'" Mr. Grant said. "When you stand, you're mobile."[3]

Given that in most social gatherings individuals can choose their partners, we shall have to analyze how participants go about choosing their partners. Beforehand, however, we must discuss the question: To whom are we attracted?

First, we must consider our motives for conversing with someone: Another's attractiveness cannot be determined before we know what our own expectations are.[4] Do we want to be with them "for the sake of enjoying their company"? Which would be an intrinsic reward, or do we involve ourselves with the hope of a future relationship or friendship, or even with the plans of getting some sort of reward as a result of conversing with that person?[5] In other words, I may want to enjoy Susie's conversation because of her wit or friendly attitude; I may want to talk with Pamela with the hope of a future date—or even of marriage;[6] and I may consent to entertain Fred today because he will ultimately have a say in my promotion. All these prospective partners can be said to be "attractive," but the attributes which make each of them attractive are obviously very diverse. I do not care about how ugly, condescending, or boring Fred is as long as there is a chance that he will root for me. I do not care if Pamela is a little silly as long as there is hope she will consent to a lengthy date with me next week. But the only reason why I want to converse with George and Susie is the immediate and intrinsic pleasure of their company.

In this chapter we shall primarily consider what makes people desirable companions in themselves and momentarily discard the concern with future and extrinsic benefits. Individuals are essentially attracted to people who, in their minds, are associated with rewarding experiences.[7] Social psychologists rightly say that individuals are mostly looking for engaging people who will recognize them for what they are, that is to say, for what they think they are. As we said in a previous chapter, guests want to be supported for the performances of the role–identities they choose to present as their ideal-selves. Guests look for people who say yes to their claims, who smile and laugh at their stories, who recognize their status, who answer to what they say, who, in a word, approve of them, even if they must disagree in part with them.[8]

Within these expectations there are two aspects which must intersect in one person to make him or her really attractive partners: first, as we said above, one wants approval to come from competent, important, and desirable people. Guests are flattered if the stars of a gathering support their performances. One wants *valuable* support. But—and this is the second necessary component of attractiveness— one wishes others to be actually *willing* to grant support.

First, one looks for valuable partners. Their support is valued in proportion to their power within the specific area in which one also hopes to be approved. The more outstanding or rare these others are, the more numerous are those competing for their approval. Candidates are all there lining up to get a nod, a smile, maybe a compliment from the star, the king, the secretary of state, the mayor, the big business executive, or the rock singer. The problem is that these stars, in turn, are also looking for approval from people they value: the film actor will look for Vincent Canby, the journalist will be interested in conversing with Walter Cronkite, the secretary of state will be interested in Henry Kissinger's opinion on his last speech, the model will look for Richard Avedon, and so on.[9] This is true, of course, at every level of the socializing classes. In a small town, the star may be a lawyer, the manager of the supermarket, the radio station director, or the principal of the high school. And a social stratification will be found among the guests of the gathering according to local power and status. This means that in every case, if we want to interact with specific individuals, we must have the proper credentials. The higher the power and status of our intended partners, the higher must be the seekers' status and power. In other words, what is known as the *matching principle* is operating here. Everyone in the party usually ends up conversing with someone who possesses a relatively equal degree of attractiveness. When equality of attractiveness is reached, it leads to a feeling that we are supported by people we are also capable of supporting, because we are as attractive to them as they are attractive to us.[10]

How do we know, before engaging another person, that this individual will bring the valued support we seek? What creates in our minds the association mentioned above between an individual and a rewarding experience?

The first source of this knowledge is, of course, past experience. If we had had a pleasant time with someone in the past, we may logically expect the same to happen again. Each time I meet an anthropologist friend of mine, I already know that he will have interesting stories and opinions to tell me and that he will show interest in what I am doing. Past experience, however, may be treacherous. Some pleasurable conversation may have happened by chance. Once Steve met a man who was extremely interested in operas. Steve is not, but he had just seen *Cavalleria Rusticana* the day before and Steve and his partner spent a good half hour commenting on the music, the performers, the costumes, and so on. A few months later they met again and Steve's partner immediately introduced the topic of opera, speaking particularly of the *Barber of Seville* which he had seen recently. He was quite disappointed when Steve told him he had not been to the opera since they had last seen each other. This time their engagement was quite short. There are other cases between two individuals in which past experience has included many varied topics they think each knows rather well and that they have enough in common to foresee renewed pleasure in each other's company.[11]

Many people are not satisfied with the idea of repeating past experiences; in their efforts at climbing the social ladder they always look for higher rewards. They want to better their self-image and wish to perform for increasingly more powerful and attractive partners. They are guided by the hope of future gains more than by the memory of past enjoyment. Not only do they not fear encounters with strangers but they actively seek them. They are faced, however, with the problem of determining who among the strangers will be rewarding companions. If one had no past experience with George or Susie, what makes one believe that they possess qualities which make them desirable partners?

Some of these virtues are visible or at least one thinks they can be discerned by some visible signals: sensuality, beauty, elegance, style, cheerfulness and maybe civility, kindness, and a certain way of looking from which individuals feel the other person likes them. Other traits, such as bedroom expertise, wealth, status, occupation, knowledge, artistic skills, could be known only if one has been told.

Knowing other people's attributes in advance has many advantages. It makes the selection process much easier and avoids lengthy and fruitless explorations when there is nothing to explore, or, if there is really something to be found, we avoid beating around the bush for an hour before eventually finding the proper topic. Many people may have only one or two interests in common, and it takes a long time to discover mutual passion for Etruscan jars or for printing mistakes in *incunabula*. If others possess elaborate skills or qualities out of the ordinary, it will be helpful to know it. At the beginning of the conversation, our expectations will be translated into an evident admiration which will challenge our partners to perform at their best. Peter Berger, in his *Invitation to Sociology*, has observed: "We find it hard to be anything but clumsy in a gathering where we know people have an image of us as awkward. We become wits when people expect us to be funny, and interesting characters when we know that such a reputation has preceded us."[12] Previous information also helps individuals to see things in others that they otherwise would not have noticed; this phenomenon is known as the principle of selective perception. If we are told in advance that George has a wonderful command of the English language, we will notice his easy and elegant conversation. We might otherwise have concentrated our attention on the man's strange tie. Likewise knowing that Mary is an expert on Middle East problems will help us appreciate the wisdom of her remarks about the Iran-Iraq war. On a similar note, some people are insensitive to other people's elegance in dressing or physical assets, unless their attention has been previously awakened. My friend Susie has beautiful emerald eyes, but I had never noticed them before I was told so by a mutual friend.

High reputation, however, has its drawbacks. It may raise our expectations to such an extent that we are disappointed when we confront the reality. The "most intelligent woman" or the "wittiest man" may seem "just ordinary" to us when we meet them. It may be that we met them on their bad days, but it's nevertheless a mark against them that they have not lived up to their reputations, and they will not easily reestablish them on successive encounters. This is well known to jealous individuals who may use excessive praise while speaking of their enemies. There is no better way to precipitate their disgrace. The audience will soon discover that the overly praised person cannot foot the bill. The Romans used to say that "The Tarpeian Rock (from which criminals were thrown to their deaths) is close to the Capitoline Hill (the political center of Rome)." Individuals do not need to be introduced as tennis champions because they won the local club cup. I still remember a young man who was introduced to me as the greatest living painter. I soon discovered that he was just one of the many anonymous painters who fight in New York to persuade an off-off-off-Madison Avenue gallery to show some of their creations. A more modest and specific introduction would have elicited my interest and curiosity: There is nothing more exciting than to empathize with the efforts of an artist who looks for self-expression and recognition.

One may wonder why we have listed sensuality among the virtues which may make other people's company enjoyable. Apart from the hope of establishing a basis for a more intimate encounter in the future, social intercourse between two sensuously oriented individuals may grant them vicarious satisfaction and lead to an exciting flirtation. Sensuality manifests itself more in presentation and in behavior than through a specific physical type. It shows in a certain way of holding our bodies, in glancing at others' bodies, in trying to make eye contact with them, in revealing our bodies, in attempting to touch others either with the hands or with some other part of the body, in introducing certain topics of conversation, and so on.[13] When Georgette entered the reception room the other day I could sense she was up to something: the signals were evident in her deeply sun-tanned cleavage, her skirt unbuttoned to show her legs, and her searching eyes, which soon met those of a nonchalant tall young man in very tight jeans, who casually rested an elbow on the mantelpiece. He half smiled at her. She smiled him away, and rather than go to him directly, moved into our small circle and soon was telling us that she was just back from the Bahamas. At my inquiring whether the sun was already warm enough for sunbathing there, she pulled her blouse up to her chin, looking around to assess the impact, especially upon the young admirer: "You see, the sun was quite efficient," she whispered laughing in my ear. When I passed by a few minutes later—having got myself a fresh drink from the bar—she was already in the corner chatting with the young Apollo.

Beauty—whatever its precise definition may be—is one of the most desired attributes. Everyone would like to be beautiful and is attracted to the beauty of others. However, beauty is a highly relative quality. At a social gathering where most people are unattractive, any mildly handsome men or women will seem desirable partners and may soon be surrounded by candidates for their company. Canons of beauty differ greatly from one century to the next and from one culture to another. But even if one makes concessions to the relativity of standards, there are some components of beauty that somehow transcend centuries and frontiers. A body silhouette that is both firm and slender, has well-proportioned limbs (shapely legs with thin ankles and wrists, long fingers), and a slender neck, together with regular features, rather large eyes with striking pupils, attractive hair, smooth skin with no fatty deposits, and so on, are elements which, put together, make a person appear beautiful. Such refinements may be found in the Venus de Milo, the Apollo Belvedere, a Botticelli Madonna, an Ingres odalisque, the Adam of Michelangelo's Sistine Chapel ceiling, a Japanese geisha, a Bali dancer, Garbo's film work, or ballet dancer Baryshnikov.

Beauty is a mark of the extraordinary; beauty is scarce and as such is valued and envied. Beautiful people are supposed to be fascinating, to have made experiences out of the ordinary, to be promised high rewards or successful careers and rich marriages. Several studies have shown that people believe them to be more honest and better sexual partners.[14] They seem to be more confident, outgoing, and perhaps have learned to enjoy themselves more in other people's company, since most of the time they meet with approval and admiration. Being beautiful and successful, they are not supposed to be envious of others' success. They can afford to be kind.[15] For all these reasons they are highly desired partners.

These suppositions, however, are not as universal and deserved as appears at first. Beauty may evoke feelings of jealousy.[16] Beauty in individuals may have been given so much importance by their relevant others (parents, relatives, friends) that individuals have become overconscious of it, uniquely preoccupied with their external appearance, and may have neglected to develop any other potential skills. It is as if the advice "be pretty and shut up" had been internalized by them. The result may be an extremely self-centered, arrogant, empty, ignorant and even silly individual, infatuated with her or her own image, incapable of attention to others.[17]

Beautiful people seem to like parties, because their beauty guarantees them having a good time, but unless they also possess those qualities which permit them successful careers, or good marriages, and happy families, their lives between parties will be even more miserable than those of common mortals.[18] Even their social lives may not be as rewarding as they would like because, once they have elicited a few compliments from their admirers, the conversation runs short. In Italy, several times I met a very beautiful young woman who was always avidly listening to men compliment her attractiveness, but after a couple of more or less original compliments, one was at bay to find any topic of conversation. Gossip about the other guests was the only and last resource. Once she complained about a common friend, a quite well-known politician, whom she thought was really a poor conversationalist because each time he would see her the only topic he could think of was the weather. "Isn't that ridiculous?" As a matter of fact, the gentleman was a most fascinating partner in conversation, at least when he had the proper vis-à-vis.[19]

According to the stereotype, Parisian *concierges* are said to be very curious about the whereabouts of "professional beauties" and to cry over their often unhappy lives: "They have every reason to be happy and look! Third suicide attempt!" As a matter of fact their beauty may have contributed to their unhappiness; it may in fact have deprived them of most of the things which make a happy life, such as empathy for other people's lives and experiences, and the will and perseverance needed to develop useful skills and succeed professionally. It is a constant temptation for beautiful people to rely on their figures, on their rippling muscles or splendid legs, on coquetry, or on self-assurance.

I always admire the beautiful women who make a career despite traditional expectations. One of them was the late Lady Jackson, better known under her maiden name as Barbara Ward, who for many years was the editor-in-chief of *The Economist*. The contrast between the image that our society has forged of a knowledgeable British economist, on the one hand (male, short, slightly overweight, bald, with a wrinkled colorless suit, stained by the tobacco from his pipe), and this frail, handsome, elegant, vivacious, blonde woman was both rejuvenating—because of the feat—and disturbing—because it demonstrated how much talent is being wasted in other cases, when parents and teachers follow the "be pretty and shut up" principle.

If they also have something to say, beautiful people will be particularly rewarded at social gatherings. Their beauty will make them the cynosure of all eyes and their multifarious interests and skills will provide them with endless topics for conversation.

Often linked with beauty but, in fact, quite different from it is elegance. At social gatherings one likes to converse with elegant people for several reasons. First because one is flattered to receive some attention, approval, and compliments from people who so evidently possess a sense of taste. Second, elegance is largely deter-mined by culture and culture in turn is dominated by the upper classes. Consequently fashionable elegance is a sign of social status. Through elegance one perceives the hidden power of the individual and one is thrilled to be in the company of powerful people, possibly even more thrilled if others are watching. There is also a third and not so evident reason why elegance is attractive. Elegance unlike beauty is not what sociologists call "ascribed" but is achieved. One was not born with elegance but had to work at it. Unlike beauty, which can be impudently displayed in front of others without much merit on one's part, elegance shows that one appreciates the others' presence and has made some effort at pleasing them. Therefore, far from being impudent, elegance is a sign of conformity, if not of humility. It demonstrates a certain concern for others' expectations. We like to engage elegant people, because they possess two desirable qualities in a partner: that of being considered socially valuable and that of showing concern for their potential partners' judgment. A fair exchange can be made: They want us to be interested in them and they show a general interest in us.[20]

This general interest in others, of course, does not neces-sarily produce successful conversation. We sense in them a desire to please, but we are not sure that we possess the qualities which would make us attractive in their eyes. Our hesitations will be reduced, how-ever, if guests show, apart from their elegance, signs of openness or cheerfulness, which seem to make them pleased with almost any en-counter. A friend of mine who has no claim to physical beauty, and never pretends to any high degree of elegance, immediately radiates such cheerfulness and contentment at being in the presence of other people, that whoever has met her in our house, remembers her as a wonderful companion. Her open sociability manifests itself in her inquisitive eyes, the attention she gives her partners' stories, in her laughing at the proper time, in her speaking to the point, and in an inexhaustible resource of witty anecdotes.

Other people are not as cheerful but we feel them to be very civil and kind. We sense that we shall not be threatened by them. It seems they will not turn us away, but rather will make an effort at being supportive. It is very encouraging, especially at the beginning of a party, if one does not know many of the guests. Civility and kindness, however, may carry with them some slight after-taste of insincerity. Does this nice man support me because he likes me and my conversation or is he nice to me because, before coming to the party, he was told I am an idiot? One does not like to be the victim of another's charity. We would like others to be genuinely interested in us and not to have to make a great effort to be so. I remember once discussing with Ivan Illich the merits of a common sociologist friend whom I praised for being really "*désinteressé*," which in French means both unselfish and disinterested. I had meant "unselfish," but Illich, choosing the second meaning of the word, retorted: "Yes, and this is the trouble. I do not like 'disinterested' people. I am interested in your being here and I know you are interested in working in my center. This is why we have something to tell each other."[21] We all know that when, in a conversation, someone pays what we think might be a perfunctory compliment, we reply: "Oh no, but you are very kind," thereby probing the other's sincerity. We hope that our partner will tell us: "This has nothing to do with kindness. It is simply the truth!"

Sensuality, beauty, elegance, cheerfulness, and to some extent, civility and kindness are visible attractive attributes. Many others are not visible but audible. We know them through the media, gossip, or the information given by friends, hosts, and the other guests.

Some individuals are national or international heroes and stars. We have heard of them on television, we read about them in newspapers and magazines, and we get great kicks out of conversing with them even for only a few minutes. Most of the time, however, the guests we meet at social gatherings are more local in their accomplishments and a tip from someone may be necessary for us to know that here is the manager of the New York City Ballet, the director of the Museum of the Legion of Honor, the conductor of the Pittsburgh Symphony Orchestra, the British ambassador to the United Nations, or the manager of Eastern Restaurants, Inc. All these titles may contribute to make their holders more or less attractive companions, but would not suffice if we cannot also find some common ground for exchanging ideas and mutual support. Their high status may make them snobbish stars who do not speak to common mortals. Quite different is the case of the people whom our hosts introduce as artists, actors, writers, or composers. Unless they have acquired national and international fame these people need the support of the public. Two of my acquaintances are composers. One of them is famous and did not even think of discussing music with me (until he learned my father was a music critic). He was only interested in my tie. The second one is still trying to get the attention of music connoisseurs and is of very easy access. He listens carefully to anything that may help him make some progress in his art or in the public reception of it. One reason why we like to converse with creative people is the hope that they might discover and value in us some buried disposition for their art or for creativity in general. Here again the law of reciprocal awakening plays a part.

Less intrinsically attractive are the individuals famous for their knowledge, unless we ourselves are particularly interested in the same fields of knowledge and therefore can exchange information with them, compare judgments, and support and discuss each other's interpretations and hypotheses. If we are ignorant in their areas of specialization, we will find ourselves in the position of beggars, at best of interviewers, as we ask questions we hope are appropriate. The answers may prove interesting, even rewarding, if they are given with grace. The very fact that we are deemed worthy listeners may be flattering; it means that we possess our own brand of attractiveness, since the learned specialist of Pacific whales or African antelopes finds pleasure in having us as an audience! Once I heard a conversation between an ornithologist from Sri Lanka (then Ceylon) and a woman who knew nothing about tropical birds but was enjoying the ornithologist as he tried his best to describe to her the wealth of colors in the feathers of his bird friends and their musical courting practices. He was unconsciously imitating the dancing of the male bird enticing his female partner and the woman's eyes were riveted on his face, following enthusiastically the artful demonstration. Note, however, that in order to be attractive listeners, it is not enough for us to show real interest in what others say but we must also possess some attribute making us worthy of their effort. If either of these conditions fails, the conversation will rapidly come to an end. A very realistic proverb goes: "Don't cast pearls before swine." Our problem then is to persuade the pearls' owner that we are worthy of their sharing with us their time and resources, or what the French call *faire des frais.*[22]

Intelligence and wit are to the mind what beauty is to the body. Although these qualities develop through education and social intercourse, they seem to be innate qualities that cast off sparks spontaneously. They bring inner security to those who possess them and permit them to grant their companions high rewards as well as devastating humiliations. Witty and very intelligent individuals are not always good listeners. They tend to be a little too preoccupied with the piquant remark that they intend to snap into the conversation as soon as they can, and quite often they are not content with only one companion. They need an audience and often "sound off" to no one in particular. Those who encounter them may be amused but feel a little awkward at being recognized not as individuals but only as part of the general audience. To win the general applause, the witty individual may not hesitate to humiliate someone in the group. Few very intelligent people know how to resist using the others' weaknesses to their advantage. This may explain in part why scientific studies have found that intelligence is less efficient to attract other people than other qualities, namely, physical beauty.[23]

The claims to others' attention and attraction reviewed so far could be called general assets: they should make their possessors attractive to everyone. But as a matter of fact individuals have their own preferences, based upon sex,[24] experience, the roles played in life, ethical or political opinions, and so on.[25] Some prefer Republicans, others like firemen. People's occupations may predispose them to converse with others of the same or similar occupations who can appreciate their problems and achievements. For the same reasons, we may look for partners who have been in the same war, or have traveled in the same foreign countries or have lived in the same cities. We also like the people with whom we share friends.

Of all the traits that attract us to specific individuals, the similarity of opinions, values, and life orientation seems to be the most powerful.[26] We feel comfortable speaking with people who have the same religious, philosophical, ethical, or political views. How could guests obtain approval, support, or recognition from people who challenge the very basis of their daily choices? The conversation will turn into an embarrassingly cautious and hesitant succession of half-heartedly made concessions and will eventually sputter out. Individuals who are not communist themselves and have tried conversing with a hard-line communist know how no understanding is possible; vocabulary itself is a permanent source of confrontation: State control is called freedom by the communists and, in their minds liberation wars, if inspired by communism, are the true name of peace. Of course, this is not meant to say that discussions between people of different and even radically opposite ideologies are impossible. But social gatherings do not seem to offer a theater proper for these discussions. To gather any fruit from an exchange with an extreme political or philosophical adversary requires much more time than is provided in a party. Less radical and generalized differences, however, should not be a problem as long as one can find some areas of understanding. Two persons may have extremely different tastes in music but the same basic political orientation.

How do we know that others share our opinions? Sometimes we have been told. Quite often, however, one does not know for sure but guesses by looking at the others' appearance. As was discussed in Chapter 4, individuals' presentations tell something of the roles with which they want to be identified or indicate their wish to dissociate themselves from their official roles. People's presentations may also reveal their opinions and attitudes. Revolutionaries, conservatives, homosexuals, feminists, and so on, display their affiliation by choice of hairdo, clothes, accessories, jewels, and other badges. One of my students dyes her hair (or part of it) purple. It is *not* a signal of standing to the right side of the political spectrum. Once I met a priest who wore blue slacks and a turtleneck gray sweater. It was *not* a sign that he belonged to the Right to Life organization. And for a long time Fr. Daniel Berrigan has not been seen wearing a Roman collar. I have never met Joan Baez, but on her record jackets she is not seen wearing her hair as only a hairdresser can fashion, or with heavy makeup or an alluring low-cut blouse. She has chosen the "natural look," wears no makeup and her hair hangs according to the simple rule of gravity. A pin-striped three-piece suit may belong to a liberal man, but it is more likely the uniform of a conservative and is seldom seen as the clothing of a radical.

In interpreting these dress codes one may be influenced by stereotypes that owe their existence to evidence that is not entirely fool-proof. Before confessing our radicalism to a woman who is assumed to be an extreme leftist, we may want to test her out beforehand, if at least we want her to stay and converse with us for a while. A typical mistake made by traditionalists is the supposition that unattractive women are more likely to be feminists than beautiful ones. One may think that unattractive women need to translate their lack of success into a contemptuous ideology. But no scientific evidence has surfaced to justify the hypothesis.[27] One must then be cautious about making assumptions about opinions of others, especially because similarity of opinion plays such a great role in creating attraction between people, more than many other traits, notably more than people's status and prestige.[28]

Of all the possible incentives that may attract guests towards others, the belief or knowledge that these others have a high opinion of them is apparently the strongest,[29] on the condition, of course that these people do not also possess traits that make them strongly unattractive. But if they are reasonably attractive, the addition of their admiration or high esteem of the guest will permit them to win the competition for the guest's company. If James knows or senses that Pamela finds him interesting and if Pamela feels that he finds her beautiful or amusing, James will have a good time conversing with her, possibly more so than he would conversing with more famous or beautiful people whom he does not know or from whom he does not sense a particular warmth.

To conclude this discussion about what makes people attractive partner choices, it seems that in decreasing order the following list could be established: high evaluation of ourselves by another, similarity of values and opinions, cheerfulness and openness, beauty, elegance and social status, intelligence and wit, and—if it is what we are looking for—sensuality and sex-appeal.

What makes the choice difficult at times is that few people possess the whole range of attractive attributes. Some individuals are particularly well-endowed and could be called social "stars," to borrow the concept from Dr. J. L. Moreno.[30] Everyone is attracted to them and even after hours of social intercourse they do not reveal any weakness. Needless to say, these people are few. This is fortunate for us—the normal people—who would otherwise be unable to compete. There are also what we could call the "sociometric proletarians," those who are chosen by nobody. In the absence of attentive hosts or of kind guests, they remain alone in front of the buffet or stuck with someone in the same category for the whole duration of the party. We do not meet great numbers of these unfortunate "social proletarians" at social gatherings because they are not often invited. The people whom we usually meet at parties are neither the (too rare) stars nor the (uninvited) social misfits, but "regular" individuals with a mixed bag of qualities and shortcomings. We want to converse with the interesting professor, but he gets carried away in his monologues; we are attracted to the great politician, but he is often dull and never gives anyone any real personal attention. As we mentioned above, those who think highly of us are not always those whom we particularly like and if we want the company of cheerful people, we may have to put up with their sometimes "tasteless" stories. Beautiful people can be vulgar, pretentious, or ignorant to an intolerable degree. Given the mixed distribution of attractive and unattractive attributes in most individuals, it is our responsibility to decide what we really want from others for the evening and what we may develop out of it. In short what part of our souls do we want to reward?[31]

One may also refuse to choose. Guests could then establish agendas based on the assumption that they will be unable to find rewards for all the aspects of their souls at one time, and so they seek successive rewards. McCall and Simmons properly write: "As no single performance can satisfy all a person's needs and desires, a series of qualitatively different performances must be stated in order to cover all these needs."[32]

Having decided with whom we want to interact, we must consider whether there are obstacles to our engaging them.

There are circumstantial obstacles. The persons of our choice could be already engaged and we hesitate to intrude unless we feel really sure we will be accepted. Our hesitation will be all the greater if the individuals with whom our target partners converse are very attractive themselves. We may feel unable to compete, afraid of being politely ignored or even rejected. If we are not acquainted with our attractive targets, the pain of rejection will not be too severe. We may console ourselves with the thought: "They don't know what they are missing!" But the humiliation of a rejection will be very painful if our intended partners choose to pursue their duo with their present companions, in spite of the fact—or, even because of the fact—that they know us.

Similar rejection may occur even when the other persons are not already engaged. They may want to remain free for a possibly more rewarding partner. Of course, one will be granted a few words of greeting. Few people are so rude as to inflict a direct cut. But after a short, dull exchange of banalities, one is made to understand that the encounter is over. As we just said, the more we are attracted to a desired partner the more we fear the rejection. This fear in turn may cause us to be awkward and embarrassed, to blush and stutter, and be utterly boring. To speak the language of the stage, we "miss our entrance" and it may be impossible to reestablish any level of credibility. We must retreat after having uttered a few incoherent words.

To avoid embarrassment, we often stay clear of people whom we crave to approach for fear that they will ignore or reject us. Quite often we also disguise our fears and our avoidance behind some judgment of contempt: "You did not talk to Pamela? Well, you're right. I didn't either. She is so silly." "I did not want to speak with Harvey. He is quite handsome and elegant, but he has no sense of humor." In the Aesop's tale of the fox and the grapes, the fox declares that the grapes are too green for his taste and good only for boors when, in fact, they were too high for his reach![33]

There is another reason for hesitating to interact with very attractive people. Unless we know that they find us also very attractive, we may fear an imbalance in the conversation (and in the relationship which may follow). We would become too dependent on the attractive partner.

"Paradoxically," writes Peter Blau, "the very attributes that make a person an attractive associate for others also raise fears of dependence that make them reluctant to acknowledge their attraction."[34]

One can sometimes see at parties men (and women) who dance around a star waiting on the star hand and foot. Does the star wish a cigarette? Here it is. A light, the match is burning before the star asks for it. A drink. Here it is on a silver platter. A different drink? OK. Strong enough? Too strong? Whatever you say! Is it too hot? Too cool? Windows are open or closed according to the whim of the star. Are you tired? You would like a ride home? A cab? I have my car. You live in Long Island? All right, it is not far. You prefer to stay now? Good! How is your seat? Uncomfortable, maybe? This one is better. You like Sally's earrings? It is so easy. A phone call to Tiffany! The star of the day may ask anything; the infatuated admirer has become a slave. Other people see the danger before it explodes and resist the temptation before it is too late. One may object: but nobody compels us to become so dependent and enslaved. Can't we be normal even with the stars? Quite often the answer is no. Stars have been educated to have slaves and find it quite normal that everyone does their will in every detail. A star–slave relationship is the only one they can understand and if the partner is not subservient, he or she is immediately dropped as unfriendly. "I like to have male friends," said one such character once. "I want them to be always ready if I need them. But the rest of the time I want them to leave me in peace. I belong to nobody." But of course she wanted her friends to belong to her! And she lost them one by one.

Other deterrents to approaching attractive people are more extrinsic, that is, they stem out of our foreseeing some negative consequences (cost) that may derive from an immediately rewarding interaction.

We may fear, for instance, third parties accusing us of ambition or presumption if we have dared to talk to the president (of the United States or of the corporation), the general manager, or the chairman of the board. Is the reward worth the cost?

We may also later be accused of having poor taste if we converse with people who in the opinion of our relevant others have poor ratings. A friend will tell us after the party: "Your poor taste showed and you made a fool of yourself by talking to that cheap gigolo. And worse, everyone could see that you had a good time!"

The accusation may also be one of treason or infidelity to our "team," if we are seen engaged in a lively and apparently pleasant sparring with a political or ideological enemy of our team. Flirting in sight of our spouses or lovers or in the presence of someone who without fail will report it to them will bring with it scenes that make the momentary pleasure not worth the trouble.

The reader may think that individuals should not be so sensitive to the judgment of others and enjoy themselves without so much calculation. Well, individuals follow their own rules and make their own calculations. We imagine that if those who react negatively to our behavior were pure strangers with absolutely no power over us, we would not be bothered. But—apart from the fact that we never really know for sure whom we might need one day—there are also people who can make life either pleasant or very miserable for us, especially those constituting the small circle of our family and close friends. One would have to have a skin as thick as an elephant's to sustain the permanent reproaches of those who are part of our daily intimate circle. As Peter Berger justly puts it, "the social control of what German sociologists have called the 'sphere of the intimate' is particularly powerful."[35]

Assuming that guests have made up their minds about whom in the gatherings are the most attractive partners, how do they go about actually choosing whom they will engage? It seems that they, unconsciously, balance the potential rewards and costs of engaging a prospective guest. S. Moscovici writes:

> Thibaut and Kelley assume that each individual has at his disposal a sort of internal "clock" or scale which determines the comparison level which indicates the profit which he might obtain if he engaged in a re-

lationship alternative to the one in which he is engaged at present. If this profit is greater, he abandons the current relationship; if not he stays with it.[36]

This is true not only of relationships but also of the more episodic encounters in a social gathering; guests may, more or less consciously, reason in this way: Pamela and George are attractive, but they might reject me or show little support. Fred is boring, but for this reason he is available and may be ready to listen to me.

In balancing the costs and the rewards, individuals are also guided by their own goals. An individual anxious to move up the social ladder and to get recognition from the most prestigious people in the gathering will take more risks than other persons who have given up self-promotion, either because they are satisfied with the level they have reached, or because they do not perceive much chance of moving to a higher rank. The less ambitious are seen engaged in peaceful conversations mostly with their friends and past acquaintances, while the competitive individuals try their luck with everyone, especially those who seem more challenging. They do their best to "foot the bill," and retreat with grace when they find out it surpasses their potential. They have the common sense not to complain. They know the rules of the play. Not everyone can be a match for Liza Minelli, Gianni Agnelli, intelligent Stephanie or the charming David Heartpound. An acquaintance of mine hates to eat by himself while traveling alone abroad. When in a restaurant he looks around and if there is an individual or a couple who look interesting to him, he goes and asks them: "May I sit at your table?" The worst they can say is: "No." "So what, if they say no?" says he, "I go somewhere else." Other people are devastated by the idea of being rejected. They prefer to play it safe. They tend to underestimate their attractiveness and have a tendency to choose partners of lower "sociable" status. At a party they speak to the elderly, the very young,[37] the least attractive men and women, and those who are visibly alone. In doing so, they avoid rejection and humiliation. They even make a lot of people happy. A third group may try some kind of compromise between the two extremes. At the beginning of a party they use the safer approach, but as the gathering develops and internal controls are relaxed, they move more boldly and push their way toward higher targets.

Whether the guests try a prudent approach or a risky one, their success or failure is determined by the limits set by the matching principle. We cannot hope to bring pleasure to those who do not perceive us as their equals; equality of attractiveness is necessary not only to bring rewards to others but also to obtain ourselves the pleasure we derive from bringing them these rewards. Conversely, we do not enjoy ourselves very much if we get support and praise from people whom we do not admire or for whom we have no respect. Even if we never gave this principle much attention, even if, for ideological reasons of equality we refuse it as elitist, it is likely that most of the time people are guided by it in their choices. If individuals know they are not particularly high in the common ratings of a certain crowd which they must occasionally visit, they do not usually choose as partners in this crowd the most highly desirable people. In a study of dating it was found that attractive subjects choose more physically attractive and more popular dates than do unattractive subjects. It appears that the subjects in this experiment were governed by the "matching principle."[38] The results of this experiment were confirmed by other studies.[39]

The matching principle does not operate in a vacuum. It may lead individuals to choose certain people in a specific gathering and to avoid them in another setting. In other words, we introduce into our calculations not only constant but also variable factors.

In a social gathering individuals not only compare their own attractiveness with that of potential partners, but also they check whether the gathering offers them some or many possibilities of finding what could be for them better matches. I have learned that I should not try to converse with Cecily when the bank colleagues of her husband are present; she reserves her company for them and if, by chance, I succeed in approaching her for a while she is absent-minded, perpetually looking around while answering in a distracted manner, and inevitably leaves me as soon as she can find some better anchorage. But the same dear Cecily is all sugar and honey, very attentive and considerate if in the party my only competitors are the grocer and the insurance clerk. This sounds silly. But a little observation permits everyone to collect dozens of similar examples. Instead of saying while coming back home: "Strange how Cecily was cold and unpleasant tonight at Bob and Mary's. Just two days ago at Ethel's she was so nice," compare the guest list at Bob and Mary's with the list at Ethel's and the explanation will become crystal clear.

The choice of our partners in a social gathering is a good application of the old proverb: "Birds of a feather flock together."

Rarely shall we see individuals of a very different level of attractiveness speaking together. This is more true with respect to social prestige than with physical attractiveness. Simmel himself observed that "sociability among members of very different social strata often is inconsistent and painful."[40] The fact is not surprising if by sociability one implies modern sociability as opposed to the festivities of the past which celebrated the communal ties among all the members of the group, rich or poor. These modern gatherings reflect the structure of the outside, larger society, not so much in its compartmentalization, which its festive unity conceals, but in its rank order. More precisely each social gathering is composed of individuals of a comparable social status. If individuals move up the social scale—and this is expected in an achieving society—they also become eligible to attend parties of a status level corresponding to their new social position. One may protest the injustices and the vanity connected with status inequalities, but they are so built into the fabric of society that they cannot be ignored. All the pieces of research quoted in this chapter point in the same direction: Without some kind of power and competence, we cannot hope to attract others; this is true of both the larger world as well as of those microcosms which represent it, the social gatherings. Even those who want to introduce more equality into society cannot attain their goals without first having reached positions of power, be they intellectual or political, technological or artistic. Their personal problem, of course, will be: once they have started to play the game of individualistic competition, will they still be capable of compassion?

NOTES

1. G. J. McCall and J. L. Simmons, *Identities and Interactions* (New York: The Free Press, 1978), p. 71.

2. Certain seats are usually avoided in a grouping of seats, particularly those located at the end of a row or of a semicircle, unless the semicircle is so small that it permits a general conversation. In the following graphs each seat has been marked with either HD, D, or ND, meaning highly desirable, desirable and not desirable.

ND   D   D   HD   D   D   ND

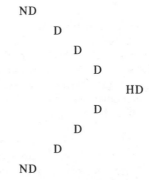

The individual in the center can easily speak to either his or her right or left. He or she can also monitor a conversation between all or several of the other individuals. This last possibility is barely offered to those seated next to the center, and not at all available to the extremities of the row or semicircle. The intermediary positions offer a choice of at least two possible partners. Those at the end can easily be left out if the conversation is somehow generalized; if the interaction is split into pairs, those sitting on the ends can have only one possible partner. In the case that the end person's only neighbor chooses to speak to the other person sitting next to him or her, the end person is left stranded. At a recent party we observed how one seat remained unoccupied for at least half an hour, until someone got the idea of moving it and using it to close the open circle:

0 0 0	0 0 0
0 0	0 0
0 0	0 0
0	0

Arrangement 1   Arrangement 2

(0 is not occupied)   (0 is occupied)

Compare with A. Bavelas, "Communication patterns in task-oriented groups," in Leonard Broom and Philip Selznick, *Sociology* (Evanston, Ill.: Row & Peterson, 1955), pp. 211–213.

    3. Enid Nemy, "New Yorkers, etc.," New York Times, April 4, 1979, Sec. C, p. 2. See also Enid Nemy, "When Trapped by a Bore, Don't Just Stand There," in New York *Times*, December 19, 1979, Sec. C, p. 15.

    4. A person's attractiveness highly depends on the type of activity we want to share with him or her. We concentrate here on what makes human beings attractive as companions in a social gathering. If the activity were that of attending a concert or a play, sailing, sitting on the beach, going away for a weekend, starting a love affair or getting married, the qualities making the others attractive would be quite divergent and each time different. One cannot determine a person's attractiveness in the abstract.

5. "The basic criterion is whether individuals are oriented towards an association as a means to some further end, as when they request a neighbor's help, or as an end-in-itself, as when they simply socialize with him" (Peter Blau, *Exchange and Power in Social Life* [New York: John Wiley and Sons, 1964], p. 58).

6. Spouse selection is quite different from date selection or selection in a social gathering. Spouse selection is based most often on age compatibility, racial and religious similarities, equality of social status and educational level, and so on. See Alan C. Kerckhoff, "The Social Context of Interpersonal Attraction," in Ted L. Huston, *Foundations of Interpersonal Attraction* (New York: Academic Press, 1974), p. 63. According to another study, attractive individuals, as opposed to less attractive ones, are not expected to be better parents. Though attractive "targets" are expected to have more socially desirable personalities, viz. to be better spouses and sexual partners, and to marry men of higher occupational status, and experience greater social and professional happiness in comparison to the unattractive target females, the attractive targets were also expected to be more vain, egotistical, materialistic, snobbish, and likely to request a divorce and have an extramarital affair as well as be unsympathetic with oppressed peoples. See Marshall Dermer and Darrel L. Thiel, "When Beauty May Fail," *Journal of Personality & Social Psychology*, 1975, v. 31, n. 6, pp. 1168–1176.

7. "Attraction is the anticipation of rewards," writes James T. Tedeschi in "Attributions, Liking, and Power," Huston, op. cit., p. 209. He refers himself to A. J. and B. E. Lott: "A Learning Theory Approach to Interpersonal Attitudes," in A. G. Greenwald, T. C. Brock, and T. M. Ostrom, eds., *Psychological Foundations of Attitudes* (New York: Academic Press, 1968), pp. 67–68.

8. "But the category of reward most involved in forming attachments is that of role support, the expressed confirmation or legitimation accorded to a performer by an audience(s) for his claims concerning his role identity" (George J. McCall, "A Symbolic Interactionist Approach to Attraction," in Huston, op. cit., p. 226).

9. Since highly desirable individuals are the targets of many others, they can afford to be choosy and withdrawn in order to discourage those with whom they do not want to interact. If someone they feel appropriate is in sight, they then sweeten their demeanor. Some other individuals who are not particularly attractive, however, imitate the behavior of the stars and by adopting a cold, distant look, hope to make others believe that they conceal in themselves some unknown treasure.

10. "At the core of human attachment is reciprocity—shared behavior—and reciprocity is its own reward," and "as a personal characteristic, reciprocal responsiveness may well prove to be a more powerful determinant of attractiveness than many of the personal attributes studied in the attraction literature." (Thomas Lickona, "A Cognitive-Developmental Approach to Interpersonal Attraction," in Huston, op. cit., p. 34).

11. On this we follow George McCall in his criticism of the reinforcement theory of attraction: It is the anticipation of rewards that is important in making someone attractive, not "the reinforcing effects of rewards received" (George McCall, "A Symbolic Interactionist Approach to Attraction," in Huston, op. cit., p. 229).

12. Peter Berger, *Invitation to Sociology* (Garden City: Doubleday Anchor, 1963), p. 101. Berger continues:

Intelligence, humor, manual skills, religious devotion and even sexual potency respond with equal alacrity to the expectations of others. This makes understandable the previously mentioned process by which individuals choose their associates in such a way that the latter sustain their self-interpretation.

13. The *Kamasutra* of Vatsyayana teaches men how they can recognize the sensuous disposition of a woman towards them. Specific attention should be given to a woman uncovering her limbs.

14. See Ellen Berscheid and Elaine Walster, *Interpersonal Attraction* (Reading, Mass.: Addison-Wesley, 2d ed., 1978). And "Beauty and the Best," in *Psychology Today*, 1972, vol. 5, pp. 42–46.

15. Several studies have shown that beautiful people are supposed to possess more socially desirable personalities. See, for instance, Ellen Berscheid and Elaine Walster, "Physical Attractiveness," in L. Berkowitz, ed., *Advances in Experimental Social Psychology*, vol. 7 (New York: Academic Press, 1974).

16. Beautiful people may arouse jealousy and resentment. In an already mentioned study, unattractive participants did not judge the beautiful targets as having more desirable personalities. (See Dermer and Thiel, op. cit., p. 1173).

17. In his *Memoirs*, Prince Alphonse Clary, speaking of nineteenth-century professional beauties, writes:

There is no doubt that such ladies were exceedingly beautiful but also rather full of themselves. When one came to know them better one might discover that some of them were also very pleasant or indeed clever and interesting, but others were insufferably vain and would often behave like naughty children. I was still very young, probably just out of school, when I was a guest at a great house in Bohemia. Also present was a famous English beauty on whom the middle-aged gentlemen were fussily dancing attention. Our host possessed a collection of particularly fine antique Meissen coffee cups which were kept in a display case. In honor of the famous guest these were for once put in use. The beauty was standing in the middle of the room, cup in hand, and when she had drunk her coffee she looked around, saw no table near her, and simply dropped the cup which shattered on the floor. I was aghast—what would our host say? But he knelt down before the lady with the words: "This is the most beautiful day of my life—the most beautiful woman in the world has broken the most beautiful cup in the world in my house!" Prince Clary, *A European Past* (London: Weidenfeld and Nicolson, 1978), pp. 201–202.

18. One of these drawbacks is that their very visible and attractive beauty excuses their admirers to look into their deeper, less visible, personally achieved assets: "I have a girlfriend who is gorgeous" explains Susan Brecht to

an interviewer, "and she's going through a lot of traumas because of it. Men are attracted to her because of her looks, and she gets frustrated that that's why they date her. No one cares that she has her master's degree . . . " (Leslie Bennetts: "Beauty Is Found to Attract Some Unfair Advantages," New York *Times*, March 18, 1978, p. 10).

19. Physical beauty increases immediate attractiveness and permits one to predict who is going to be the target of dates or of conversation at a party; it does not, however, predict the duration of a relationship which supposes different and deeper personal assets. Stendhal used to say that to establish a love affair, beauty in a man saves him only a couple of weeks, meaning that many other assets are more important. On the evolution of attraction, see George Levinger, "A Three Level Approach to Attraction: Toward an Understanding of Pair Relatedness," in Huston, op. cit., pp. 100–120.

20. Contrary to the common sense idea that adornment is selfish, Simmel writes: "One adorns oneself for oneself, but can do so only by adornment for others . . . adornment is the egoistic element as such, it singles out its wearer . . . but at the same time, adornment is altruistic: its pleasure is designed for the others, since its owner can enjoy it only insofar as he mirrors himself in them; he renders the adornment valuable only through the reflection of this gift of his. . . ; the aesthetic phenomenon of adornment indicates a point within sociological interaction—the arena of man's being-for-himself and being-for-the-other—where these two opposite directions are mutually dependent as ends and means." Georg Simmel, *The Sociology of Georg Simmel*, Kurt H. Wolff, trans. (Glencoe, Ill.: The Free Press, 1950), p. 339.

21. We must here disagree with James T. Tedeschi's following point: "The definition of attraction as an expectancy that an actor will *altruistically* provide benefits of various types and values . . ." (Italics, ours). No doubt there is an element of self-restraint in the granting of the benefits we collect from our social companions. They must be *willing* to recognize us as valuable partners but not out of kindness; it must be out of some kind of necessity. We want them to be somehow *compelled* to bow before us in an attitude well translated by the familiar French expression *chapeau!*, meaning "I feel compelled to raise my hat when confronted with your . . . skills, value, achievement, etc. . . ." See James T. Tedeschi, "Attractions, Liking, and Power," in Ted L. Huston, ed., op. cit., p. 200.

22. Literally "make expenses" for someone. The partner is considered worthy of one spending for him or her if not money at least efforts at being interesting and witty.

23. "Students with exceptional social skills and intelligence levels were not liked any better than were students less fortunate in this regard. It seems, then, that it is helpful to be beautiful if you wish to inspire passion in your contemporaries" (Ellen Berscheid and Elaine Walster, "A Little Bit About Love," in Huston, op. cit., p. 375).

24. Experience as well as empirical studies tell us that females request more intelligent, considerate, and outgoing dates, whereas males request more frequently that the dates possess physical attractiveness (Elaine Walster, G. W. Walster, and K. Dion, "Physical Attractiveness and Dating Choice; A Test of

the Matching Hypothesis," *Journal of Experimental Social Psychology* 7 [1971], 173–189).

25. This being determined, every individual could be rated with a double instrument: (1) a grade average given by a panel of judges and (2) a coefficient of variance, indicating whether the judges agreed on a similar coefficient or whether they had a great variety of judgment. Some people are equally attractive to every observer. Others elicit great passions or great hatred.

26. ". . . [a]ttraction to another varies directly with his or her perceived similarity . . ." (George Levinger, "A Three-Level Approach to Attraction: Toward an Understanding of Pair Relatedness" in Huston, op. cit., p. 103).

27. See: Philip A. Goldberg, Marc Gottesdiener, and Paul R. Abramson, "Another Put Down of Women?: Perceived Attractiveness as a Function of Support for the Feminist Movement," *Journal of Personality and Social Psychology*, 1975, vol. 32, pp. 113–116.

28. According to William Griffitt ("Attitude Similarity and Attraction," in Huston, op. cit., p. 296), the prestige of an individual does not make him more attractive in the eyes of a "judge" if the other knows this individual's attitudes. Attitudes are predominant.

29. William Griffitt refers to several studies that prove that the others' evaluation of the subject have even much more effect on the subject's response than the knowledge of the others' attitudes (art. cit., p. 294).

30. See J. L. Moreno, *Who Shall Survive?* (Washington, D.C.: Nervous and Mental Diseases Monography, No. 58, 1934).

31. Affective and intellectual components of attraction can be theoretically distinguished. See Gerald L. Clore and Donn Byrne, "A Reinforcement-Affect Model of Attraction" in Huston, op. cit., pp. 149–151. It seems to me that the affect component of attraction is not very differentiated. Either we feel attracted to someone or not, while the intellectual component is susceptible to many articulate nuances. I can feel violently attracted to a human being full of sex-appeal and I can judge him or her to be "attractive," "friendly," "modest," and so on . . . but also "vulgar," "ignorant," and—according to my standards— "immoral." The question of deciding (intellectual judgment) whether the other is "attractive" or not does not rest upon the other, but upon my judgment.

32. G. J. McCall and J. L. Simmons, op. cit., p. 162.

33. "The Fox and the Grapes" is the most famous fable of the Greek poet Aesop. The Fox perfectly sees the beauty of the grapes but denigrates them since they are out of reach. Similarly it does not seem that the high attractiveness of an individual prevents others from perceiving it, even when they themselves are unattractive. But unattractive women (not men) hesitate to perceive or to label other unattractive individuals as such. See G. Tennis and J. Dabbs, Jr., "Judging Physical Attractiveness," *Journal of Personality and Social Psychology*, 1975, vol. 31, pp. 513–516.

34. Peter Blau, op. cit., p. 43.

35. Peter Berger, *Invitation to Sociology* (Garden City, N.Y.: Doubleday Anchor, 1963), p. 77. Berger continues:

... because of the very factors that have gone into its construction in the individual's biography. A man chooses a wife and a good friend in acts of essential self-definition. His most intimate relationships are those that he must count upon to sustain the most important elements of his self-image. To risk, therefore, the disintegration of these relationships means to risk losing himself in a total way. It is no wonder then that many an office despot promptly obeys his wife and cringes before the raised eyebrows of his friends.

In "The Rating and Dating Complex" (*American Sociological Review* 2, 1937, p. 731) Willard Waller writes:

A girl's choice of whom she falls in love with is limited by the censorship of the one-sex group. Every boy that she dates is discussed and criticized by the other members of the group. This rigid control often keeps a girl from dating at all. If a girl is a member of a group in which the other girls are rated higher on the dating scale than she, she is often unable to get dates with boys who are considered desirable by her friends. In that event she has to decide whether to date the boys that she can and choose girl friends who would approve, or she must resign herself to not dating.

36. S. Moscovici, "Society and Theory in Social Psychology," in J. Israel and H. Tajfel, eds., *The Context of Social Psychology: A Critical Assessment* (London, New York: Academic Press, 1972), p. 72.

37. "... [t]here are broad statuses in our society, such as that of old persons or the very young, that sometimes seem to be considered so meager in sacred value that it may be thought their members have nothing to lose through face engagement, and hence can be engaged at will" (Goffman, *Behavior in Public Places* [New York: The Free Press, 1963], pp. 125–126).

38. See I. Silverman, "Physical Attractiveness and Courtship," in *Sexual Behavior*, September 1971, pp. 22–25.

39. For instance: B. I. Murstein, "Physical Attractiveness and Marital Choice," *Journal of Personality and Social Psychology*, 1972, vol. 22, pp. 8–12; B. I. Murstein and Patricia Christy, "Physical Attractiveness and Marriage Adjustment in Middle-Aged Couples," *Journal of Personality and Social Psychology*, 1976, vol. 34, pp. 537–542; B. I. Murstein, *Who Will Marry Them? Theories and Research in Marital Choice* (New York: Springer, 1976).

40. Georg Simmel, op. cit., p. 47.

7
ENGAGING OTHERS

In a film about Jane Goodall and the chimpanzees she studied in Kenya, we see a chimpanzee wandering alone in the forest after losing her family. The chimp was desperate. She knew death would come soon to her and her baby: No creature can live alone for long in the dangerous forest. After another night of anxiety and hunger the chimp resumed her blind, hopeless search. Suddenly a deep exciting feeling gripped her: the scent, yes, the scent of companions. She moved faster, looking to the right, to the left. She started to run and soon, out of breath, stopped; there they were, not her family, but similar faces: five, six, seven, ten, strong and healthy chimpanzees, with their familiar faces and their elegant moves. However, a new fear took hold of her. She did not know them. Would they accept her, the females who jealously guard their sexist males who in turn welcome only the young and the pretty? The head, the chief, might not want two other charges in his care. She sat still, cuddling her baby, looking as modest as she could, but hoping she appeared attractive, too. Long minutes passed. Then the big male grumbled and, turning his large head toward her, at last, nodded. Trying to control her overwhelming joy, she walked slowly toward him and stopped humbly next to him. He put his big hand on her shoulder. She was definitely adopted. Safe.[1]

Even though a party is not as dangerous, the fear that seizes us when we enter a crowd of strangers seems at times as extreme as if we were entering a dangerous, life-threatening jungle. Of course, this is not the case with family gatherings, in which everyone is known to everyone else, but is more true of the modern gathering which is largely made up of strangers. As a consequence we will focus here on the problems that arise when we attempt to engage these unknown others. More than anything else our attempts are thwarted by the fear of possible indifference or rejection. The dread of coldness or refusal by other participants does not mean starvation and death, as for the chimp, but it directly conflicts with the desire for recognition and support, which, more or less consciously, motivated the guests who came to the party.

There are several issues involved in engaging others at a modern gathering. First, while it is true that every guest at a private party is entitled to engage any of the other guests, the hosts are usually needed to facilitate introductions. But, as we will demonstrate later in this chapter, sometimes hosts do not introduce their guests, or, once the first introductions have been performed, guests cannot expect the hosts to continue helping them. How, then, will they engage other people? Guests are well aware of the other guests' theoretical accessibility, but they know or sense that other guests also possess the right to decide whom they will admit into their company. Therefore, one cannot engage others without receiving first a clearance sign. Also, in the later part of this chapter we will examine the logistics of how guests proceed to engage others when they are alone or when they are already engaged with another person.

As we have said, the fear of rejection is a primary obstacle to engaging others. It is a fact that outright rejection is infrequent in social gatherings. But quasi-rejection, which includes a perfunctory exchange of polite banalities, is often found. This is a consequence of a right we all possess: the right to decide whom we will admit into our company and more especially to whom we shall communicate our inner thoughts, feelings, opinions, and attitudes.[2] We only offer these parts of ourselves to those whom we trust or at least suspect will bring us support and recognition in return.

We will examine our right to select companions later in the chapter. Here, what must be stressed is that social gatherings are precisely organized to provide access to people whom we would otherwise never have had a chance to engage. However, the ability of social gatherings to create mutual accessibility does not completely eliminate our right to choose.

This rule *fully* applies in an anonymous crowd. No one has any right to our company there and we may deny it to everyone or to any specific individual whom we do not wish to engage. There is no obligation to stop our car to pick up a hitchhiker or to engage in conversation with someone sitting on the same bench at the botanical garden. The same is true of today's large street festivals or fiestas. And this principle also applies, to some extent, to very large receptions where everyone and anyone is admitted: for instance, to the crowd which fills the American Embassy in London, Rome, or Paris for the Fourth of July celebrations. The only exception we can think of are the European or Latin-American and specifically German or Brazilian carnivals. Those who attend, especially if they have put on the proper carnival attire, explicitly tell the other participants that they are available for engagement, for dancing or drinking with them, and so on.[3]

When the guests at a party evidently constitute a selected crowd, then our accepting the invitation from the hosts is somehow a waiver of our right to privacy and selectivity. All guests, in principle, grant the hosts and the other guests the pleasure of their company. The more selective the party—we said earlier that selectiveness usually, but not always, corresponds to the number of guests—the less right others have to deny their company to anyone in the party. An outright denial would mean that one didn't trust the hosts in the selection of their guests. In other words, in a private and selective gathering, guests ought to make themselves somehow accessible to all others, and, conversely, everyone is accessible to them.[4]

As Erving Goffman says, this general rule of accessibility is made more specific—and pressing—through the ritual of introductions.[5] Introductions have a double function: first, they provide the guests with some information about each other in order to facilitate their ensuing engagements. We shall deal with this aspect in further chapters. The second function is to make explicit the mutual accessibility among the guests and to give them the opportunity to engage in a ritual of mutual acknowledgment.

Introductions can be general or specific. By a general introduction, we mean an introduction performed between one individual and several of the guests who have already arrived. The name of the newcomer is proclaimed to the existent gathering, followed by the name of every other guest. The newcomer moves around indulging in a ritual of mutual acknowledgment with everyone: handshakes, bowing, kissing, embracing, waving, and so on. This type of mass introduction could be called a "cheap" introduction or an introduction "at a discount." It saves the hosts time and effort. It shows that the newcomer is welcome and makes him or her feel better than had no introduction been performed at all. However, the approach is so impersonal that it does not create a specific obligation in any one of the guests towards the newcomer and they return immediately to their previous engagements without including the new guest. We have seen newcomers, who, having been treated to the mass introduction, and having finished the round of acknowledgment rituals, found themselves alone and had no recourse other than going to the bar and getting a drink. If they were lucky they could start a conversation there with one of the lonely souls who usually hangs around the bar or the buffet.

Introductions can also be specific. The hosts or one of their assistants can take the newcomers "by the hand" and accompany them to *each* of the already formed pairs, trios, or groups. These introductions are not limited to the more or less audible utterance of the name, but a brief conversation starts each time and mention is made of the possible common interests existing between newcomers and the other guests. This greatly facilitates the real insertion of the newcomers either into the last group to which they were presented or to any of the previously visited ones. The care that the hosts have taken, making a personal sacrifice of time and thought, creates in every other guest the obligation to be ready to engage the newcomers. This type of introduction is more needed when the newcomers are indeed new in town or new to the already gathered clique. It will make the difference for them between a boring or humiliating experience and a very enjoyable party. Such treatment makes them much more confident in their right to approach the other guests, and it also helps them to choose from among those with similar interests or status.

For the very reason that specific and personal introductions make individuals much more accessible, they might not be welcomed by everyone, especially by those who think of themselves as having a higher rank or at least a higher power of attraction. They may resent the obligation created by the introduction to welcome people they do not particularly value. This is quite possible. But is this not an unavoidable pitfall of all socializing? Since no one is expected to remain for the duration of the party with the same partner, the suffering will be short enough.

More justified would be the displeasure of some important

participants of public gatherings and receptions whose presence is less the result of a choice than of a professional obligation. The president, the director, the manager, the mayor, and so on, have no choice but to attend. One cannot say that by coming to the party they had subscribed to all its obligations, including that of being totally accessible to everyone and to welcome all those introduced to them. Before introducing Johnny to the general manager, it might be politic to ask the latter whether an introduction of Johnny is welcome, which will avoid poorly concealed displeasure on the part of the general manager and embarrassment for Johnny.[6]

As we mentioned earlier twice, mutual acceptance is expressed by a ritual—for instance, a handshake, signaling the passage from the relationship of strangers to that of acquaintances.[7] One may wonder why a ritual of acceptance is needed. The answer is that many things that go without saying go even better when they are said. People in social gatherings are supposed to acknowledge, recognize, and respect one another's presence. The ritual assures everyone else that they intend to respect the established rule. The ritual does even more. As Peter Berger well observed,

> One feels more ardent by kissing, more humble by kneeling and more angry by shaking one's fist. That is, the kiss not only expresses ardor but manufactures it. Roles carry with them both certain actions and the emotions and attitudes that belong to these actions.[8]

Similarly, a ritual of mutual acknowledgment increases the feeling of mutual acceptance. There are variations in the rituals of mutual acknowledgment. Handshaking comes from the times of chivalry when the right hand was extended, first to show that no weapons were held, and that, second, by entrusting one's hand to the other, the drawing of a sword was prevented. Certain countries have forgotten the knightly origin of the ritual and permit both females and males to engage in it. However, in the United States many women still hesitate to shake hands, especially with men. In other nations, bowing the head or even the upper part of the body, possibly with joined hands, indicates a humble acknowledgment of the other person's dignity. Hand kissing is a medieval practice. It is a gesture of submission to someone of higher rank: king, queen, elder, religious dignitary, and so on. It is limited nowadays to the greeting of a married woman by a man; sometimes a young woman will kiss the hand of another woman if the other is older, but these practices are found only in rare European circles and are almost unknown in the United States. Recently the New York *Times* published a photograph of King Hussein kissing the hand of Mrs. Giscard d'Estaing while Queen Nur-el-Hussein and the French president watched. The image was deemed exotic enough to merit being published by the *Times*, which had not otherwise mentioned the encounter between the two leaders. I once watched with amusement a colleague who had just arrived from France and had been invited to a party at my university. When introduced to wives of the president and other dignitaries of the school, he bowed and kissed their (unprepared, somehow resisting) hands. The surprise in their eyes, the blush on their cheeks, their embarrassed looks, expressed puzzlement: "But, what is this? What's happened? Is this a declaration of love?" In many countries of Europe and Latin America, embracing is a frequent ritual. It may be used by both men and women. It does not necessarily imply a high degree of affection, but simply joy at meeting someone. Kissing is yet another game. It usually expresses a deeper degree of affection. Heterosexual men seldom kiss each other except in Russia, or, if they are close relatives, in Italy (more seldom in France and Spain). The United States in the past decade has seen an increase in the number of women kissing their male friends in public, as a greeting ritual.

These various rituals are usually accompanied by brief but intense eye contact as a manifestation of trust. To offer individuals the privilege of looking into our eyes and to be able to sustain their inquisitive look without blinking or diverting our eyes, is a sign of trust and sincerity.[9]

As the meaning of all rituals is ambiguous, so are the rituals of greeting. They may be observed with intentions different from those they are supposed to convey. It is impossible to refuse a proffered hand. It would be an offense not only to the individual, but also to the host and the other guests. No one prevents people, however, from doing their best to avoid guests they do not want to engage. As the following pages will make clear, people do so by avoiding eye contact, that is, avoiding the situation where they are compelled either to dismiss unwanted acquaintances or to admit them into their company. Avoiding eye contact, unfortunately, does not work in all circumstances. For instance, the party may be quite small or one may have arrived early when only a few guests are present. One cannot hope to avoid the unpleasant encounter by addressing the hosts. The hosts need to remain free for the welcoming of their guests, and sooner or later, one will have to speak to one's "enemy." In these cases one chooses the most impersonal topic of conversation and hopes for the best.

If many guests are around when an individual arrives and if that person has been introduced to the guests in a very general way, the newcomer is faced with the opposite problem: not of being compelled to talk to someone, but of finding someone to engage. Before we come to this thorny matter, however, we must deal with a case more and more prevalent today (*O tempora! O mores!*) when no introductions whatsoever are performed by the hosts. It happens not only at the semi-public receptions of city hall or the embassies, but at very private parties. This negligence does not have its full impact when all or most of the guests are mutually acquainted. As soon as they have greeted the hosts, they mingle in the crowd and find in it many possible companions. But today in what we have called modern gatherings, this is not often the case. These gatherings, as more or less faithful microcosms of the larger society, most often bring together people who are largely unacquainted. This considerably increases both the anxiety of the guests who wonder how they can approach all these unknown people and the responsibility of the hosts in monitoring their party. However, quite often the hosts overlook the fact that their guests are unacquainted, probably because they unconsciously presume that all their friends are known to each other.

Robert was recently invited to a cocktail–buffet dinner by William, an old acquaintance. Remembering previous similar parties at his house, Robert was certain he would know many of the other guests and rejoiced in advance at seeing them again. As he was about to press the forty-first button in the elevator, he saw that it had been done. When the elevator stopped, another gentleman motioned to leave the elevator, but let Robert—who is older—go first. Upon entering, Robert and the unknown gentleman greeted the host. Ignoring Robert totally, William started a conversation with the other gentleman. Robert could not believe his eyes. He knew William as a very polite and friendly man. He considered forcing his way back into the duo and claiming his right to be introduced. However, given his curiosity about party behavior, he just stood still, eager to record the sequence of events. First, a butler stopped and took his order for a drink. Then William's fourteen-year-old daughter passed by, offering a dish of small sandwiches; she then went her way. Robert was looking around to spot some familiar faces, but he could not recognize anyone except his host's mother, who was wandering about as perplexed as he was. Robert greeted her and started some small talk which soon focused on whom had been invited. The old woman did not know any of the guests and apparently her son was absolutely indifferent to his stranded mother, as well. Soon, however, a crowd of habitués began to arrive—and even to pour in. Robert found many old acquaintances and had not even the time to speak to all those he knew and liked. His discomfort had been, therefore, very temporary. It might have lasted much longer without anyone at hand to help.

At a recent party I found myself in an intermediary situation. I knew a dozen of the hundred guests. No introductions were performed and apart from a couple of newcomers in town who were looking avidly for some anchorage, I engaged only the few people I already knew. The party was private, but large and not very selective. It was evidently a collection of all the people to whom the hosts owed some obligation. In such a case, self-introduction is almost impossible: Why start talking to this one or that one, having no idea who they are or what there might be in common? As already mentioned, our only chance in that case is offered by the people who are new to the community, if we succeed in spotting them. Quite often they can be identified because they constitute a couple and remain together, not facing each other but looking together either at the other guests, or at the paintings, or at the buffet arrangements.

Not all introductions are performed by the hosts. Once a party has already started and everyone is conversing or moving through the crowd, guests often introduce their old friends to people with whom they have become acquainted or to those they judge could make good matches with their friends.

Except for the cases in which an interaction is the consequence of an introduction, we are often in the situation of having to approach others and engage them. Even if an engagement has followed an introduction, we will have to shift partners at some point and we cannot just expect that the hosts will always be available to help initiate new engagements. All we can justly wish for from them is that they tell the other guests who we are. It is up to us now to engage them.

Before engaging other guests, one assesses their degree of accessibility. Certain categories of people are more accessible and there is no problem in approaching them. Others are less accessible either because of their higher power or because of situational conditions.

We have already discussed the matching principle and its consequences for the relative accessibility of people in social gatherings. When guests contemplate interacting with others, they consider—given their own social power—whether they make a good match with them. An important element of the guest's assessment is a weighing of the competition they must confront in the gathering. No two parties are identically composed and our relative power and attractiveness largely depends upon with whom we must compete. Every party is a new game.

Some categories of people, independent of the circumstances, are more accessible. Among them, Erving Goffman lists the hosts of the party, their immediate family, the very young, and the very old.[10] The first took the initiative of organizing the gathering and doing the inviting. The latter two categories do not possess a high level of power; this makes them less attractive, less in demand. They welcome anyone who shows interest in them.[11]

Apart from personal accessibility there is what we could call situational accessibility. Certain individuals may be already engaged with someone else or, on the contrary, may stand alone; if alone, they are, of course, much more available. We cannot take it for granted, however, that the lonely man or woman will welcome our company. Like everyone else, they, too, somehow want to be courted for the pleasure and honor of their company. This observation leads us to the second basic principle which presides over mutual engagements at social gatherings: As we said above, the duty of being accessible does not deprive guests of their right to privacy and to manifesting their acceptance of new companions.

To start an interaction with people—alone or in a group—without having been first accepted by them is an act of aggression. Even if the aggression can be construed as a sign of liking or appreciation, the target individuals may want to protect themselves from being acquired and possessed by others. Guests may resent the assumption that they are so desperate for company that they will avidly converse with anyone at all.

As a sign of their autonomy, guests have the right to control their personal space; and they may object to an invasion of their immediate space by others without consent.[12]

The space around us is structured: It contains various circles or chambers, both physical and symbolic. These are two different kinds of spaces. The same physical space can in certain circumstances be invaded by others without resentment on our part, while in other circumstances we object to it. In a bus or subway train, people can be extremely close together without their proximity having any meaning for human interaction. But physical proximity in our house or bedroom, even when standing many feet apart, is considered an intrusion, if done without consent.

Most intimate is the space which is found between our skin and our clothes. Its invasion supposes a very decisive permission from the person (the permission can be implicit: for example, the silence of the hesitant partner to the prudent and slow invasion of the seducer's hands. At each step, the latter carefully watches the partner's reactions before moving on). Next in line is the bed. To admit someone into bed usually grants total access to one's body. Sitting on the bed is already a lesser invasion, but is still quite intimate. Next in the decreasing order of intimacy is access to our bedroom, which indicates, however, a high degree of friendship. Then comes our apartment or house, the garden, the entrance. We may hesitate to admit a salesperson into our house, and may speak together on the porch instead.[13] When we are on the street we maintain a barrier around us that permits penetration only for select reasons. This personal street space varies considerably according to the average density of the place. There is no objection to someone who passes close by in a busy street. But someone walking on the opposite sidewalk of an empty street who crosses apparently without motive, except that of being next to us, is viewed with suspicion. In any space, be it the desert or a garden party, the personal space increases or decreases according to the density of the people. In an empty movie theater we object to someone coming and sitting next to us, or even two or three seats away from us in the same row. If the number of patrons increases, we won't object to people sitting closer and closer to us, until, the theater being almost full, the last to arrive does not find any seat other than the one next to ours. But we might vigorously protest if the newly arrived individual interprets the physical proximity as permission to initiate a conversation or a sexual advance.

In general, entry into someone else's private space must be preceded by a "knock at the door," followed by a "come-in." This is the reason why a successful encounter with someone is initiated from the front and not from behind or from the side. The frontal approach allows the recipient of these attentions to control what happens better than if they were to occur outside view.

In situations other than social gatherings it might not be enough to "knock at the door" in order to be granted access; we might have to explain why we request an audience. But in a social gathering no motive has to be offered, since our presence itself at the party indicates our intention to enjoy the other guests' company. It is therefore enough for us to manifest our hopes of engaging someone and to wait for a sign from that someone that we are welcome.

How do we manifest our intentions? We used the image of knocking at the door. In a social gathering there are, strictly speaking, no doors upon which to knock, but the equivalent is done by approaching another person's personal space. We do not invade it, however; we remain at the border and accompany our moves with an interrogative gaze.

When intending to engage someone, people use two kinds of gazes: the cognitive gaze, and the soliciting gaze. The cognitive gaze does not convey—at least immediately—an intention of interaction. It is directed at the other in order to find out who the other is. "Do I know you?" is the question the stare is meant to ask. It is not a curious or assessing stare to which the target person could object. People accept being looked at for a possible recognition. This cognitive gaze concentrates on the face of the other, since it is the part of the body by which usually people are best identified. An assessment gaze on the contrary might concentrate on the silhouette, on a man's rear-end, or a woman's breasts (and the face, too, but not exclusively). The assessment gaze is relaxed and sometimes ironic. It reduces the other to the status of an object. The cognitive gaze, on the contrary, is accompanied by some facial tension, showing the effort made to reach into one's memory. It manifests an interest in the identities of others, not in their external presentations, such as their looks.

Take the example of Mike and Larry. According to outward signs, it is not clear whether Mike recognizes Larry who is repeatedly staring at him. If Mike is willing to interact with Larry, he will probably answer with a smile and a nod, meaning, "Oh, yes, I know you!" If he does not recognize Larry or does not wish to interact, he simply gazes back with a perplexed look, intending to say: "Yes, I understand you think we know each other, but as far as I can figure it out, I don't think so." In this case, if Mike recognizes Larry but has decided not to show it, he controls his facial expression perfectly, because any "slip of the face," giving off his recognition, will demand that an interaction follow. To go on denying the acquaintanceship would be an uncivil cut.

It is also possible that Mike may not wish to exclude an interaction with Larry, but he might want to delay (or at least convey the impression he wants only to delay) the engagement, because, for instance, he is presently busy. He then responds to Larry's cognitive gaze, by a nod and a smile, but before Larry has had the time to express his wish to interact (through a soliciting gaze, for example) Mike immediately expresses his temporary nonavailability: "Hello, you're not leaving right away, are you?" he might say while walking briskly away, or even better: "Hello, how are you? I must see you some time today. I'll be back," the last uttered in a confidential tone. Then Mike might disappear to his very important business.

Let us suppose that Mike has acquiesced to Larry's cognitive gaze, and does not manifest any wish to postpone an interaction; then, the cognitive gaze of the caller, Larry, is transformed into a soliciting gaze, meaning: "Can we talk?" Mike, the target person, at this point would usually make a move, stretch out his hand, turn his body toward the caller in order to say: "Yes, the road is clear." These various moves are here called *clearance signs.*

The reader may think that reality is not so complicated and does not include so many elaborate steps. As a matter of fact, reality might be even more complex and include several more intermediary moves, at least in some cases. What is true, however, is that the various steps are performed in very rapid succession and most of the time we are unaware of the details. Do dancers think about all the movements they make with their feet, legs, bodies? No! The same is true of the habitués of social gatherings.

There are, of course, many variations on the basic theme. Imagine for instance that the target, Mary, does not recognize the caller, Jane, but in spite of her hesitation, grants clearance to Jane. The caller, Jane, may then say, "I see you do not recognize me. But we already met three years ago. . . ."

What is essential is the clearance sign, however it has been arrived at. The clearance sign is what the lonely chimpanzee had so long waited for and what saved her life. This is what we look for from potential partners in a social gathering before we penetrate their personal space. At least it is what we are expected to be looking for. Needless to say, many people are not so scrupulous or attentive. They brutally pitch into others and compel them to converse with them.

As we said above, the fact that we may be alone does not excuse others from performing the ritual of requesting from us a clearance sign and waiting for it. Perhaps we are alone because we are waiting for a specific partner. Most of the time people who are alone in a party engage in some kind of activity: They look through the window or at the paintings and bibelots; they may stand in front of the buffet. We have observed that in order to approach them, guests often start engaging in the same activity, then make some kind of impersonal comment which their target may ignore or pick up. The target's "pick up" is a clearance sign and the two start a short conversation which may be soon interrupted by a more formal mutual recognition. A few weeks ago at a large reception where I had already spoken with all those I knew or was interested in, I went to a table where small sausages and a large baked ham were offered. A man accompanied by a woman was busy cutting the ham. I waited a minute or two, then thinking he had finished, picked up a piece of the ham. Both the man and the woman laughed. The piece had been reserved for the wife who had not yet taken it. The three of us laughed together at my mistake and we started a long conversation which they welcomed. Having just arrived in New York, they did not know anyone at the party and really were waiting for something to happen.

In most cases, others are not alone but already engaged in conversation. Before intruding, we first assess the situation. Do the two or three companions give signs of being a little bored with each other, or are they sincerely involved? Whether an interruption would be welcome can be determined not so much by the tone of voice or the facial expression but mostly by the eyes. It is quite frequent to see two persons who are anxious for any distraction. However, to avoid giving the impression that they are stuck together, they feign great interest in what their partner says, laugh, raise the volume of their voices, and so on. But they betray themselves through their eyes. While talking and laughing they look around—sometimes anxiously—in search of relief. If, on the contrary, two or three individuals are intensely looking at each other, they signal that they are very much involved and would not welcome an intrusion. Besides, by not looking around they shield themselves from seeing anyone who might figuratively be knocking at their door. Another sign of involvement is a low-voice conversation.

Individuals who are in search of partners look for a group where the conversants, or at least one of them, signals availability by looking around. In groups of three or more, there is often one person who is less involved. For example the outsider, Jane, has placed herself within the less involved person's radar range and sends to that person, Mike, a cognitive or a directly soliciting stare. If Mike, the target individual, is not interested, he pretends not to have seen the outsider and concentrates on his companion(s).

Suppose Mike has not shown signs of welcoming Jane the outsider's move; it does not mean—not always, at least—that he does not want to engage her later. Jane therefore repeats the same tactical moves once or twice. But the cost of a third denial is too high, unless rewards from the interaction will compensate for the embarrassment, as they would in the case of a very special "star" and if the expectation is that the star will also enjoy her company. Perseverance is likely if the already engaged individual is the only person Jane knows in the gathering and is apparently her only chance to interact and get introduced to other guests. Once Robert was conversing with a foreign journalist when he spotted Elinor, an old geography professor, whom he had met a couple of times in the past. He wanted to pursue and finish his conversation with the journalist and managed always to look elsewhere when Elinor was trying to penetrate his radar range. After a while, however, as Elinor was moving again and again into his visual space, Robert could not ignore her any longer and greeted her. He then introduced her to a few guests, since, as he had guessed, Elinor did not know anyone in the reception. Elinor's repeated soliciting of Robert's attention was the price she chose to pay for getting introduced.

After we are given a clearance sign by an individual who is already involved in a previous interaction, we do not forget, while moving toward the individual, that we are entering not one but two personal spaces. Having performed the rituals linked to the invasion of the first space, we then enter into a second ritual, that of acknowledging the presence of our friend's companion. And this is done quickly if we want to avoid giving the companion the impression of being treated as a nonperson.

The above is one example of how delicate a matter is the irruption into an existing interaction. Before concluding the chapter, we shall examine various cases of enterings into existing duos and try to determine what strategies will bring the maximum rewards to all the participants, to those who formed the initial duo as well as to the persons who want to join them.

A typical sequence can be seen at the beginning of the school year in a college cafeteria. Judith, a sophomore, is talking with Kathy, a freshman. She delivers hundreds of wise pieces of advice to Kathy, who takes courage in sipping from her Pepsi can. Then Winston suddenly appears. Judith jumps to her feet and greets Winston with warm embraces, kisses, and laughter: "Did you just arrive? Where have you been? Sit here and tell me everything!" And, totally ignoring Kathy, the two old friends start the most animated conversation. It does not occur to Winston nor to Judith that Kathy feels abandoned.

Sometimes we spot an acquaintance conversing with a very attractive partner, and we think of using our acquaintance in order to be introduced to our friend's partner. The intention may be legitimate but the tactics for actualizing it are not easy. Such a maneuver often ends up in a comic disappointment. In a college mixer, I observed the following sequence: Sally, a vivacious but not very pretty sophomore, had spotted her friend Ann talking with a handsome and elegant man. She was not interested in conversing with Ann, whom she sees everyday, but was crazy to meet the unknown man. Without giving much thought to how she might bring about the desired result, she approached Ann and greeted her as if she had not seen her in years. Ann's answer was rather cool; she felt compelled to introduce Sally to James, the handsome senior. The latter grinned, as Sally beamed excitedly at him and, while ignoring her friend, started talking, joking, and performing for James. He tried to bring Ann back into the conversation by commenting on Sally's volubility. Then, suddenly, he said, "Well, girls, it was nice meeting you," and he left, leaving Ann angry and Sally disappointed. Sally, upon reflection, blamed herself. She intruded without being given a clearance sign. Her greeting to Ann was exaggerated and did not conceal that she was only interested in James. She did not accept the topic of conversation established by Ann and James but imposed hers. To top it all, she simply ignored Ann. James felt that his rewarding exchange with Ann, to whom he was attracted, was over. And since Ann was left with a friend, he could exit without being rude.

The preceding story rests upon the higher attractive power (at least at first sight) of Ann over Sally. Let us suppose now that it is Ann, the more attractive of the two girls, who spots Sally, talking to a man who is unknown to her (James). If Ann is very civil she will use what is presented above as a second solution, that is, she will request from her friend, Sally, a clearance sign before joining in. Ann gambles on the chance that James will quickly shift his attention from Sally to her. If he does so, it will then be Ann's choice either to eliminate Sally from the conversation, covertly or overtly suggesting her departure, or to involve her and thus keep her friendship. But whatever Ann does, she has won James's attention and it is unlikely that James will leave the two women to themselves; he will tolerate Sally's presence since there is little he can do about it, in order to go on conversing with Ann. If he is really civil, he will also try to acknowledge Sally's continued presence. Now what about Sally? Upon Ann's arrival, she can, of course, stay. But she could also use Ann's approach as an excuse to take a civil leave. That way she avoids competition with Ann and does her a favor.

Once, during a party, I observed a middle-aged gentleman named Steve, talking privately to Patricia, a vivacious and attractive 30-year-old journalist. After a while, a second man, Samuel, elegant and apparently younger than Steve, walked toward Steve and a little abruptly—that is, without the subtleties described in this chapter—addressed him: "Hi! How have you been since I saw you at the concert?" Steve, made more perceptive and loquacious after a couple of drinks, snapped back: "Do you really want to talk to me or are you more interested in this pretty woman? OK. See you later." Patricia and Samuel were a little abashed but pleased—Patricia because of the compliment and Samuel because he now had the sole attention of his new partner. But Samuel was nonplussed at the idea that this scheme had been so easily exposed. Why did Steve leave? Several explanations are possible. First, Steve is a friendly, realistic gentleman who knows that no one can monopolize attractive guests. He had had a good conversation with Patricia; he had enjoyed it, and was glad to offer the same opportunity to someone else. It's also probable that once he guessed Samuel's intentions, he did not want to be used as a pretext and preferred to make that clear and then to retreat. Another explanation could be that Steve, having assessed Samuel's higher level of attractiveness, did not want to remain in a group where he might have played second fiddle. Perhaps Steve thought his engagement with Patricia had lasted long enough, not according to his taste but according to Patricia's or his wife's taste. Samuel's arrival was then a good opportunity to dissolve a pleasant but slightly dangerous situation.

Another scene worthy of examination was a situation which occurred in a college night club. Joe was there, apparently having a good time with Elisabeth, a very popular red-headed junior. They drank whiskey sours after having danced slowly cheek-to-cheek. Suddenly Charles popped up, seemingly from nowhere, pretending he had just discovered Joe's presence, although Charles had watched Elisabeth from behind the cigarette machine with interest for several minutes already.

"Hi!" shouted Charles, "how're you doing?"

"OK," said Joe slowly. "Nice to see you."

Joe immediately turned to Elisabeth and said, "Beth, why don't you now make the phone call you told me about. I just have to say hello to Charles. But come back! You promised me the next dance!"

Nipped in the bud, Charles became white with anger and made little effort to answer Joe's affable remarks. He was furious at Joe for sending Elisabeth away and at himself for being so clumsy. He knew he was not as handsome as Joe, but given his wit, would have had a fighting chance to win Elisabeth's attentions if Joe had not sent her away. And this was probably just what Joe understood and feared.

Another evening, I observed someone who used a more refined strategy. Jonathan approached Tom, who was drinking with Janet, an attractive brunette. Before even speaking to Tom, Jonathan said to Janet: "Please do not go, I only intended to say hello to Tom." He then said a few words to Tom and to the latter's relief, Jonathan left for the bar. Later on as Tom was momentarily alone, Jonathan maneuvered back towards his friend. He complimented him on his date, asked for her name, and requested to be introduced to her. Tom was flattered by the compliment and even if he was not enthusiastic about introducing Jonathan, he had to do so for civility's sake, when Janet came back.

In all these examples, the principle which promotes success is always the same: Before intruding into an existing interaction, outsiders are expected to control their narcissistic impulses and to look at the situation from the point of view of each of their intended partners; having guessed what gratifications the prospective partners expect to get from their interaction, the would-be intruders, in every instance, choose partners whose own expectations will easily combine with the gratifications they seek.

In concluding this chapter, let us point out that two basic and apparently contradictory norms have emerged. While we expect that the guests will be accessible, as a result of the hosts' selective invitations, we cannot assume that we are welcome conversants to all of the other guests; therefore we must proceed with caution, waiting for a clearance sign.

The tactics used by the guests in a social gathering work well when individuals try to approach people of approximately the same degree of attractiveness. In other words, the law of mutual accessibility does not eliminate the matching principle. But a problem arises, at this point, for all the guests, because many of the other guests in a modern gathering are strangers to them. We may have engaged someone to whom we soon discover we cannot bring much reward. This is unavoidable. It explains why people so often shift partners, preferring a strategic retreat to an unproductive exchange. In this case the shorter the engagement, the better for both partners. It is the role of what we call the conversation's "opening bids" to discover whether or not an engagement promises to be fruitful. This will be the topic with which we will open our next chapter.

NOTES

1. I take this story from the film *Miss Goodall and the Wild Chimpanzees*, National Geographic Series, 1966, by Hugo and Jane van Lawick. I have told the story to the best of my recollection.

2. On the intimacy of conversation in modern parties, see the quotation of Oscar Lewis in Chapter 3, note 15.

3. The conditions of "Engagements Among the Unacquainted" are well analyzed by Erving Goffman in Chapter Eight of his book *Behavior in Public Places* (New York: The Free Press, Macmillan, 1966), pp. 124–148.

4. Erving Goffman writes (op. cit., p. 135):

And, as implied, social parties and gatherings in private homes bring into being open regions where participants have a right not only to engage anyone present but also to initiate face engagement with self-introductions, if the gathering is too large for the host or hostess to have already introduced them.

Goffman then refers to an excerpt from (*The Laws of Etiquette*, by "A Gentleman" [Philadelphia: Carey, Lee and Blanchard, 1836], p. 101), which we quoted above, p. 67, note 16.

5. Goffman, op. cit., pp. 120–121.

6. Erving Goffman quotes Emily Post's *Etiquette* (New York: Funk and Wagnalls, 1937): "You must never introduce people to each other in public places unless you are very certain that the introduction will be agreeable to both (ibid.)."

7. The concept of *Rites of Passage* has been developed by Arnold Van Gennep. Van Gennep has shown how every change in the social position of an individual is made known to the whole group of interested individuals (including the subjects of the change) through a ritual. See Arnold Van Gennep: *The Rites of Passage*, trans. Monika B. Vizedon and Gabrielle L. Caffee (Chicago: University of Chicago Press, 1960).

8. Peter Berger, *Invitation to Sociology* (Garden City, N.Y.: Doubleday Anchor, 1963), p. 96.

9. There are variations in the ritual. For instance, hand-kissing when performed by "gentlemen" of tradition is preceded by a very short eye-exchange and is performed by the man bowing deeply enough to avoid raising the woman's hand more than a few inches. Younger and less respectful individuals—for instance young Italian bachelors—might, on the contrary, take the woman's hand into theirs and raise it to their lips' level while exchanging with the woman a long, penetrating, and flirtatious stare.

10. See Chapter 3, "Sociability, Festivity, and Society."

11. Accessibility is not linked directly to age but to social power. In societies that accord high status to old people, it would be very difficult to approach them. The same would be the case if the child were the future king or the Dalai Lama. The relative accessibility of old people is the consequence of a society which esteems economic production and technological progress above tradition, experience, and wisdom.

12. There are, of course, exceptions: the stars of a party, whatever is the source of their power, can usually get away with their intrusions. But if their being a star (because of money, beauty, position, or some other attribute) facilitates the first move, it does not help them to hold a rewarding conversation. It may even hamper it, as we said in the last chapter, by making them presumptuous, oblivious of others and their interests, and so on.

13. The porch, however, is not a public space. Paula Deitz writes, in an article for the New York *Times* (Design Notebook: "The Lure of a Porch in Summer: Privacy and Pleasure," June 28, 1979, Sec. C, p. 10):

> Although outdoors in the fresh air, the porch is a midpoint between inside and outside, governed still by the rules of the home but with formalities of its own ... When a person is alone on a porch it is assumed that he wishes not to be interrupted. Others may join him, but it is not considered polite to intrude unless he makes a sign. ...

8
CONVERSATION

As Georg Simmel has pointed out, "in the case of the party the task itself is essentially nothing more than identity negotiation."[1] More precisely it is the function of modern gatherings to permit and encourage the sociable conversations that provide identity negotiation and support.

Of course conversation can be used for other purposes: to propagate ideas[2] or give news about the members of the family.[3] But in a modern gathering, conversation is essentially meant to permit reciprocal recognition and support. Simmel says that talk exists for its own sake or rather to permit the "purest and most sublimated form of two-way-ness."[4] The topics themselves do not matter much. They can be changed rapidly. What is important is conversation itself, as long as it permits the exchange:

> Hence even the telling of stories, jokes, and anecdotes, though often only a pastime if not a testimony of intellectual poverty, can show all the subtle tact that reflects the elements of sociability.[5]

The subtle tact demanded by sociable conversation was always expected in the past, though, of course, it was often forgotten in reality. People have always shown a tendency to draw attention to themselves and ignore their partners. Today, reciprocity and tact seem more than ever in danger of being put aside, because the uncertainty of our identities makes individuals overly preoccupied with themselves and unattentive to their companions. The generalization of this narcissistic attitude is linked by Charles Derber to the isolation of modern humans who, in the absence of a comforting community, can only count upon their enterprises for finding social recognition:

> In America the individualistic psychology underlying conversational narcissism is one of broad self-absorption created by cultural and economic individualism and the emergence of the "self" cut adrift from an enduring community.[6]

In this chapter, after having identified the problems involved in conversation, we will review how individuals start conversing together, how they agree on conversational topics, how they shift from one topic to another and how, in all this, they either grant each other identity support or withhold it.

Identity negotiation is an exchange in which the two (or more) partners concede to one another the identity support each wants. As said above and is well expressed in the following passage by George J. McCall and J. L. Simmons, identity support is not approval for the performances of our socially defined roles, but is rather support for people's idealized views of themselves:

> [Role-support] . . . is the expressed support accorded to an actor for his claims concerning his role–identity. This support is not *simply* for his claim to the right to occupy the social position in question or for the conventional rights and duties of the accompanying social role, although role-support includes these points as a minimum. Nor is role-support to be equated simply with prestige, status, esteem, or social approval of one's conduct in a given social position.
>
> It is instead a set of reactions and performances by others the expressive implications of which tend to confirm one's detailed and imaginative view of himself as an occupant of a position. Role-support is centrally the implied confirmation of the specific *contents* of one's idealized and idiosyncratic imaginations of self.[7]

Identity negotiation can be extremely easy if both partners— for whatever reason—are ready to grant it without resistance and delay. It can be an arduous task, on the other hand, if one or both of the partners are slow in granting the expected rewards. In other words, conversation can be as simple as the buying of a visibly labeled utensil in a shop where the terms of the deal are pre-settled and accepted without even a word, or it can be as strenuous as the prolonged haggling over the price of a carpet in an oriental bazaar. In the latter case, the two partners may reach a breaking-point several times during the negotiation and be on the verge of splitting apart. However, their respective interests in the money or the carpet may bring them together again.

In sociable interaction, the ideal conversation is located in a precarious in-between. It is neither a taken-for-granted exchange of approval nor an all-out-war ending up in a rupture. While conversation usually results in a friendly exchange of rewards, quite often this outcome is reached only after a sustained struggle between the partners. Why should a conversation include an element of fight? There are two different reasons: first, individuals may be reluctant to grant recognition to their partners, and second, a reward obtained too readily is not really rewarding. Let us examine these two reasons.

For whatever motives, the partners in a conversation may be on the defensive and consequently reluctant to let each other win easy points. The reason for this reluctance may be sheer narcissism. It is also possible that one of the two conversants has formed a negative image of the other person. The latter in turn, feeling hostility or contempt, will not easily reward the partner. One will make the other "pay" for that cold attitude. Each partner then feels compelled to perform quite hard in order to extract from the other some kind of approval. The conversation then takes the form of a fencing match. It is polite, but cold and tense. There is the permanent threat that one of the fencers, tired of fighting without scoring, may quit. If both partners, or at least one of them, want the match to go on, however, they will have to stop the struggle and encourage each other. A relatively mild case of a covert fight is displayed in the following exchange:

Robert: And what are you doing for a living?

Joseph: I am a stockbroker.

Robert (impressed and a little jealous): Hard work, but likely a little monotonous.

Joseph (uncooperative): Not at all! And you?

Robert (proud): I teach business analysis at the Harvard Business School.

Joseph (impressed, but seeking revenge): Quite an interesting job. How long have you been there?

Robert (matter-of-factly): Three years.

Joseph (I have got him: he is only an assistant professor): How is the teachers' market nowadays?

Robert (on the defensive): Not too good. (Attacking): But when one is inside the fort one knows the rules of the game. . . .

Joseph (challenging): Yes, publish or perish. What about you?

Robert (triumphant): I just signed a contract with Random House for a new text book.

Joseph (still hoping): Good! It is your first book?

Robert (slightly embarrassed): Yes. One must start somewhere. (Fighting back): And you—have you published something?

Joseph (modestly victorious): Yes, several things; you may have heard of the last one, *The Stock Market Explained to Everybody* by Joseph and Paul Murphy?

Robert (beaten and vengeful): Well, no, I am sorry, but you know at Harvard we use only scientific literature . . . that is, no trade books.

There is no reason for the fight to stop. However, at one point the partners may want to acknowledge the combative skills they respectively demonstrated, if nothing else. This, too, is a kind of recognition.

The second reason for conversation to include an element of struggle is that true rewards are necessarily earned. People do not want us to treat them like children or weaklings, incapable of meeting the challenge of a sophisticated performance. They have barely begun with a preliminary jump and we stifle any higher jump by praising them prematurely for their prowess. People want to be given the opportunity to prove themselves, to demonstrate their best abilities. Paradoxically, then, civility requires us to be slow in giving approval and to invite the other to convince and impress us. Eventually we will have to yield, to declare "touché." But not at the first skirmish.[8]

Our partners must be persuaded that they are facing a tough interlocutor. The stronger the partners, the higher we can hold the rod for them to jump over. We should make the challenge as tough as we think they are capable of bearing. Similarly, one way of giving more value to our approval is to be choosy. Discriminate approval means that we know the field, that we are competent judges. Slight criticisms of details enhance the compliment we finally make. Meg, the first guest to arrive at Pflaumen's party, in the McCarthy story cited earlier, understands this when she is requested to check the perfection of a cocktail Pflaumen has concocted for the occasion: "He was disappointed always if you pronounced it perfect. He wanted to tinker with it a little, add a dash of Cointreau or Curaçao at your suggestion. "You're absolutely right," he would agree at once, "I knew it needed something," and, picking up the shaker, he would hurry out to the bar . . . When he came back the drink would taste exactly the same to you, but Pflaumen's satisfaction in it would be somehow deepened."[9] We do not like blanket approval. It may mean several of many things and none is really flattering. It may mean: "I don't want to bother discussing it with an ignoramus like you. Whatever you say is OK." or, "I am really totally ignorant of the things you speak of." In the first case, the approval is an hypocritical rebuff and if we have any sense, we'll realize that it is a sign of deep contempt. In the second case, what use do we have for the approval of an incompetent? On the contrary, a slowly granted and discriminate compliment is the best reward for which we can hope. Singers can be thrilled by the bravos of the public, but still they anxiously await the judgment of the severe theatre or music critics in the morning newspapers. They dismiss with a shrug the adulation of a young journalist who is courting them, but will be rewarded in reading: "The voice, which twenty years ago was a magnificent instrument at the service of an undeveloped artist, actually has gained in warmth and emotional expressiveness over the years. On Sunday it improved in quality as the night went on and the moderate tremolo that had caused a few misgivings early in the program tightened down to a nice vibrato."[10]

Discrimination in judgments, occasional criticism, or struggles are not the goals of sociable interaction. All aim at something more positive. Deeper than the opposition between the partners is their fundamental readiness to grant, at some point, the desired approval and to do it willingly, freely, before the other party has compelled them to surrender. This means that they may not pursue the fight to its utmost limits. We stop it before our partners surrender or, on the contrary, before they say: "OK, you asked for it, I will force you to concede the recognition that you did not want to grant me graciously." In every conversational struggle there is a critical point when we stop challenging or arguing, a time when we reverse our attitude, smile and acknowledge our partner's "victory." This possibly grants others a recognition that is not totally merited but by doing so, we avoid the embarrassment of having destroyed their self-images or of being compelled to concede their victories. A few months ago, at some friends' house, Jack met an older man he did not know and who indicated some interest in operatic music. Jack, a passionate admirer of Rossini, started discussing some details in Act III of *Il Barbiere di Siviglia*. He suggested that the New York Opera Company had misinterpreted the intent of the composer. His interlocutor politely challenged his views, giving his own analysis of the scene and the way it had been played by the famous troupe. Insensitive to the clues given by his partner ("Be careful, young man, I think I know what I am talking about"), Jack persisted in his criticism. The old gentleman then mentioned various documents (newspaper reviews of the premiere, writings of Rossini himself, and so on) to substantiate his views. Jack, stubbornly still resisted and called the host Mark, another opera buff, to give him support. To his great surprise and dismay he heard Mark say: "Well, Maestro, I believe you directed *Barbiere* divinely and I particularly appreciated your going back to the authentic interpretation of Act III."

In other cases our obstinacy leads us to win. But winning by humiliating others is a self-defeating way of scoring. Pauline was discussing the political situation of Afghanistan with George, who displayed some knowledge of the country but did not appear to know the latest developments as presented in the New York *Times* and the *Journal of Eastern Political Affairs*. Pauline expressed her own evaluation and George agreed only in part, maintaining a different interpretation based, said he, on first-hand knowledge. Pauline suspected that the so-called first-hand knowledge was really only second-hand, outdated, and superficial, probably the result of a short sojourn as a tourist. At this point she might have stopped the exchange, rewarding George for having traveled so far away, which showed an adventurous spirit and a healthy savings account. But she pushed her challenge further:

"When was it that you were there?"

"Six years ago."

"Well, a lot has happened since! (first rebuff) How many days did you stay? (provocative)"

"Ten days."

"Hm, that is something but still not very long. Do you speak Afghan? (a little nasty)"

"Of course not! (you are pushing things a little too far)"

"Then where did you get your information from?"

"From an American doing business there."

"Well, my experience is that most people in business know nothing outside their economic transactions. They spend their time with other English-speaking foreigners at cocktail parties and swimming pools."

George had nothing to reply. From the rank of international expert, Pauline degraded him to that of a foolish tourist. But, having destroyed George's image, Pauline could not expect much from him in return. The conversation was forced to a close, while it could have been enjoyable. If guessing that the first topic of conversation was going to be a flop, Pauline, after having given a limited recognition to George, could have suggested another topic.

Success in conversation will be reached only if the partners avoid forcing each other to concede defeat. Thus, it is in the conversants' mutual interest to grant recognition of the others' ideal images once they suspect that they might not sustain any further scrutiny. The endangered partners will like their companions for their discretion. The partners' gratitude—often silent—will be their companions' reward.

Erving Goffman writes that in an encounter "each participant is expected to suppress his immediate heartfelt feelings":

> Each participant is allowed to establish the tentative official ruling regarding matters which are vital to him but not immediately important to others, e.g., the rationalizations and justifications by which he accounts for his past activity. In exchange for this courtesy he remains silent or non-committal on matters important to others but not immediately important to him. We have then a kind of interactional *modus vivendi*. Together the participants contribute to a single over-all definition of the situation which involves not so much a real agreement as to what exists but rather a real agreement as to whose claims concerning what issues will be temporarily honored. Real agreement will also exist concerning the desirability of avoiding an open conflict of definitions of the situation. I will refer to this level of agreement as a "working consensus."[11]

The civility of conversation is more easily maintained if the partners have succeeded in establishing between themselves some commonality, a basic understanding made of similarities of experience, ideas, or tastes, which will keep them together when their mutual challenging may become a little tense. In other words, before engaging in discussion, partners may try to discover whether they might not constitute some or several "teams," making them accomplices within the larger crowd, bonded by their common fate to support each other. The commonality may stem from a city where both were born, a similar ethnic origin, the same religion, the same college, or the same occupation. It could be travel in the same countries, similar misadventures, or illnesses. God only knows how long two individuals with stomach ulcers can sit together, exchanging feelings and tips on symptoms, remedies, and diets. The common basis is even more solid if it extends to similar philosophical or ideological orientations. These shared ideas will permit a movement into politics and religion which would only lead to argument without some basic agreement. The common basis is not necessarily constituted by essential life experiences or ideas. What counts is that each of the two partners be linked to this common basis by some emotional attachment. Two individuals who find out that they are enthusiastic fans of the Yankees can move through many different topics and quite often disagree and come close to a fight. However, their common admiration for the baseball team will bring them back together. This would not be the case if one of the two conversationalists had only a vague interest in baseball. In other words, a feeling of commonality, that is, of constituting a team can develop only if the two partners feel a similar intensity of identification with the quality which makes them similar.

On her way to a party, Margaret read on the front page of the *Daily News* that the Lions had severely beaten the Jets. Rejoicing in the opportunity to tease her husband who was a Jets fan, she joined the party where she met Matthew, an admirer of the Lions. Her remarks made him believe that he had found a sister soul and for ten minutes he took off exalting his favorite team, recalling details from old matches. Several times Margaret tried to introduce new topics, using Detroit, the automobile, the recession, and the gas shortage as tentative bifurcations. She succeeded on the gas shortage only to find out that Matthew had views totally opposite to hers. The latter, sensing the tension, tried to ease it by coming back once more to the Lions. Margaret finally declared that she could not care less about the Lions and football and that she had mentioned it only because of her husband's passion. As for her, she was a dentist and her hobbies were tennis and seventeenth century choral music. At this point the conversation had to stop. The two, in fact, had nothing in common, since Matthew was a computer programmer and apart from football, liked science fiction and poker.

If an acquaintanceship is still new, and is not established on the secure basis of many common values, sentiments, opinions, or experiences, and if—because of some mutual attraction—the partners are interested in maintaining and developing their relationship, they will likely avoid arguing, stopping rapidly when disagreement rears its ugly head. They might prefer to try their wits not against each other but against categories which constitute what we could call their anti-teams: patients or hospital administrators if the conversants are both doctors, professors if they are both students (and vice versa), civilians if they are army officers, their bosses if they are salaried workers, and so on. They may also compete in a friendly way by showing a sense of humor about themselves or their ascribed teams.

If we want recognition we need more than partners who are merely well-disposed. As suggested above, we need also individuals who can give us qualified, competent signs of interest, of approval, or of admiration. Sometimes we engage people precisely because we know their areas of interest and expertise (see Chapter 6 on choices), but quite often we find ourselves in conversation with individuals of whom we know next to nothing. In order to succeed, we must know the areas in which the others are competent. Apart from permitting us to build with our partners common affective bonds, this discovery will permit us to get competent approval for our performances. This double benefit will be attained by what will be called in this chapter the *opening bids*.

Not only the others' areas of competence but also their level of competence in these areas must be discovered. In two of the previous examples of conversation—on the opera and Afghanistan—both partners showed some knowledge of the common area, but failure came in part from the great difference in expertise.

The discovery of others' areas of competence is not an easy task. First, because individuals' identities have many facets and we may know or discover only a partial aspect of a new acquaintance. We then embark in a conversation on shoes or tennis, with which we associate our partner, but in which we have a very limited competence and interest, while we unwittingly ignore the possibility that they, like us, collect early stamps. The problem then is to discover in other people aspects which are compatible with our own interests. The problem is compounded by the fact that our partners may have built of themselves images which are quite different from those suggested by their official roles, definitions, and competence. To compel them to speak about computers when their real passion is Beethoven, just because they are computer programmers, will be felt by them as some kind of an offense to their "real," that is, "ideal" selves.

Only when we think we have discovered the others' ideal-selves, or rather one of their ideal role–identities, compatible in turn with one of the various facets of our ideal-selves, do we feel inclined to reveal ourselves to them. We then engage in a performance which will reveal who we are, in front of individuals, who, we think, are not only adequate but also interested judges.

When we present partners with a definition of ourselves, we need sometimes to accompany this declaration with some explanation of what it means. Many people ignore the meaning of role titles or of institutions. James, who is a newspaper columnist, was once asked by Helen: "Is this a good job? You know, my husband is also on a newspaper. He works in the photo department and he is always complaining. What about your job?" Well, it was not easy for James to explain that the two jobs have little in common and that any comparison would be vain. Helen was wise enough not to ask why, sensing some kind of hazard. She moved prudently into the area of inflation, which permitted the journalist to make very plausible remarks and predictions.

Also, an explanation may be needed because, while the official definitions of occupations may be clear, they may not reveal their holders' real achievements. Someone may be stereotyped by others as a doctor. But this introduction does not specify that the doctor was just appointed head of cardiology at Mount Sinai Hospital. One is labeled a technician in the coal industry, but this does not say that the person has invented a revolutionary way of liquefying coal. One is introduced as a professor, but the partner does not know that the individual just published a text book in economics which has been adopted in a few months' time by all the major colleges in the country. Someone is known as a lawyer, but nobody said that the person is heading the most famous law firm in New York. These achievements radically modify the images conjured by the bare mention of an occupation and totally transform the images that the holders of these roles form of themselves.[12] Others should know more details if a rewarding conversation is to take place. No doubt we should use some prudence in mentioning our achievements, but again to conceal them will prove even more dangerous. Sometimes when we find ourselves in a group of three or more persons, one of the individuals with luck will intervene to apprise the others of our real identity, freeing us from appearing pretentious.

Our partners will not disclose their identities if we do not offer them a reciprocal knowledge of ourselves, of our areas of interests and of our levels of expertise. This will permit the partners to choose not only the facets of themselves they should present to us, but also the quality and contents of their performances. It will also help partners to avoid making mistakes which would be embarrassing for them as well as for us. If Jack had known that the old gentleman had directed the staging of the Rossini opera, he would have been more prudent in his discussion of its interpretation. Our duty of disclosure is greater today than in the past.

In past centuries all famous people in town were known to everybody. If not already known, a newcomer would have been properly introduced by the host. But, given today's sectorialization of human activities, not everyone knows the face or even the name of famous specialists and artists. If, then, a conversation moves into an area where we are recognized as a specialist or where we play an important role, it is courtesy on our part to tell our partners, before they have a chance to utter some blunder. If one conducts the Cleveland Symphony Orchestra or is the executive director of the Ford Company, the person will say it before the conversation moves too far into symphonies or criticisms of large industrial companies.

If what we said about our ideal selves is true, not only our socially defined roles (like our occupations) need to be revealed, but also we must disclose anything that may permit the others to understand what kind of people we think we are and want to present. This is done by mention of our readings, of the movies we like, of the TV programs or announcers we favor, of our hobbies, of the types of sports we indulge in, the countries we would like to visit, the musicians or the artists we love, and so on. A disclosure of our real, that is, ideal, selves however is as problematic as the discovering of another's ideal self. Our ideal self is itself multifaceted, and without knowing others' possible identities, we are at odds as to what side of ourselves to show. It will be the task of the "opening bids" to explore the grounds and to make the first, prudent steps which permit the mutual discovery of two compatible ideal selves.

Opinions and values are cherished treasures that we do not

like to disperse too easily. They might also clash with contrary opinions and values of others, bringing an interaction to a crisis and possibly a halt. There are, however, lightly held opinions that we might display at the beginning of a conversation to start something interesting, with the option of retreating or modifying our assertions if we encounter too much resistance. A good example of this is given in the first sequence of the Woody Allen film *Manhattan*, where a group of four young people loudly—but not seriously—clash over their likings and dislikings of pieces of avant-garde sculpture. It soon becomes clear that they attach much more importance to their new acquaintanceship than to the artistic bickering which started it. Some people think that they would waste time if at one point in the conversation they did not engage in discussing the burning issues of the day, at least those on which they have formed strong convictions. They do it at their own risk. If their interlocutor shares the same values and opinions, they may embark on a very smooth and pleasant conversation. This in turn may be the beginning of a happy relationship. But if the values and opinions of the two interlocutors are in direct opposition, the engagement will not, of course, last. The willingness to incur the risk will primarily depend upon the decision of both partners to prolong their engagement or not. If, for whatever reason, they want the conversation to continue (because they are seated next to each other and there is no real alternative, because they do not see any other guest to engage in conversation with, or because they are deeply attracted to their partner for reasons other than ideas and opinions), they will conceal their values and opinions. Or, they may present them in a prudent and tentative way.

Summarizing the preceding analysis, it appears that when individuals start a conversation, they are faced with a double and contradictory necessity. They must discover the identities of others and must make evident their own. However, given the multivalence of these identities, much leeway is left to them. Individuals must then present others with a variation of themselves which is compatible with their partners' identities. But how can each of us know what in us is compatible with the others' identities without knowing first who the others are?[13] In other words, the two presentations are mutually dependent: they precondition each other. We somehow tell our partners: "I would like to show you a side of myself which you will like and which will also be compatible with some aspect of yourself. Please tell me something useful." The other will answer: "I would love to oblige you, but how can I present you with this desired facet of myself, which will be compatible with you, if you do not tell me more about yourself?"

In order to overcome this apparently insoluble vicious circle, two persons who meet for the first time, or who may know each other only superficially, will resort to a strategy of slow mutual disclosure, which is made of prudent and vague questions and intentionally tentative answers. Erving Goffman perfectly describes the "guarded disclosure" which occurs during the opening bids:

> When individuals are unfamiliar with each other's opinions and statuses, a feeling-out process occurs whereby one individual admits his views or statuses to another a little at a time. After dropping his guard just a little he waits for the other to show reason why it is safe for him to do this, and after this reassurance he can safely drop his guard a little bit more. By phrasing each step in the admission in an ambiguous way, the individual is in a position to halt the procedure of dropping his front at the point where he gets no confirmation from the other, and at this point he can act as if his last disclosure were not an overture at all.[14]

Individuals do not start conversations in total darkness. Others' physical presentations give us clues on their sex, age, income, real or intended social class, national or regional origin. We may even make guesses about their value orientations if, in our eyes, they dress and act in a conservative, or up-to-date, or even possibly provocative manner. But we really need to listen to them if we want our guesses either to become certitudes or to be discarded as stereotypes. Sometimes our first questions are helped by some unusual badge or piece of jewelry. By asking their origin, we may have our partners say something about their "teams" and what they like. It is likely that these symbols have for them a very special meaning and an emotional value: While everybody must wear clothes, nobody is compelled to wear badges and jewels. In the absence of such "conversation pieces," we have to use our own resources. Some people start trying to discover their partners' occupations. This may have to be known at some point, but as we have often mentioned, occupations are not necessarily a very good indicator of what individuals are and want to be known for. If, on the contrary, some individuals identify very strongly with their jobs, they will find an occasion to tell us. Of course, we cannot ask them: "Who are you, I mean not socially, not professionally, but really, in your own eyes?" Most people would be very much embarrassed. Some have never formed—even unconsciously—a very definite image of who they want to be. But even those who have built a more structured image of their ideal-selves, have never had the opportunity of giving themselves a formulation or even alternate formulations. They would be embarrassed by the question and beg us to give them a few days before they could tell us. More conducive to some step-by-step discovery are the questions, Where do our partners reside, and how long have they lived there? By residence we do not mean the exact address. This may be asked later, if the conversation has been very rewarding and we hope to develop with our partners some more permanent relationship. By residence we mean the city, the town, and above all the neighborhood. Almost everywhere the neighborhood has acquired a specific social image in the eyes of the community-at-large or within a specific circle of its population. There is the old neighborhood where the traditional families live, or the rich new development, somehow despised by the former, but where only the well-to-do can reside; across the tracks run-down tenements shelter the unemployed and the transient; on each side of the highway south a large social housing project is inhabited by the workers of the paper mill and the furniture factory. Between the old neighborhood and the social housing project lie the single houses two generations old, owned by local merchants, artisans, and municipal employees. The answers of our partners will give us our first approximate idea of where they stand in society. Equally as significant as the indication of our partners' residences are the comments, the tone, the body language which accompany their answers. These will tell us whether they feel totally at ease with their neighborhoods and the implicit images the locations convey or whether they do not really accept the images. In trying to counteract the conclusions we may have reached, they may try to project an image of themselves which is different from that implied by their residences: "I am not that rich (he wants to say 'I am not *nouveau riche* like the rest of the neighborhood') but when I got my position at the paper mill (of course not that of a mere machine operator) it was the only place I could find." Or: "It is not exactly the place where one would like to reside, but I was told that they have the best high school." Or: "It is the only neighborhood in the city where one finds high ceilings and plenty of light, which are essential for my wife's painting." These comments, and their possible nonverbal accompaniments (smiles, embarrassed hand gestures, and so on) tell us a lot about our partners and their ideal-images. They tell us also how they perceive us. Maybe the self-consciousness about their place of residence results from their impression of who we are. They may sense or fear that we ourselves belong to the "old aristocracy" in town. It is our task at this point to encourage or discourage this perception of ourselves. We will encourage an inflated impression if we think that we can sustain such an image through our coming performances (we will have to explain where we ourselves live) and if we think that such an image will be conducive to a rewarding exchange. Otherwise we will modify the image by mentioning some modest attribute, such as how many of our very good friends live in the same neighborhood as the interlocutor and that we often visit them there. We may, of course, tell our partners where we reside and add any comments which will help them to get an idea of how much we identify with the images our neighborhood conveys, taking into consideration what we have guessed of their own intentional images.

After the question on residence, a question on our partners' birth place may bring another round of information. We may learn the origin of their families, their ethnic or religious affiliations. These data help us to avoid unwelcome, ethnic jokes and the like. They possibly permit us to find some common grounds for talk, perhaps a common ethnicity, if only partial, or a common knowledge of some foreign country. Prudent discussion of the political, economic and cultural situation of a foreign country gives us a hint of the others' range of knowledge and interests. It may indicate also their ideological orientations. In all this, both partners usually start making ambiguous statements, which can be interpreted one way or the other. This will permit them to retreat in case one interlocutor manifests very clear-cut opinions about which the other would not compromise.

Robert: It seems to me that the situation in Brazil is really improving (typical ambiguous statement: It may mean that the economy is improving; it may mean also that the political situation is better).

Mike: Well, I don't know what you mean. Do you think that jailing people without warrant, torturing and killing them is a sign of progress?

Robert: Of course not. But I had the impression that precisely these practices were considerably decreasing. (We have reached a basic agreement on human rights, even if we may disagree on the exact degree of violation in Brazil today.)

An alternative answer to our mention of progress in Brazil could have been:

Mike: You bet. They have a 10 percent increase of the G.N.P. per year. They pay it with a little dictatorship, but it is worthwhile, don't you think?

Robert: Well, it is a matter of values. If one gives precedence to economic development. . . .

Mike: Of course. But do you think that democracy is possible where 80 percent of the population is poor and illiterate?

The ambiguous statement has permitted the uncovering of the other's preferences. In the first case, Mike stated his opinions rather abruptly and we understood that it was some kind of "take it or leave it." In that specific case we accepted it without resistance, since we shared our partner's commitment to human rights. In other encounters we may reach a point where our partners' values and ours clash so openly that, in the absence of an alternate subject where we could agree, the only solution is to abandon the conversation. In the second answer the partner was more cautious in formulating his praise of the economic progress of Brazil and did acknowledge that people may differ on what is the most important criterion of progress. He succeeded, however, in politely maintaining his conservative stand.

Frequently our conversation will not move so far away from the United States. Comparisons may be suggested between different states or cities, in terms of political or cultural differences, entertainment, sports, cost of living, job opportunities, and so on. These topics will encourage our partners to mention their areas of interest: We hear them then mention the Red Sox or the Pittsburgh Symphony Orchestra, the Space Museum or the new wing of the National Gallery of Arts, the Astrodome or Disneyland. The subject of job opportunities will indicate the category of workers with which they identify and may lead us to uncover our present and past occupations.

Education is a subject which may come spontaneously or be suggested by the previous questions. The level of education reached by our partners, the schools they attended, the subjects they studied, the degrees they may have obtained, speak for themselves and suggest further revelations. And as before, when we spoke of the place of residence, the comments indicate not so much the social image of individuals as would appear in the statistics of the Department of

Education, but serve to convey their personal or ideal images. Are they apologetic about having dropped out of high school or proud of having taken a tougher road to success and fortune? Is she proud that she could pay her way through the county's community college and thus get a better job in the city welfare office? Does he mention that he had been accepted by Vassar and Yale but had to attend modest Wagner in order to stay closer to his ailing father? Does she pretend that she could have earned her Ph.D. in physics at Princeton if she had not quit after her M.A. in order to marry Jeff, with whom she was so madly in love? The regret we perceive in this last statement tells us that our partner sees herself as a potential first-rate scientist. This may not be the moment to press questions about her job, which probably does not reflect such a gratifying image. We might on the contrary explore her future plans, which may include some research or even, who knows, a return to school in order to obtain the longed-for Ph.D.

Quite often our partners will not be so guarded at a social gathering, eliminating a battery of questions to determine their ideal selves. Many individuals—sometimes with the help of a couple of drinks—are very straightforward and greatly facilitate our task. As Peter Blau observes, the risks our partners take may win them our admiration: ". . . taking risks is a method of impressing others in its own right. Superior competence is impressive, and so is outstanding courage."[15] There is a danger, however, in presenting an image so clear-cut and inflexible that it might not be compatible with any of our possible identities. It may appear that there is little we can share with this individual; we won't even have to uncover our own cards and will look for an opportunity to take our leave as soon as we can politely do so. Is this not, however a rash decision? Possibly. George McCall and J. L. Simmons observe that discovering in others possible anchorage grounds for a mutual accord "takes a good deal of time" and that the impression gathered in a first encounter may be misleading.[16] Since, however, first impressions are hard to correct, we may prefer to avoid rushing to disclose our identities.

If our partners are slow at uncovering their hands, we may help them by disclosing something of our own selves. But we play our cards slowly, one by one, starting with those which do not give too sharp and definitive an image of ourselves. We are able to modify it in proportion to what we discover of the others' own images. It is like focusing a camera in which two images must be superimposed;

but just as we think we have succeeded in superimposing the first image upon the second, the latter moves away and we must work again at catching it. This slow discovery permits us to modify, at each stage, the interpretation that others may have assigned to our previous performances. If we think they have formed an exaggerated view of who we are, some modest statement will rectify the impression. If we sense that they tend to look down on us, an allusion to some esoteric experience or to an unsuspected area of expertise will shed some doubts on their too rapidly formed ideas of who we are. A classical means of protecting ourselves against the negative impact of a declaration of opinion is that of disclaimers.

> A disclaimer is a verbal device employed to ward off and defeat in advance doubts and negative typifications which may result from intended conduct. Disclaimers seek to define forthcoming conduct as not relevant to the kind of identity challenge or re-typification for which it might ordinarily serve as a basis. Examples abound and serve to make the abstract concrete: "I know this sounds stupid, but . . ."; "I'm not prejudiced, because some of my best friends are Jews, but . . ."; "This is just from the top of my head, so . . ."; "What I'm going to do may seem strange, so bear with me." "This may make you unhappy, but . . ."; "I realize I'm being anthropomorphic. . . ."[17]

The disclaimer permits us to retreat if the partners manifest some surprise or antagonism towards the statements which follow. If, on the contrary, the partners agree with the statement, it is the disclaimer which can be dropped. "Yes, I agree, the more I think about it, the more I'm convinced of it."

When individuals think it is appropriate to disclose some area of personal expertise they are usually cautious to avoid, especially at the beginning of an interaction, alluding to fields in which they have only a very remote interest. Otherwise we might become associated with them in the mind of our interlocutors for the whole duration of the gathering and even for the whole time of the mutual acquaintanceship.[18] Gregory had indulged in a little stamp collecting when he was young. Once he had the imprudence to allude to it as he started conversing with a foreigner: "Oh, yes, your country has printed such a nice series of stamps with tropical birds. I still remember the one with the multicolored parrot!" Since then Gregory has become for his interlocutor the stamp collector. This was also due to the fact that the two partners in the interaction had not found any other common field of interest.

Conversely, the fact of already knowing individuals should not entirely absolve us from the necessity of better discovering them. A first encounter may have left us with the wrong image. The ideal image that people are perpetually building and rebuilding may also have changed since we met them. We remember the ironic way in which a young woman spoke of a common acquaintance, named Henry. "Each time I meet Henry, the only things he manages to speak to me about are the termites in my roof!" she says. Henry is a very distinguished and knowledgeable gentleman who had formed an image of the young woman as a good housekeeper preoccupied with the condition of her house. He had not inquired any further into the very rich background of the woman, who, at college, majored in philosophy. Even when we meet with old acquaintances, that is to say, *especially* when we meet them, if we want to conduct a mutually rewarding conversation, we should again sound them out and try to discover a new side taken by their always striving ideal selves.

Once two individuals discover each other and their mutual fields of interest, they can settle for a while on a common theme of discussion: movies, politics, restaurants, ballet, a foreign country, a book, flying experiences, hobbies, children's education, auctions, exhibitions, modern art, theatre and the like. When I said "they settle," I do not mean that there is always or even most of the time a real agreement between the partners. Usually one of them starts speaking on the topic and the partner follows him. If there is an evident imbalance of age, knowledge or social status, it is usually the more powerful individual who determines the topic. If no power difference is manifested or acknowledged, it is the more active of the two companions who will—often unconsciously—make the selection.

To establish a good conversation the partners need some basic common interests. These commonalities not only provide the emotional link which will keep them together through the vicissitudes of their interaction, but will also serve as a common territory of which both know the geography. To evaluate the pleasures and the dangers offered by the "territory," to recall and compare experiences incurred there, permits the partners to speak, each in a way which is meaningful to the other. This common territory can actually be a country, a city, a province; it could as well be a war experience, climbing a mountain, a foreign culture with its celebrations, its foods, and its manners, a film and its actors, or even a common past lover.

We do not always have the good fortune, however, to find a

common territory with our companions in social gatherings. Difficulties result from what Peter and Brigitte Berger and Hansfried Kellner call the "pluralization of the social life-worlds."[19] While in traditional societies everyone had the same experiences which had the same meaning for all of them, modern humans develop along parallel tracks in the midst of contrasting interpretations of reality. Not only are the ideologies different and opposed, but their formulations—due to social clan and national variations—can be extremely different. To be a socialist or a liberal may mean as many different things as there are individuals who declare themselves to be unique. We have seen above the consequences of this social indeterminism for the definition of the self. We mention it here to signify the difficulty of finding a common territory and language with our companions at social gatherings.

In the absence of a common territory, what can the conversants do? We may consent to play the role of listener and let the others develop subjects in which they are competent. The listeners need not be entirely passive. They can show their interest by looking attentively at the talkers, by smiling or laughing if the occasion calls for it; they can ask questions if certain points seem obscure, and so on. The talkers are then rewarded. The listeners have also gained something. They have compelled their companions to show more of their cards without uncovering too many of their own. They can measure the interest that the talkers have in them by the efforts they make at telling their stories well and with humor. We like people to go to some effort on our behalf. Traditionally women have been trained to play apparently self-effacing roles in which they flatter the male ego by avidly drinking in their stories, and staring at them in silence with admiring eyes.[20] These interactions often end up with the talkers "confessing" that they have never had such an interesting "conversation."

Even if the partners have found a topic of common interest, they may feel, at some point, that they have extracted from it all they could. It is also possible that one of the partners feels less at ease with the topic, or another partner senses that it is his or her companion who no longer fully enjoys it. The partner's reactions have become dull. The person starts looking around, and now answers in a noncommittal way and contributes little to the conversation. We then feel the need to change the topic. But in the case that our partner is not reacting at all to what we are saying, we are left in the dark, not knowing which direction to take. We then try to remember allusions made by the partner in the phase of the "opening bids." Maybe then, our now disinterested friend signaled some area that if tapped could help him or her to become a little more loquacious. At any rate, we do not lose anything by trying.

Paradoxically it is easier to shift topics if it is the other who is doing most of the talking. Of course, we are not supposed to stop the partner abruptly and say: "Let us talk about something else." There are civil ways of doing it. It is done first by acknowledging something the other said; having rewarded the other, one then adds: "Speaking of . . . horses or Picasso or Las Vegas, do you know that. . . ." This does it, unless our companion was so deeply involved in the subject that any intervention would be resented. For instance, Mary had been speaking about her late mother who, in spite of her passion for (horses, Picasso, or Las Vegas) had lost, little by little, all interest in the material world and become a devout worshipper of Krishna. At this point, before making the transition to the horses, Picasso, or Las Vegas, one will comment at some point on Mary's mother, her illness, and her conversion, before prudently moving to one of the favorite passions of the late gentlewoman. This means that, before shifting to another topic, we grant our companions some "support-responses," as Charles Derber calls them.[21] We will return later to the various types of support-responses; we only mention support here as an element in a "shift-response," that is, in a response which is intended to introduce a new topic. This support is an essential element, if we want our companions to be in a good mood, and ready to listen to our coming statements. However, the support element of the shift response is often reduced to such a rhetorical minimum that it conceals rather than reveals support: "Speaking of . . ." or "A propos . . ." or "By the way. . . ." Quite often there is no relationship between the previous topic and the new topic which could justify the rhetorical "A propos." The latter is just lip service paid to civility by a narcissistic talker.[22]

Conversational narcissism is often manifested in modern social gatherings, particularly in the episodic exchanges occurring at cocktail parties. Then the individuals, knowing that they will have little time to impress their partners, seldom have the patience to give them many support-responses. They rush to shift-responses, in order to immediately impose whatever topic they hope will give them an advantage. Charles Derber writes that the more individuals are narcissistic, the more they use shift-responses over support-responses and the earlier they do it in each engagement.[23]

When two narcissistic individuals meet at a social gathering, they both try their best to impose topics which permit them to shine in the conversation: showing their knowledge, cracking jokes, making fun of common anti-teams, dropping names of prestigious people and places. If only one of the two is narcissistic, and is a brilliant talker, and if the other companion is of the listening type, the talker may carry on a conversation which is rewarding for both partners. But this is far from being the normal case. Most people are not attentive, rewarding listeners. If they cannot participate in the conversation, they somehow fade away, become absent-minded and look around for possible alternate partners.

Narcissism can go one step further: narcissistic individuals not only impose their own topics, but they actually know only one topic of conversation: themselves. Whatever you say, they will retort: "Oh, yes, it reminds me of . . . my childhood, my first day in school or in college, my relation to my mother, my first boy/girl friend, my, my, my. . . ." Endlessly they like to talk about how they feel now, how they felt yesterday, about their internal conflicts, their sufferings, their joys, their loves, their hates, their analysts, and so on. They do not object to your participating in the conversation, as long as you play their game, that is, comment on their affairs, or ask them questions on further details and nuances that they will reveal in answering. They relish wallowing in front of you in these personal and often intimate matters. If you manage to pull them out of themselves for a while, they will become annoyed, bored, impatient, and will soon look for another "friendlier" audience. Somehow for them the outside world does not exist, or exists only in relation to themselves. If a war is threatening, if a new tax is contemplated, if someone is sick or has gone bankrupt, if underpaid workers are going on strike, they care only if they themselves feel threatened or struck. Such individuals never show any interest in what others say, and do not ask any questions in the course of a conversation, except if they need that piece of information related to their own interests or feelings. They never ask questions about what may be of interest to their partners. They do not "scratch their partner's back" in order to have theirs scratched in turn. Needless to say, they do not bring any reward to their listeners. As for themselves, inattentive as they are to the personality, values, opinions of their partners, they are likely to give of themselves images which will not elicit any admiration and support from the partners: paradoxically, narcissism achieves the opposite of the desired result.

From the allusions made so far, it appears that much conversation is made of narcissistic monologues. A little observation in parties will show that real life is quite different from plays and novels where people answer questions asked by others or make remarks which respond to what others have said. Most of the time, in real life, a person's speech is preceded by an explicit or implicit rejection of what's been said, followed by: "I personally think . . ." or "I remember. . . ." The speech which then comes is sometimes so far away from what the other had said that total confusion follows, since the audience may believe, at least for a while, that the intruder was continuing the subject discussed beforehand. Not less confusing is the habit of asking questions and not listening to the answers. An acquaintance of mine regularly rattles off one question after the other, passing from subject to subject:

"Where did you go during the summer, Charles?"

"I went to Turkey and Italy."

While Charles was saying "Turkey" George exclaimed:

"My! what a beautiful ceramic plate you have got here. Where did you buy it?"

"Well, in Turkey."

"In Turkey? Why didn't you tell me you went to Turkey?"

"That is precisely what I was trying to . . .".

But before Charles could finish the sentence, George had interrupted:

"I thought you went to Italy. Didn't you send me a postcard from Venice?"

"Yes, indeed; from Turkey we took . . .".

Charles could not finish his answer; George was already embarked on another question that in reality was another monologue, since his questions were not intended to elicit answers. Some people listen to their companion's speech in an absent-minded way, pick up a few words, start thinking about what kind of speech they could make, and after the topic of conversation has already moved into a totally new area, solemnly utter their views on the abandoned theme. Once in a university cafeteria, a professor of economics and a group of students were eating and commenting on the ongoing inflation. At one point the professor seemed to lapse into a deep meditation. In the meanwhile the conversation moved to films and someone suggested going and seeing *Wild Strawberries* at the nearby theater. "How much is the seat?" asked a freshman. Two dollars was the answer. At this point the economics professor came to life and said: "Two dollars for wild strawberries . . . that is not expensive, unless it is for half a pound." This sort of distraction is representative of what often happens in conversation. One is so accustomed to this occurrence that most of the time one does not even notice it.

Someone I recently met at a party, who senses the danger there is in losing control of the conversation, tries to guard the territory at all times. To shut out any possible penetration of the field by the "enemy," he fills up any gap in his speech (when trying to remember a detail or looking for a word) with a continuous humming. If by chance he must stop humming to clear his voice, and if you succeed in interrupting him, he looks at you with a completely puzzled, disoriented expression. Without understanding what you might have wanted to say, and after a little stuttering, he resumes his endless speech. If you try again to stick in a word or two, he abruptly warns you, "Don't interrupt. I have not finished."

A variant of the previous pattern is what we call the "Russian dolls" story. Russian dolls are sets of hollow wooden dolls which can be divided into halves. Each doll fits completely inside the next bigger doll until the largest contains them all. After having started a narration, say about a trip to Italy (lower-half of the largest doll: the upper half will come at the end of the story), the speaker remembers an episode in Palermo (second and smaller doll, lower-half only for the time being) where she was courted by a young man while eating *pollo all'arrabiata*, which permits the introduction of Sicilian and Italian cuisine into the conversation (third doll, lower-half). This, in turn, reminds the narrator of Sicily's complex history: "Do you know one can still find people of Norman stock in Central Sicily?" The development about the Norman people, their blue eyes and blond hair constitutes the fourth story (fourth and hopefully smallest lower-half). At this point, if you take the question about the Normans seriously and start to answer, you are stopped immediately: "Wait, I have not finished my story! Of course not; because all of the lower-halves of the dolls require their respective upper-halves, starting with the last and smallest one: the invasion of the Normans, followed by (third doll) the completion of the description of Italian food, which takes us back to the lunch with the young gallant Sicilian (second doll) who followed the talker all around Sicily (it makes a real big doll) and finally the largest doll must be put together by commenting upon Sicily, and how Italy at about those times was so beautiful and hospitable, and so on. The narrator, tired by such a long journey, is no longer alert enough to listen to your own experiences of Sicily, although you might have been there a dozen times and know it much better than she does: "Well, she concludes, "it was nice talking to you. Now I think I need a drink."

A conversation is a tennis game in which the players send back the same ball they have received, not playing a new ball with each stroke. To acknowledge another person's very words is one of the best ways to draw his attention to what we are saying ourselves. Actually, sometimes people are so surprised to find someone who pays attention to what they say that they are embarrassed to have been taken seriously. They retreat: "Well, . . . yes . . . that is what I said . . . at least I must have said it . . . Carter should have bombarded them . . . let me think it over a little more . . . ". Awakened by the attention he or she was shown, your partner now will want to show you equal civility and will start considering seriously what you say. Derber distinguishes various degrees in the support that people can grant each other.[24] The minimum degree is made of what he calls "background responses," like "Hm," "I see," "You say," "Of course," and so on. These background responses usually suffice to keep the conversation going. However, at times the story is too dramatic to be supported by such a weak response. For example, she says her father suffered an infarct and her companion comments: "I see." Derber says also that slowness in granting support is actually a denial of support.[25]

What people are in fact expecting from their partners in conversation are supportive assertions,[26] like: "this is interesting," or "I never thought of it," or "this is the most intriguing story I ever heard!" Supportive questions are even more rewarding: "When did this happen?" or "Have you told your boss (colleague, friend . . .)?" or "Was it the first time you experienced such a thing?" or "Could you tell me where I could (do, buy, find, hear, see . . .)?"[27] Another way of supporting our partners is to laugh at their funny stories even if we know them already. On the contrary, a sure way of embarrassing and antagonizing speakers is to tell them "Oh, I know this one already!" or "Are you sure the story is about the Irish? I thought it was about the French." How often have we observed a situation similar to what occurs below with Jack and Jane. While Jack's busily preparing his own story, his friend Jane painfully strives to have her joke heard. Before Jack is even through with his story, she shouts, "Good ... great ... but now listen to this one!" The latter's victory over her predecessor is shortlived, because he is soon given the same treatment by someone else. Some individuals are even so anxious to take the floor, that, in hearing another's story, they start laughing before there is anything to laugh at and, having paid this misplaced tribute to their baffled companion, they feel entitled to take over.

When we are the victims of a narcissistic individual who does not grant us any support, we become nervous and multiply our efforts at getting attention, either from our partner or from potential new companions. Individuals who have often experienced rejection or indifference when they speak, may take the habit of interjecting into their speech requests for support, such as: "you see," "you know," "isn't it?" and so on.[28]

Civility does not require us to forever support a partner's monologues. Conversation is supposed to be an exchange. This requires that, at one point, listeners stop listening and shift to new topics, where they can contribute their own stories, experiences or ideas. The shifting will be all the more acceptable if we preface our introduction of the new topic with a word of support for our companion, or if we obviously graft our interventions on something that our companion has said.

Literature gives us examples of good conversation more often than does reality. We read dialogues between people who listen to each other and on the spur of the moment can concoct a thoughtful or witty reply. To this the protagonist answers no less provocatively. Literary conversation is a rapid succession of statements, short stories, piquant remarks, or interrogations which answer each other. Again, the comparison of the tennis game comes to mind. Each move is not part of a prolonged personal performance—during which another's speech is regarded as a temporary disturbance, but is each time invented on the basis of what was said before. Good conversation is a matter of attuned responses. To get an idea of what conversation could be, we suggest that the reader look into the table conversation between Lady Narborough and her guests in Oscar Wilde's *The Picture of Dorian Gray*. We quote here only a short passage:

"Is it true, Mr. Gray?" [that Madame de Ferrol had four husbands]

"She assures me so, Lady Narborough," said Dorian. "I asked her whether, like Marguerite de Navarre, she had their hearts embalmed and hung at her girdle. She told me she didn't, because none of them had had any hearts at all."

"Four husbands! Upon my word that is *trop de zèle.*"

"*Trop d'audace*, I tell her," said Dorian.

"Oh! She is audacious enough for anything, my dear. And what is Ferrol [her latest husband] like? I don't know him."

"The husbands of very beautiful women belong to the criminal classes," said Lord Henry, sipping his wine.

Lady Narborough hit him with her fan. "Lord Henry, I am not at all surprised that the world says that you are extremely wicked."

"But what world says that?" asked Lord Henry, elevating his eyebrows. "It can only be the next world. This world and I are on excellent terms."

"Everybody I know says you are very wicked," cried the old lady, shaking her head.

Lord Henry looked serious for some moments. "It is perfectly monstrous," he said, at last, "the way people go about nowadays saying things against one behind one's back that are absolutely and entirely true."

"Isn't he incorrigible?" cried Dorian, leaning forward in his chair.

"I hope so," said his hostess, laughing.[29]

Observe that in this passage there is only one slight exception to the rule of the "tennis exchange." Lady Narborough did not pursue Dorian's remark about the heartlessness of Madame de Ferrol's husbands; she went on speaking about the marriages to "four husbands" which seemed to have excited her considerably. That is not, however, a real exception to the rule because her "heartless husbands" theme had not been introduced by her, but by Lord Henry. She cannot, then, be accused of persisting in her own topic and ideas. Perhaps she did not want to acknowledge openly Dorian's rather gruesome description of the embalmed hearts hanging from Marguerite de Navarre's girdle. She is, after all, a "refined lady." She succeeded in ignoring this detail (maybe as a slight lesson to Dorian: some things should not be mentioned) without really changing the main line of conversation. After she had expressed her judgment on having four husbands: "It is *trop de zèle*," each rejoinder picks up exactly what the previous speaker has said. *Trop de zèle* leads to "*trop d'audace*," which is itself echoed by the adjective "audacious" and the question concerning the last husband of Madame de Ferrol, leads to a scathing remark about husbands of very beautiful women. This remark was taken by Lady Narborough as an allusion to herself and she hit Lord Henry with her fan for his "wickedness" which is "recognized by the whole world." Lord Henry then uses the word "world" to suggest that he may not have such a wide reputation. But Lady Narborough maintains her disguised compliment and Lord Henry cynically acknowledges that this is true. This cynicism escapes neither Dorian who underscores it, nor Lady Narborough who wittily expresses hope that Lord Henry will never stop being wicked.

The contents of this conversation may look a little light. This is not our point. What is significant is the reciprocal quality of the exchanges. The reciprocity, the attention to what others say, and the willingness to share the air are attitudes displayed by Wilde's characters.

Why is it that reality seems so far from fiction? Is it because writers possess long hours to write and rewrite their dialogues until they near perfection, while such leisure is not granted to the participants of a party? Might they not be quick enough to graft a witty remark onto the last sentence or word uttered by their partners? Is it because Wilde's characters have established their positions in life and are less anxious than our middle-class contemporaries who struggle to promote themselves—and consequently are more able to relax and listen? Or is it because Wilde describes a dinner party in which all the guests know they will be seated together for a relatively long time and do not feel they must rush to have their say, unlike the participants of modern receptions who constantly shift partners and cannot wait and wait for their turn to speak?

These three explanations probably must be combined. One should also observe that in the conversation described by Wilde, total reciprocity is not attained. Only four of the many persons dining together participated in it. The rest listened. They constituted the audience. This happens frequently when the number of those who converse together goes beyond three, four, or five. This in turn suggests that different rules apply to different numerical arrangements. Duos differ from trios and from larger groupings. It will be the intent of the next chapter to investigate these different situations.

NOTES

1. George J. McCall and J. L. Simmons, *Identities and Interactions* (New York: The Free Press, 1978), p. 146. The authors refer to Georg Simmel's pages on sociability (*The Sociology of Georg Simmel*, Kurt H. Wolff, trans. [New York: Free Press, 1950], pp. 40–57).

2. Social gatherings do not offer good opportunities for long political and ideological declarations because the episodic character of most exchanges precludes it. However, the very fact of expressing one's values, even in a short statement, may considerably influence one's partner and the mood of the gathering. Many individuals arrive at a party with the wish to "fit in" and they do not challenge the positions and opinions that seem to prevail in the gathering. However, in order to exert such influence, one must have acquired a recognized status in a gathering.

3. The "family" can be the extended family itself, or a tribe, a clan, a clique, an office, or a group of business executives and their spouses.

4. Georg Simmel, op. cit., p. 53.

5. Ibid.

6. Charles Derber, *The Pursuit of Attention: Power and Individualism in Everyday Life* (Boston: G. K. Hall, 1979), p. 6. One should accept these generalizations only with a grain of salt. America has not the privilege of conversational narcissism, which I have personally encountered often in Europe. Maybe narcissism is the necessary consequence of the emergence of the self and the only way to kill conversational narcissism would be through a revolution which would suppress all conversation! The only answer to narcissism is civility and civility cannot be imposed by force.

7. G. J. McCall and J. L. Simmons, op. cit., pp. 70–71.

8. As J. Huizinga pointed out, even solitary play—the play of a child for instance—is an effort at winning against some difficulty or resistance. It makes play "tense" (*Homo Ludens* [New York: Roy Publishers, 1950], pp. 10–11). Huizinga observes that play and contest or fight are etymologically related in many languages (ibid., pp. 40–42). "'There is something at stake'—the essence of play is contained in this phrase" (ibid., p. 49). In the rest of the book, Huizinga often returns to this equivalence between play and contest, fight, competition, and even war.

9. Mary McCarthy, "The Genial Host," *The Company She Keeps* (New York: Simon and Schuster, 1942), p. 142.

10. Donal Henahan, "Concert: Birgit Nilsson Sings a Benefit at the Met," New York *Times*, Nov. 6, 1979, Sec. C, p. 8.

11. Erving Goffman, *Presentation of Self in Everyday Life* (New York: Doubleday, 1959), pp. 9–10.

12. "Each role–identity of each individual thus has two aspects, the conventional and the idiosyncratic. The relative proportion of these two aspects varies from person to person, and from identity to identity for the same individual. Some people add little to the role expectations they have learned; others modify and elaborate culturally defined roles to such extreme extents that the

roles become unrecognizable to other people and the individuals are regarded as eccentric or mentally ill. Most of us, fortunately, fall somewhere between" (G. J. McCall and J. L. Simmons, op. cit., p. 68).

13. See George J. McCall and J. L. Simmons, op. cit., pp. 181-182.

14. Erving Goffman, op. cit., pp. 192-193.

15. Peter Blau, *Exchange and Power in Social Life* (New York: John Wiley and Sons, 1964), p. 40.

16. George J. McCall and J. L. Simmons, op. cit., p. 181.

17. John P. Hewitt and Randall Stokes, "Disclaimers," in Jerome G. Manis and Bernard N. Meltzer, *Symbolic Interaction, A Reader in Social Psychology* (Boston: Allyn and Bacon, 1978), pp. 310-311.

18. Erving Goffman writes:

The individual's initial projection commits him to what he is proposing to be and requires him to drop all pretenses of being other things. As the interaction among the participants progresses, additions and modifications in this initial informational state will of course occur, but it is essential that these later developments be related without contradiction to, and even built up from, the initial positions taken by the several participants. It would seem that an individual can more easily make a choice as to what line of treatment to demand from and extend to others present at the beginning of an encounter than he can alter the line of treatment that is being pursued once the interaction is underway (op. cit., pp. 10-11).

19. Peter Berger, Brigitte Berger, and Hansfried Kellner, *The Homeless Mind* (New York: Random House, 1973), Chapter Three.

20. In a study of conversation, Don H. Zimmerman and Candace West of the University of California at Santa Cruz, found that women do not interrupt men in conversation, while men do it often. "Sex-Roles, Interruptions and Silences in Conversation," in Barrie Thorne and Nancy Henley, eds., *Language and Sex* (Rowley, Mass.: Newbury House Publishers, 1975).

21. Charles Derber, op. cit., p. 32.

22. Ibid., p. 33.

23. Ibid., p. 25.

24. Ibid., pp. 30-31.

25. Ibid., pp. 32-33.

26. Ibid., p. 32.

27. Women have been socialized to be more attentive and supportive. This may explain why they are reported to ask more questions than men. Glenn Collins, in an article for the New York *Times* (November 17, 1980, p. C19), "Men's and Women's Speech, How they Differ?", reports that according to a study conducted by Pamela Fishman, a sociologist at the University of Santa Barbara, women asked nearly three times the number of questions that men did in 52 hours of recorded conversation of mixed couples.

28. Derber, op. cit., p. 33.

29. Oscar Wilde, *The Picture of Dorian Gray* (Harmondsworth: Penguin Books, 1950), pp. 204-205.

9
DUOS, TRIOS,
AND GENERAL DISCUSSIONS

If we exclude the dinner parties at which all the guests sit around the same table, most conversations in social gatherings are held in small groups of two or three persons. This is particularly true of the modern gatherings, in which all participants are eager to have ample opportunities to air their ideal selves. Consequently before approaching the problems involved in general discussions—which are the exception—we shall analyze the more common combinations of trios and duos.

Among the small joys of life, there is hardly one greater than being engaged in conversation with someone who is attuned to the same themes that excite us; and of all the numerical combinations that can be found in a social gathering, the duo seems to offer the greatest rewards. This is not always so, of course. Like the tongue, which is the origin of the best and the worst things, according to Aesop, duos have their seamy side. Before coming to this, however, there are many positive things to be said about duos.

One of the first advantages to being the only two in a conversation, is that we can expect someone else's full attention. In a larger constellation of people, unless we are the central star, we receive only limited, if any, attention. Like Caesar who said he would prefer to be the first citizen in Capua rather than the second citizen in Rome, we find more reward in being the object of one person's total attention than in conversing with ten important people who are only vaguely aware of our presence. Having a lively exchange of experiences and opinions with our partner gives enormous support to our self-images. Why should we entertain doubts about ourselves, when this intelligent person tells us—sometimes explicitly, or at least implicitly—that what we say is worth listening to and that the listener deems us important enough to give us optimum performance in return? To this we should add the minor advantage of being exempt from the difficult and strenuous effort of giving our attention to two or more individuals. As we shall repeatedly see later, this is a type of exercise that very few people have mastered.[1]

There is another basic advantage to being a pair: Two can more easily reach mutual understanding without additional people raising obstacles. Even when others crowd near us, they seldom hear what we say to one another in a duo. There we are somehow sheltered from the curiosity, the reservations, or possible criticisms of others. We constitute a kind of enclave, within which we can grant each other mutual support on the basis of our mutually consented norms and values. We know that if our conversations were heard by a third party, the latter would possibly challenge a name, date, place, pronunciation, detail in a story, and maybe the story itself. But as long as the two of us remain together we are protected from outside scrutiny and we feel more comfortable in offering unrestricted mutual support. Each of us may suspect (or know) that what the other says is a little distorted or inflated and that our stories would have to be censured if a third person were to join us. But we are grateful to our companion who "understands" us so well. Given the laws of civility and reciprocity, the partner expects the same in return, and is not intent on detecting our occasional but insignificant flaws. The listener encourages us to express a bold image which we like to think is closer to our genuine selves. The friendly inattention of our companion when we don't remember a name, or a place, or when we make a slip of the tongue, is courteously repaid by our similar inattention to his or her own mistakes. Could we be accused of having created "a society of mutual admiration"? Possibly so, but why not? Accomplices? Yes, in a way, but is this not the preliminary condition for identity negotiation and support?[2]

The participants of the duo may often seem to offer too generous encouragement. First this may be due to the fact that individuals may be somehow incapable of judging others' performances. One may not have the background data that would permit discrimination between truth and fabrications. I once met a man who introduced himself as the last descendant of an old Hungarian aristocratic family. He knew so much about his "ancestors," their deeds, and their alliances that made him cousin to several reigning royal families, that one could not help being impressed. His presentation and behavior were in perfect agreement with his "identity." No one had ever doubted the veracity of his claims, at least not until an acquaintance of mine, a genealogist, told me in great secrecy that the famous exiled gentleman was American-born, and the son of a shop-owner in a small town in the Midwest. Very early in life he had developed an interest in genealogies, had learned foreign languages in an impressive manner and had adopted the identity of the descendant of an aristocratic family which had been extinct for many decades. The beloved count has no trouble in getting support for his cleverly acquired new identity from all those who are not expert genealogists themselves. Our ignorance of the background of our partner is not always so radical. However, our partner may have discovered the limitations of our information and as a result may profit by obtaining a not entirely merited approval from us.

It may also be that, while knowing the background very well, we have detected in the other guest a pathetic desire for recognition. Knowing how little of it the poor person usually gets, either on the job or at home, we console and stroke the other's wounded self-image while thinking: "Of course, I know what I'm hearing isn't exactly the truth, but why embarrass my partner with a confrontation?"

What appears to us as "not being exactly the truth," may have been said very sincerely by our partners. In presenting their ideal-selves, they show what they consider their real, true selves, which daily routine performances do not manifest adequately.

Quite often we also sense that other guests have potentials stored in reserve that they do not know how to manifest or present in a convincing way. A heartless judge would simply give them a poor grade and move on. We may want, on the contrary, to encourage awkward performers, and give them enough time to show us a wide sampling of performances. Once we have supported their acts long enough, we can then start withdrawing our approval if confronted with particularly inadequate performances. In doing so, we may have won a friend, who was grateful for both the encouragement and the discriminate approval. Our friendly support may be crucial in helping our partners to manifest potential abilities they had hardly suspected they possessed, and thus further define their ideal selves. This result would not have been reached if we had not patiently supported their hesitant first steps. This required the privacy of the duo.

In Chapter 1 we discussed the possibility of individuals acting as slaves towards others in order to profit from these other persons' favors. Few people like to do this in public view. But because they feel free from scrutiny in a duo, people tend to be bolder. People may like to perform for someone they know lacks the expertise or knowledge to criticize them and in a duo it is possible to receive incredible praise from a companion who wants to go on enjoying our company. This in turn may make partners more interesting or attractive in our own eyes.

At times when the duo members are equally attracted, they benefit equally from their separation from society. They both can put aside rational evaluations and engage in a joyous exchange of jokes, senseless stories, smiles, and laughs. In such a case the duo may easily give way to a flirtation or even a courtship.

Because of the seriousness of its intent, courting can at best be given only a brief start at a party. It requires time and intimacy. It is usually carried on after the party and elsewhere. On the other hand, flirting is a party game and quite often does not last beyond the party. "The play-form of eroticism is coquetry," wrote Simmel.[3] Because of its very ambiguity, flirtation is half-private, half-public, even though what the partners exchange is often not for public consumption. To outsiders, the exchange often looks silly. It revolves around personal aspects of mind and body that may have no universal value but are noticed and appreciated by the partners. The flirting may consist of extremely refined and elegant comments on each other's particular intellectual and moral constitutions. Or it may dwell on tickling allusions to each other's looks, to the alarming sinuosities of his or her body, to the welcome seductiveness of a garment, or to the hope of eventually seeing the partner in less modest attire. Flirting is also half-public. Its public character is intended to manifest the totally nonserious character of the enterprise. It takes the appearance of children playing: "Let's suppose that I'm Tarzan and you're Jane." It is full of maybes, of hesitations about one's own intentions; the speech is such that it could be interpreted one way or another.[4] Take the flirting exchange between Emma Woodhouse and Frank Churchill in Jane Austen's *Emma*:

"You are comfortable because you are under command," [says Emma].

"Your command?–Yes."

"Perhaps I intended you to say so, but I meant self-command."[5]

In flirting the "perhaps" does not necessarily mean "yes," unlike in the previously quoted joke.[6] It can really mean "no," as it does in the case of Emma:

> Emma . . . gave him all the friendly encouragement, the admission to be gallant, which she had ever given in the first and most animating period of their acquaintance; but which now, in her own estimation, meant nothing, though in the judgment of most people looking on it must have had such an appearance as no English word but flirtation could well describe.[7]

And, indeed, it is a flirtation. Everyone thought so: "Mr. Frank Churchill and Miss Woodhouse flirted together excessively."[8] But the public character of their exchange limits its meaning, and Emma, who is much less involved in the flirting than her suitor, resents making an exhibition of herself for the other guests: "Your gallantry is really unanswerable. But (lowering her voice) nobody speaks except ourselves, and it is rather too much to be talking nonsense for the entertainment of seven silent people."[9]

This statement puts an end to the flirtation because Emma clears the ambiguity with the word "nonsense," and thus rejects the possibility that their conversation might mean any serious intent. Frank Churchill understands it and devaluates his previous declaration ("Three o'clock yesterday? That is your date. I thought I had seen you first in February.") He had meant that he had fallen under Emma's command the very first time he had met her. Now he reduces the compliment to a mere statement of facts: "'I say nothing of which I am ashamed,' replied he, with lively impudence. 'I saw you first in February' . . . ."[10]

Why, if people are attracted to each other, would they want to engage in ambiguous statements? First, because the individuals who initiate may be uncertain about their partners' disposition towards them and the more they feel attracted, the more they would be devastated by a cold shoulder or a rejection. They then want to keep a ready-made exit for themselves: "I was not serious, of course. I was just kidding."

"Flirting," writes Peter Blau, "involves, largely, the expression of attraction in a semi-serious or stereotyped fashion that is designed to elicit some commitment from the other in advance of making a serious commitment oneself. The joking and ambiguous commitment implied by flirting can be laughed off if they fail to evoke a responsive chord or made firm if they do."[11]

At this point others may show they are interested in their gallant partners. By showing some encouragement to the companions, they prompt the latter to proceed further, still with prudence, until successive and deeper commitments totally clear the road for their own commitment and involvement.[12] Then the flirtation may become a love duo, a mutual courtship. This in turn will suggest a less public stage. It is the time when the partners may either disappear for a while into the garden or readily take their leave from the party, in search of more appropriate and discreet surroundings.

Seldom does flirting end up in a sexual relationship as in the case described above. People usually enjoy flirting for the fun of it. They do not want the flirtation to become serious. Why? It may be that in spite of some superficial attractiveness, one of the partners or both of them, perceive that the other would not be a good match for a serious affair. The seductive partner may appear to be so selfish or bad tempered, superficial or governed by thoroughly different values, that the companion could not imagine being really involved with that person. Another reason may be that the partners, or at least one of them, is so deeply involved or entangled in family or social obligations that he or she does not wish to seriously endanger them. This person wants to maintain the flirtation at the level of an imaginary involvement. Each gets excited knowing that the partner could entertain the idea of an involvement. However, to be sure that either partner will not take the "love game" too seriously, the game is performed in view of the public. Others can get glimpses of what is going on, and hear snatches of conversation. The conversation itself is made to sound very unrealistic and any time one member is possibly tempted to take it seriously, the partner makes some exaggerated statement that sends both partners back into a world of empty dreams. All these elements are present in the following flirtatious exchange we overheard at a recent party (the topic of conversation had been the movies and mention had been made of Lina Wertmüller's film *Swept Away*):

"What if you and I were stranded on a tropical island after our lifeboat had been overturned and everybody else had been eaten by sharks?"

"How did we get to the island, if the boat had been over-turned? You know I swim so badly."

"Of course, I would have taken you in my arms and brought you to the shore! Do you object?"

"To have been brought to the shore?"

"No, to have been carried there in my arms."

"I only object that the shore was so near."

"Well, the ocean is always there. But do we need it?"

"What we will need now is to dry our clothes."

"Good, the sun will do the job, and it will also dry our bodies. Would you be shy?"

"Shy of the sun? No. It has no eyes."

"I could pretend to look the other way."

"Yes and try to do some work, like finding food and making a couple of huts."

"A couple of huts—why a couple?"

"Well, in case we have a visitor."

"In that case I'll build his hut not too close to ours."

(At this point the woman smiled and, lowering her voice, said): "After all, we might never find ourselves on a deserted island, but there are . . . mountain refuges, discreet inns, and . . . motels."

(Her companion replied aloud): "Oh, I know one with water-beds, mirrors on the ceilings, a sex instruction manual on the night table, and a video camera in the corner to film every phase of our raging passion!"

The woman laughed and, contributing to the new mood, said: "Of course we will share the royalties."

The exaggerations, the allusions to impossible situations, the loud voice, bring back the flirtatious exchange to the level of an amusing dream and exclude any intention of pursuing a serious in-volvement.

Usually, as in this case, the flirtatious exchange ends up in a laugh and both partners go back with their spouses to a house with-out waterbeds and mirrors on the ceiling but a baby in the crib and a baby-sitter who fell asleep in the armchair. This is reality. But at the party they (at least one of them) had a good time. They escaped for half an hour into a dream world and were reassured that their actual life destinies were not their only chances in this world. There could have been other partners and other adventures. Their personalities contain a great array of possibilities which may never materialize, but their joint dreaming at the party shows what could have become true. Flirting at a party is just another way of getting encouragement for who we are, or could have been, or could become.

Being shielded from the eyes of society in a duo often yields pleasure but at times can become a source of displeasure and tension. As we said, we find pleasure in interacting with attractive, supportive companions who behave civilly in the absence of witnesses. But we may also find ourselves engaged with uncivil companions. Unimpressed with us or with anybody, these narcissistic individuals are civil only when compelled to be so. When they think they can get away with it, they do not hesitate to be indifferent to our stories, absent-minded, unsupportive, and even sarcastic. We try our best, we change topics, ask them questions that we think may elicit from them a good performance. But to no avail. They leave us at the first opportunity without a word of regret. In this case the duo has been a flat failure.[13]

Our inability to give our partners sufficient or the right kind of attention constitutes a lesser offense. But it may create deep feelings of resentment in the partners who may, however, persist in conversing with their inattentive companions because they do not perceive any possibility of engaging someone else.[14] Inattention to our partners may take various forms. As we said above, at parties some people are so preoccupied with noticing who else is there that they hardly concentrate on their present partner. Others are absent-minded, look at their shoes, straighten their tie, pull out a cigarette and look for a match. We may also give the other person the wrong type of attention. Sally, a handsome woman, was listening to Eugene and looking at him with admiring eyes. He was telling her of his recent archeological dig in Iran, amidst innumerable bureaucratic difficulties. The woman was smiling and the man happy. However, at one point we could see he became a little nervous. The woman was looking him over, assessing him, from his Italian shoes to his designer tie and his gold and ruby cuff links.

"What are you staring at?" he asked.

"Oh, I was wondering whether you dress so well when you do your digging in . . . , well, wherever it is."

"It is in Iran, and that is what I . . ."

"Well, I don't see you there in the mud with those shoes. . . ." Eugene was thrown off-balance. He was somehow flattered that his attire had brought him some approval from an attractive partner, but he had been trying to impress her with much more difficult achievements, presenting her a self-image he cherished much more deeply than that of an elegant man of the world. Needless to say, the mistake made by Sally is much more often committed by men. How many of them hardly listen to a beautiful woman telling about her artistic, literary, or business roles? While giving the woman some perfunctory support for her activities, they make a thorough examination of their partner's physical attributes, those they see and those they must guess about, trying to decide—more or less unconsciously—how much pleasure they would have being in bed with her. Women, especially today, object to being treated as sex objects. It is their right; and their demands cause men to be more cautious in their expressions of interest. There is little doubt, however, that this expected restraint contributes to the tensions arising—at least for the males—when in a duo. In a larger grouping, one could more easily indulge in one's own selective assessments of others and daydream without being offensive. In a duo we are required to be attentive, not only to the partners' presence, but to the specific performances they are offering us.

Another problem we have to face in a duo is how to handle what we think is an undue claim for support. We may be inclined to be kind, but there are statements, pretenses, or boastful stories we can listen to only with the utmost degree of patience. If we hesitate to grant our support, without the benefit of a third party who could support our hesitancies, our partners may accuse us of unfriendliness.

Assuming they have escaped all these possible pitfalls, the two partners are still not out of the woods. They may not be threatened by one another, but they are under the scrutiny of others in the gathering who resent two guests who are so involved that they no longer appear available for interacting with others. Once, the day after a buffet dinner party, I received a telephone call from Deborah, a woman who wanted, she said, to thank us for the marvelous party. Her thanks, however, were rather short and she moved quite fast into a criticism of a certain bachelor who allegedly had been so ill-behaved as to spend a great part of the evening in a duo with only one woman. The reproach was, of course, addressed primarily to us—the hosts— for having tolerated such a breach of civility. We should somehow have compelled the attractive bachelor to distribute his attentions more equally among the various women in the party. Deborah's complaint said much about her frustrations, but it also pointed out a constant expectation from the other guests in social gatherings: that of offering one's company to everyone who may desire it and of postponing the immediate gratification one might get by interacting only with a couple of attractive guests.[15]

It is not only the length of time we spend with the same companion, but our behavior which may become objectionable to others. The other guests will object to two persons staying locked for a long time in a totally absorbing gaze which practically admits no one else. No more pleasant is the "plotting sequence" in which two individuals use obscure sign language, speak in a foreign language, or whisper, with the clear intent of excluding others from their conspiracy. Flirting, too, should not exclude the rest of the party. If practiced at all, the participants are expected to do it in public view and choose several partners in succession. More generally, any mutual activity which cannot be extended to all will be disliked. In a party where—with the help of alcohol or other relaxing mechanisms (like dimming the lights)—everybody starts indulging in touching others, holding them by the waist or shoulders, kissing and caressing them, no one will object to all the guests following the general trend, especially if, in this friendly exchange, they do not monopolize to their advantage the most attractive guest in the room. But if only one person is indulging in these types of activity at a gathering, the other guests may object to what they consider a private monopolization of a desirable partner. This behavior is interpreted as an act of possession, by which people exclude others. This is also applicable to engaged and married people, who bring their partners to the party. They are expected to refrain from engaging in any behavior that cannot be extended to everybody. As has been hinted above, it is not the sexual or "obscene" character of this behavior that people object to, even if they express their disapproval in those terms. What they actually object to is being excluded. Now, given that sexual intimacy requires very specific conditions of mutual attraction, it remains an essentially private type of activity, that is, an activity we do not indulge in with everyone. Sexual intimacy, then, is by its very nature selective, that is, exclusive. This is why—except in the case mentioned above, where special mechanisms have blunted our sense of discrimination—it is not practiced in social gatherings. Duos are all right, on the condition that what is done in a duo can be replicated with any of the other guests.[16] After having been together for a while, the partners then are expected to relax their mutual involvement and somehow signal that they are also available to others.[17]

The last but not least of the problems encountered in handling a duo is that of breaking it. It is awkward to end it when the two partners agree on the termination but do not know how to go about it. It is much more difficult when one partner clings to the other either physically or morally. Sensing that their partners might want to escape them they start bombarding the partners with questions and are all the more desperate when the partners' answers become shorter and shorter.

There are interactions that we would like to last forever. However, sociability demands that we free our partners and ourselves for other involvements. Outside considerations, such as family duties, team duties, work demands, or physical exhaustion may possibly, too, require that we stop the conversation and leave the party. Assuming that in both cases, we break the duo only reluctantly, we won't have much trouble in getting our feelings across to our partners. A tone of sincerity in our voice will convince them that, if we really could, we would like to have stayed with them. Words to express our regret will come easily. But even if we have not been so delighted by someone's company, we are expected to express some regret at having to terminate the engagement. We all want to hear that our company was pleasant and that others do not rejoice in leaving us. In every language, formulas have been invented to express the desire to meet again the person one must leave. These formulas are repeated again and again, and quite often do not express our real sentiments: *Au revoir!* See you soon! *Auf Wiedersehen! Hasta pronto!* Italians, with their taste for superlatives, say sometimes: *"A prestissimo"* (see you very soon). Don't take it too seriously, as I pretended to do once; I replied: "Oh yes, I would love it. When will it be?" My partner looked at me with blank eyes, as if to say, "What do you mean?" For her, the expression *"A prestissimo"* had become a way of saying "good bye!" and in no way meant a desire for a new encounter. The emptiness of this and similar formulas suggests that if we really want to express a desire to meet our companions again, we should say it using a more personal sentence.

It is easiest to depart when we want to break away from the party altogether. Everyone knows that at one point all the guests must go and any pretext for leaving is good. If we must go rather early, we try to be more inventive: "The weather may turn nasty and we would like to reach home before the tornado," or "We promised the baby-sitter we would be back by eleven," or "We must go; Paul leaves tomorrow morning for São Paulo," and so on. It is plausible; it may even be true. Civility may have inspired the explanations and civility requires that the listeners not check their accuracy. We certainly prefer hearing them than learning that our company or party is particularly boring.

Much more difficult is our desire and even willingness to terminate a duo with the intention of going to interact with another guest in the midst of a gathering.[18] Sometimes we are helped by the hosts who introduce a new guest, permitting either the development of a trio or a civil departure by one of us. We might also be blessed by the move of an individual who manifests the desire to join us or one of us. Unfortunately, these are not always the case and some strategy must be devised. Here are a couple of common procedures: First guests engage in the ritual mentioned above by which—even if they do not completely mean it—they express the wish that sometime they and their partner will meet again, for instance, to discuss another aspect of the question or to hear about the issue of whatever problem the partner mentioned and has at heart (what will be the success of the merger, will the baby be a boy or a girl, will the daughter be accepted at Smith, and so on). If we really mean it, or at least do not strongly object to meeting our partner again, we ask for the partner's address or telephone number. Possibly the visiting card or the piece of scratch paper with the precious information will join a bundle witnessing to many other interrupted interactions in the past, but the gesture is always refreshing. Then, or rather concurrently, guests try to "deliver" their partner to someone else or at least guide the other in the direction of a new partner. Explicitly or not, we invite our partner to join a group of people among whom there is one or several individuals who might be interesting or attractive. We may ask our partner whether she is interested in being introduced to a specific person. At this point, if the partner has any common sense, she will accept the "generous" suggestion and avoid proclaiming: "But I am much more interested in going on talking with you!" If all these procedures fail, we confess our thirst or hunger and suggest a trip to the bar or the buffet. There, the necessities of handling food or drinks may take the two partners apart, and while one is busy getting a drink or putting together the bread and foie gras, the other may either disappear, or, having spotted another possible companion, start another animated conversation, clearly precluding the intrusion of a third person. If one is lucky, the previous partner will also have met another friendly guest at the buffet.

The task of departure would be made much easier if partners, instead of pressing their luck by trying all means to keep their companions within their grasp, sense restlessness with the encounter and instead express their intention of freeing their partners from their company by saying: "I really do not want to take too much of your time, when I know so many other people would like to talk with you." This remark would have given their companion the generous possibility of protesting: "You want to leave me so soon! Please do not go that fast. I still have one question. And then you must give me your address!" By mentioning that we still have "one" more question and that we want our partners' addresses, we actually accept their offers of terminating the encounter, but we do so in a civil manner that leaves both of us happy. If by chance we misread our companions' intention and wrongly assume that they want to terminate the encounter, their protest that they want to continue the conversation will be an even greater reward.

A duo does not constitute a society, observed Simmel. A trio (or a triad as his translator prefers to say) is a society. Or, we should say, a trio could be a society, constituting a system where any exchange between two members is under the impartial scrutiny of a third. By being supposedly independent of the others (or similarly tied to each of them) the third member can restore an objective criterion of evaluation and enforce rules of civil behavior.[19] By so doing, Betty prevents Sam from exploiting Fred, and stops Fred who accepts any kind of demand from acting in a servile way. The third member can play a mediating role if a conflict has already erupted or if it is about to explode. This can make the triadic situation more relaxed than the duo. All three partners feel that they are protected against possible exploitation.[20] Social control is at work.

Another advantage to the trio is that its members need not fix their attention exclusively on one another, as in a duo. The third party, while the two other partners interact, can rest a little while. Yes, the third listens, but with a more detached mind, and may play the benevolent bystander who offers a brief remark from time to time.[21]

A fourth advantage to the trio is more extrinsic; it concerns the other guests in the gathering. A trio is a more open situation, which makes collusions or conspiracies more difficult. The exchange is necessarily less personal and lends itself to the inclusion of newcomers. The other guests feel that, if they wanted, they could join the group.

A final advantage of the trio is the ease with which one can depart from it. Choosing a moment when the other partners are involved in an animated discussion, one takes leave, easily giving it an air of civility, as if saying: "You both seem to enjoy each other very much, and I do not want to interfere with your pleasant duo." The opportunity offered by the trio for an easy departure is the reason why one may often want to transform a duo that has become a little tiresome into a trio. The arrival of a third party may spur the departure of the previous companion ("I see you have found a friend, I'll leave you to enjoy each other's company") and if it does not, it will be the occasion for taking your leave.

All these are real advantages, adding flexibility to mutual engagements. But they are probably outweighed by many drawbacks or pitfalls.

By exerting more control over its members, the trio, in contrast with the duo, may restrict the possibility of giving "free" performances and of readily getting support. One cannot obtain the same degree of complicity that one can expect from a single companion. Merely by remaining silent, one of the trio may resist our act and our claims; that resistance will, in turn, make our other companion more reluctant to approve of us wholeheartedly. Both of the other two companions are afraid they will look ridiculous if they approve of everything we say. No one wants to look like a sucker. Conversely, the members of a trio cannot offer any of their companions their support too cheaply. They would blush at receiving undue rewards. Each of the three companions plays for the other the role of an objective critic.

Conversation, we said, is a fight for recognition. Triadic conversation offers no exception. It is true that the presence of a third person may lead to the resolution of a conflict, but it can also—before this stage is reached—encourage or even engender a conflict. A former duo which had stifled a potential conflict for the sake of its survival, may give way to the conflict upon the arrival of a third person. Jack and Janet hope to attract Peter, number three, to their cause. If Peter thinks he must support one of the antagonists, instead of remaining an impartial judge, the conflict will rage all the more. The defeated partner, for instance Jack, will attack whatever seems to be the basis for Janet and Peter's collusion against him: "Of course, I should have thought of it before, both of you are Catholics, or Jews, or lawyers, or Republicans or Hispano-Americans, and so on." He will also struggle all the more to reverse the situation.

A different possibility is that of a pleasant rapport existing between two guests marked by laughter and animated conversation that suddenly gets disrupted by the arrival of a third and attractive companion. The original members of the duo then will fight for the newcomer's attention and favors.[22] He or she may be the chairman of the board, the elegant model from Haiti, the well-known actor in the Broadway hit, the successful physician. In fighting for the newcomer's attention, one of the previous partners may have assets which will appeal more to the newcomer. The bank executive appeals more to the stockbroker than does the dress designer; if the newcomer is a model, he or she is more interested in the fashion designer than in the other companion the insurance broker, and if she is an actress she will more willingly interact with the film director than with a high school principal. The greater attractiveness could also be based upon age, sex, or beauty. At any rate, in the trio, one of the partners is invariably less attractive. Quite often the latter is ignored by the other two and can win back from them some attention only by fighting. Instead of bringing peace, the arrival of a third party in this case has created discord.

For whatever reasons, it is also a fact that some people are not capable of talking to two other individuals at the same time. If they find themselves in a trio, they select one of the partners and engage in a lively conversation with that person, ignoring the third companion. They probably choose one of the companions over the other without much reflection—for instance, they know one of the other two better, they know that person's expertise in one area, or they have common memories or experiences with number two. This is a dangerous game, because number three may be a very knowledgeable individual, precisely in the area discussed by the other two. More generally, it is dangerous because there is hardly a better way of making oneself an enemy than treating someone as a nonperson. A little observation of social gatherings—ranging from coffee breaks to large receptions—shows that this kind of unsocial behavior is extremely common. The slight may be subtle or it may be overt. Few people, or so it is hoped, have endured the extreme lack of civility that Paul, a friend of mine, who was a New York City politician, experienced years ago. Paul remembers the occasion as if it had happened yesterday, although it occurred during the early 1960s. He was having lunch in a hotel in Chicago, when he spotted in the hotel's lobby an old friend from St. Louis. Paul went to greet him and they chatted for a while. Learning that Paul had an appointment with a Chicago labor leader, the man expressed a wish to accompany him. Paul accepted, not suspecting that after a few minutes of preliminary talk with the union leader, his friend would take over the show and—in spite of his total ignorance of the local situation—start a conversation, comparing the labor conditions of St. Louis and Chicago, from which Paul was totally excluded. Being much younger and unwilling to offend his old friend, Paul, after a few vain attempts at asking what he thought were the real questions about the Chicago situation, gave up and remained silent. It was not until two hours later that Paul's friend announced that he had to attend another appointment and that, consequently, the conversation had to stop. He was very surprised when Paul said that he intended to stay and converse further with the union leader. What else could be discussed, thought the friend? Paul told me that until his death his friend remained totally incapable of involving two persons at the same time in one conversation.

Before reviewing the ways through which we can try to involve both our companions in a trio, let us look at what the neglected party often does or could do when placed in this uncomfortable position. The third party has three ways out of the awkward situation: they may first succeed, at one point, in forcing their way back into the conversation by making a forceful and impressive re-entry. George and Sally, for example, are speaking about symphonies although they are making all kinds of errors. Odette, a very good pianist—which is a fact unknown to her companions—is practically ignored for ten minutes until they attribute to Dvořak a piece written by Bartók. This, she thinks, is too much. "I believe you mean the Concerto for Two Pianos and Orchestra written in 1938 by Béla Bartók. He played it himself with his wife in 1943 in New York. I was still very young then, but I still remember how I was impressed by the mixture of atonality and traditional orchestration." At this point George and Sally had to wake up to the reality. For several minutes they had made a poor show of their limited musical knowledge in front of an expert whom they had managed to treat with great incivility. The ignored party cannot always make a successful comeback, however. Most are condemned to use simpler means of showing their displeasure at being ignored: one makes noise, drumming on a table with all five fingers, another asks for a cigarette, then a match, still another puts on lipstick or waves at other people, calls the waiter or stares pointedly at the ceiling or a painting. One solution, of course, would be to leave. But there are instances when leaving is not possible: when people find themselves in a group comprising a powerful individual whom they do not want to antagonize, or when the spouse or the friend whom they have accompanied to the party is having a good time and does not want to go. Quite often, too, in a modern anonymous gathering, people prefer to remain in an unrewarding group rather than blindly search for a companion in that jungle of anonymous guests. Being unable to withdraw physically from the engagement, they, at times, try to leave it mentally, for instance by pulling out an agenda and making notes in it. There is, however, more than one circumstance when even this is not possible, for example, that of the seated dinner party. Normally the arrangement should permit all guests to engage alternatively with their two neighbors. But this does not always happen. Take the following placement:

	Hostess	
Bertrand		Steve
Martha		Susie
Felix		George
. . .		. . .

If Martha and Felix are deeply engaged in a duo, and Susie and George do the same, the hostess is left with Bertrand and Steve on either side. Normally she should divide her attention between the two, or possibly engage both of them in a triadic conversation. However, it is not unheard of that one of the hosts engages only one of his or her neighbors, abandoning the other neighbor to the delights of eating and drinking. There is actually nothing else to do. We can also let our minds wander on the sociology of social gatherings.

In many other occasions there is no real obstacle that prevents us from leaving two other uncivil companions. It is useless to say that we do not need to indulge in elaborate leave-taking rituals. The shortest departure will be least painful.

One of the reasons why a trio effectively becomes a duo attended more or less patiently by a silent third party is the difficulty of finding a common topic of conversation. We already mentioned the difficulty for two individuals to find a common ground. This difficulty increases when a new member is added to the original pair.

Simmel has also observed that uniformity of mood is much more difficult among three persons than between two. The genteel complicity of the two fades when number three arrives: "the sensitive union of two is always irritated by the spectator. It may also be noted how extraordinarily difficult and rare it is for three people to attain a really uniform mood—when visiting a museum, for instance, or looking at a landscape—and how much such a mood emerges between two."[23]

In spite of its intrinsic difficulties and its pitfalls, some people succeed in making the triad a workable combination. The leader of the trio or at least one of its two more powerful components can work to include number three and make that person comfortable. When Jane, number three, joins, she is not only greeted by the individual who knows her, but is also introduced to number two. Then Jane is apprised of the topic of conversation and if she maintains any connection or familiarity with this topic, it is mentioned to number two. If she has no knowledge of the theme that has been discussed, she is rapidly acquainted with it. This is preferred to shifting immediately to a new topic. Such a shift would likely be unpleasant to number two and would suggest that number three had disrupted the previous engagement or is not worthy of participating in the former exchange. If, after a while, it appears that the newcomer has little to contribute to the existing topic, then a change will be a sign of friendliness and hopefully number two will not resist it. If the change of topics has been initiated in order to accommodate the third party, the initiator of the change is then faced with the duty of maintaining number two within the circle of attention.

At any time during a dual exchange within a triad, number three can be attended in various ways. We can for instance preface a statement by adding an explanation allowing number three to understand its meaning. We can also make of number three a witness, almost a judge of our interaction with number two. We can, for instance, comment to the third on something that was said by number two. Doing so, number one kills two birds with the same stone: number two is flattered to hear number one comment (favorably or at least discriminately) on his or her own statement and number three is pleased to be addressed and made part of the interaction. Taking number three as a witness, however, is not always possible. It makes sense only if, without being an expert, the third can be supposed to understand—even with a couple of complementary explanations— what the issues are. Two nuclear physicists discussing some very abstruse detail on the composition of the atom could hardly expect a charming but uneducated grandfather to be interested in their exchange. If the two must for some time go on talking about a complex issue in front of someone unacquainted with the topic, they (at least one of them) may try to involve the grandfather by maintaining some kind of physical contact with him, if the local rules and the degree of familiarity permit it. I still remember that during my first trip through Latin America I interviewed, among other celebrities, Bishop Helder Camara. He received me in a large parlor where many other visitors were seated. When I entered the room, the bishop was talking with a simply dressed, middle-aged woman. When he saw me, the bishop signaled me to come and sit with them and he started to answer my questions on the social situation of Brazil. The topic had little interest for that woman, at least at that level of generality. To involve her the best way he could, the bishop rested his hand on the woman's arm and then accompanied his most eloquent statements by pressing the woman's arm, at times very vigorously.

Before abandoning the subject of triadic interaction, we should mention the situation when a trio is a pseudo-triad, that is, made of a two-member team plus a third party. As long as the team acts as one, sustaining the same opinions, reinforcing each other's stories, things look more like a duo. What we said of dyad applies here, including the mutual encouragement of overstated achievements and poorly sustained performances. The situation is altered, however, if one of the team members, in arguing with number three, becomes so carried away that the partner in the team does not want to support him or her any more. The latter feels compelled—at least for a while—to dissociate from his or her team partner. The outsider feels a little relieved by the breach in the "enemies'" camp, but is then confronted with the stress developing in the team itself. Who doesn't feel sympathy for spouses who despair at their drunken partners' abusing a guest or the hosts at a party? What can they do? Begging the spouse to cool down may work sometimes. It may also spark a new explosion. For this and other reasons, in middle-class and upper-middle-class gatherings spouses and lovers usually do not stick together in social gatherings as much as space and the number of the guests permit.

According to Georg Simmel, the tension is even greater if the third person is tied to the two other parties, especially if he or she is linked to them not through some accidental and superficial bond but through a more intimate bond:

> In such a case, the third, whom love or duty, fate or habit have made equally intimate to both, can be crushed by the conflict—much more so than if he himself took sides. The danger is increased because the balance of his interests, which does not lean in either direction, usually does not lead to successful mediation, since reduction to a merely objective contrast fails. This is the type instanced by a great many family conflicts.[24]

And so, rather than face the conflicting pressures from two equally loved persons, intelligent third persons may prefer to withdraw, letting them settle their case with the help of a "stranger." The stranger can look at things from an intellectual, cold, impartial point of view and avoid the passionate feelings, the emotions, the passion necessarily aroused by ties of friendship, kinship, or love. A woman cannot successfully intervene in a dispute between her husband and her brother, nor can a man successfully intervene in a dispute between his wife and his sister, for example. This combination does not constitute a real triad that can work as such since the three individuals are emotionally involved with each other.

It is unusual to find groups of people larger than three engaged in a common conversation. However, they may be found at seated dinner parties, especially when the hosts or a spontaneous leader preside over the common exchange. In most other cases, either the group breaks down into duos and trios, or, at best, listens for a while to the monologue of a star.

Why is it so? The first and main reason is that in the absence of an orchestra conductor, no symphony is possible. If the hosts or spontaneous leaders do not take the initiative of directing the general conversation, of suggesting topics, of giving the floor to those whom they deem competent to speak on the subject while gracefully silencing a narcissistic talker, no general interaction will work. Here again, we may think that in the past hosts were more skillful at practicing the art of chairing a general conversation. The modern dissemination of democratic ideas and the hatred for any forms of authoritarianism, manifest themselves not only in politics but also in family life and in everything that is done in the house. In the absence of capable hosts, one does not see how a group of people could engage in a general conversation. What is more likely to happen is either the splitting of the group into smaller interactions or the harmonizings by a star to whom everybody, more or less, willingly listens. To win the general attention, however, the star must present high credentials. Only the excitement of listening to the talk of a great personality and the extrinsic reward of being able later to report the fact to one's peers would convince one to give up the immediate returns of a chat with an attractive and supporting neighbor. If, for a while, an ordinary guest succeeds in winning the general attention, this is usually of short duration and soon the group breaks down again into smaller units.

Not only is listening to someone of a less than extraordinary status and prestige not rewarding, but speaking to a relatively large audience does not appeal to most people. Apart from the stars whom we have mentioned, most individuals are ill at ease at formulating their opinions or at telling their stories in front of people they do not know well and of whose values, allegiances, and expertise they are largely ignorant. We risk either antagonizing some of the guests because we seem to disparage their teams, or looking ridiculous in front of people who might know the subject much better than we do. It seems that we are walking blind-folded through a mine field. And there are additional complications. Any performance offers to others a specific image of ourselves. We said earlier (in Chapter 8) how difficult it is to negotiate with one's partner a plausible and convincing presentation of oneself. When we speak in public, we may be confronted with a dozen people, half of whom we do not know—and we just mentioned the hazards of speaking in front of unknown individuals—and half of whom we do know and who know us. Each old acquaintance has already formed a specific image of us through the role we have been led to play when interacting with them. In a pluralized and compartmentalized society, there is much probability that the various images do not coincide. Even if the various acquaintances are ready to accept some minor alterations, they will resist "buying" an image too different from the one they know, to be the "true" one. The bachelor who must speak in front of his boss, his lover, his mother, and his colleague from the office, will have problems. Before his boss, he likes to display his organized, responsible, and efficient self, which is always ready to work overtime. To his lover he usually presents his creative, leisurely, carefree but faithful, fun-loving side. His mother knows him as a kind, God-fearing, righteous but slightly timorous boy, and his colleague in the office knows him as a bonvivant who works just enough to keep his job and pretends to spend every evening with a different woman. How can he say anything in front of them that will not damage at least one of these contrasting images of himself? Shall he tell them about his wild safari in Kenya last summer where he had to confront a lion if not with his bare hands, at least with an innocuous hand gun? His boss will think: "Last summer? A safari? I thought he had been working the whole summer for the company!" His mother: "My son, a lion? How funny!" His girl-friend: "What safari? He never told me. Why didn't he tell me? He must have been there with another woman." The colleague: "Kenya? Come on! You spent your weekends on the Jersey shore." The whole thing was not an out-and-out lie. But the story was seven years old when the story-teller, then in the army, had spent three days at Dar-es-Salaam and rode a jeep 50 miles into the interior where, in a special reserve, he saw a lion and was too nervous to take any photographs.

Most guests prefer private conversations where they do not have to work so hard at the impossible task of matching the conflicting images which people hold of them all at once, or of respecting the values, teams, and expertise of those they do not know in the crowd.[25]

It may happen, however, as we suggested, that certain individuals have acquired such a high reputation and so clearly defined their public images that they can choose either to reinforce further the expected images by engaging in a plausible performance, or, if they prefer, give of themselves quite a different picture which will not endanger the solidity of their publicly known selves. Thus, when Professor Barnard, the famous heart surgeon, toured Europe in the late 1960s, his heart transplants had made him so well known as a first-class and bold surgeon that he could show himself as a man of the world, even as a playboy, and thus captivate the imagination of beautiful women. Similarly, the great poet may like to speak about his flowers and his orchard or even how he likes to make himself the Béchamel sauce for his cauliflower.

All this, however, cannot be called general interaction. It is more the discourse of stars in front of a more or less captivated (or captive) audience. If nobody in this audience matches the prestige of the narrator, the latter will remain the only one to speak. What the other guests in the party can do is just ask the star questions or utter brief statements in order to start him or her off again.

These interventions are not always received with pleasure by the audience. Quite often they are not presented as helpful to the general conversation but as attempts at gaining the attention of the star. They are often the expression of a competition among the guests and since the star cannot equally reward all the questioners, he or she must necessarily give some more attention to this or that guest to the displeasure of the others. It is clear also that not everyone has the expertise to ask the proper questions. Even if the great poet Penelope leaving the heights of Parnassus and the company of Euterpe comes down to the mundane topic of training a new puppy or how she waters her cacti, not everybody can participate. Imagine now that she wants to come back to Pindar or Sappho! In general, modern activities are so specialized that we can already be glad if we succeed in finding a common topic with one or two companions. If everybody has to be involved, the topics must become less and less specific. From a discussion of contemporary painting, the partners may have to move first into painting in general, then into art, possibly into hobbies, pastimes, and baseball. The larger the number of participants the more likely the topic will become trivial: The weather is the most common topic of discussion between strangers. The weather, for that matter, can be crime in the subway or the cockroaches. It is always a trivial topic known to everyone, that is in reality known to no one, as David Riesman noted in his article "The Vanishing Host."[26] Similarly, Simmel wrote:

> But the more persons come together, the less it is probable that they converge in the more valuable and intimate side of their natures, and the lower, therefore, lies the point that is common to their impulses and interests.[27]

A last drawback of general conversation is that it does not encourage the plurality of identity negotiations that middle-class and upper-middle-class individuals expect when they come to a social gathering. To the limited or nonexistent participation often experienced in general conversation, they prefer a more active role offered by duos and trios. They also want to shift partners in order to get the maximum exposure to the other guests, who, for them, represent "the world." General conversation, then, is more likely to be found among less competitive individuals either in the lower classes or on the contrary at the highest echelons of the social stratification system.

Should we, then, conclude that general conversation has been eliminated from middle-class and upper-middle-class gatherings? We would not go so far. But the fact should be acknowledged: It seldom occurs. Middle-class and upper-middle-class partygoers prefer small groups. If, however, general conversation is to be found in today's gatherings, it must meet very specific conditions that are not easily met. The first is that the guests be somehow limited in number. It is already difficult to manage a group of six to eight persons. It requires a very strong authority to handle twelve or more guests. The second condition is a balance between the need for homogeneity of interests among the guests and the need for enough of a diversity allowing the guests some freedom in the staging of themselves: A guest list comprised of only bankers, economists or lawyers would compel everyone to act out their occupational identities and little else. A third condition would be a certain physical arrangement of the people—seated for their comfort—permitting each of them to hear and be heard. The last and most important condition would be hosts capable and willing to preside over the general discussion. And this is not easy to find, if we believe David Riesman who, in the very title of the article we quoted above, was complaining about the "vanishing" of the hosts.

Is the species really disappearing or has it suffered a mutation? Maybe the new brand of hosts does not know how to direct a general discussion. It may be also that they do not want to, because their guests prefer to find in their house a freer, more relaxed atmosphere, permitting them to be themselves with whomever they wish, without having here again to follow pre-established rules and patterns. The modern conception of parties seems to preclude the perpetuation of the hosts as presidents or department heads. What, then, are they becoming?

NOTES

1. Simmel observed: "It may be also noted how extraordinarily difficult and rare it is for three people to attain a really uniform mood ... and how much

more easily such a mood emerges between two" (*The Sociology of Georg Simmel*, Kurt H. Wolff trans. [Glencoe, Ill.: The Free Press, 1950], p. 136).

2. G. J. McCall and J. L. Simmons show a condescending attitude towards this "I'll scratch your back if you'll scratch mine" game.

> This bartering strategy is also frequently seen, strangely enough at parties and mixers that bring together a number of strangers who are likely never to see one another again. We are all familiar in this context, with the tragicomic figure who runs from person to person, presenting the same "come-on", seeking (often desperately) someone who will, for the duration, allow him to pretend to be what he is not. If he is lucky enough to encounter someone in the same fix (very often someone of the opposite sex) the two may quickly negotiate this sort of "scratch my back" understanding. The resulting suspension of critical evaluation of each other, though transparent to outsiders, allows them to gain a fleeting modicum of support for their starving role–identities (*Identities and Interactions* [New York: Free Press, 1978], p. 150).

3. Georg Simmel, op. cit., p. 50. Flirtation or coquetry, as Simmel writes, being the play-form of eroticism is often found in social gatherings, which are the play-form of society. It is a "civilized" and social way of releasing sexual impulses. Coquetry applies to both men and women. Simmel further writes: "Coquetry that unfolds its charms precisely at the height of sociable civilization has left behind the reality of erotic desire, consent or refusal . . . coquetry is the flirtatious, perhaps ironical play, in which eroticism has freed the bare outline of its interactions from their materials and contents and personal features." Ibid., p. 51.

4. The "coquettish woman enormously enhances her attractiveness if she shows her consent as an almost immediate possibility but is ultimately not serious about it. Her behavior swings back and forth between 'yes' and 'no' without stopping at either. Similarly the man who wants to remain at the level of sociability, must not take seriously either the 'yes' or the 'no'. He must not let himself be defeated by the prospect of refusal nor must he pursue an erotic purpose." Ibid., p. 50.

5. Jane Austen, *Emma* (London: Macmillan, 1927), p. 333.

6. See Chapter 5: "The Pact of Civility."

7. Jane Austen, op. cit., p. 332.

8. Ibid.

9. Ibid., p. 332.

10. Ibid.

11. Peter Blau, *Exchange and Power in Social Life* (New York: John Wiley and Sons, 1964), p. 77.

12. One may use flirting in order to ridicule and defeat another person. After the other has committed himself, the initiator of the game backs out and leaves the other hanging. Eric Berne in his entertaining book, *Games People Play* (New York: Grove Press, 1964), pp. 126–129, describes this sort of game under the name of Rapo, because the game player, a woman in the book, after having enticed the man, plays innocent, and accuses the man of being a rapist. The pur-

pose of the game—a zero-sum game—is not really a sexual gratification, but the discomfiture of the partner.

13. Simmel suggests that dyads, in order to work well, suppose stronger personalities than other numerical combinations: "Dyads, wholes composed of only two participants, presuppose a greater individualization of their members than larger groups do." Op. cit., p. 137.

14. In the eyes of Simmel, dyads are a fragile reality, because if one of the participants leaves, the whole is destroyed. Consequently each of the two companions makes more effort at keeping the other interested, "because others' departure means isolation, looks like abandonment." Ibid., p. 124.

15. At a reception I remember how a group of three scholars, co-editors of a political journal, remained together for the duration of the party, denying to everybody, including other well-known intellectuals, the pleasure of their company.

16. Erving Goffman, *Behavior in Public Places* (New York: Free Press, 1963), pp. 166–170.

17. A few pages further on Goffman writes:

> ... it is characteristic of occasions such as social parties that partici-
> pants have a right not only to initiate face engagements but also to
> enter ones that are already in progress. Here participants, in order to
> demonstrate how thoroughly they have been lifted up and brought to-
> gether by the party, may feel obliged to admit newcomers to their con-
> versation easily. "Open" topics of conversation may thus be maintained
> in preparation for newcomers. A conversation that by its tone forbade
> the entrance of new members would be improper. Consequently, we
> can understand the strategy sometimes employed by those who would
> converse about intensely involving private matters in a public place:
> instead of huddling together in a furtive conspirational way, they affect
> a style of matter-of-fact openness (ibid., p. 173).

18. Ibid., pp. 188–190.

19. If the third element of a triad is a nonpartisan, he or she can be a mediator, says Simmel: ". . . because of the nonpartisan, each party to the con-flict not only listens to more objective matters but is also forced to put the issue in more objective terms than it would if it confronted the other without media-tion," op. cit., p. 147.

20. Simmel writes:

> From the conversation among three persons that lasts only an hour to
> the permanent family of three, there is no triad in which a dissent be-
> tween any two elements does not occur from time to time—a dissent of
> more harmless or more pointed, more momentary or more lasting, more
> theoretical or more practical nature, and in which the third member
> does not play a mediating role . . . such mediations do not even have to
> be performed by means of words. A gesture, a way of listening, the
> mood that radiates from a particular person, are enough to change the

difference between two individuals so that they can seek understanding, are enough to make them feel their essential commonness which is concealed under their acutely differing opinions, and to bring this divergence into the shape in which it can be ironed out most easily (ibid., p. 149).

The mediating role is easy if the third party is not linked to the other two, but very difficult if he or she is personally involved with either or both of the others. He or she will be crushed. (Ibid., pp. 150–151).

21. Simmel also contemplates the case in which the third member of a trio uses his or her relatively superior position for egoistic interests; for instance, a person might draw advantages from one or either other party, because each of them, needing his or her support, may compete for their favors. He refers to this comfortable position as that of the *"tertius gaudens"* (ibid., pp. 154–156).

22. This is an example of the tertius gaudens position. Simmel, narrowing further the example, writes: "This (the tertius gaudens position) applies to one of the most common cases—namely the competition between two persons of the same sex for the favor of one of the opposite sex" (ibid., p. 156).

23. Ibid., p. 136.

24. Ibid., p. 150.

25. The preference for breaking down the audience into more homogeneous groupings (homogeneous as far as the image of the individual is concerned) is called "audience segregation" by Erving Goffman:

> By audience segregation the individual ensures that those before whom he plays one of his parts will not be the same individuals before whom he plays a different part in another setting (*The Presentation of Self in Everyday Life* [Garden City: Doubleday, 1959], p. 49).

26. David Riesman, Robert J. Potter, and Jeanne Watson, "The Vanishing Host," *Human Organization* 19 (1960), p. 24.

27. Georg Simmel, op. cit., p. 112. In another passage Simmel writes: ". . . because the mass is not the sum of the qualities of individuals, but only of these fragments of each of them in which he coincides with all others, these fragments can be nothing but the lowest and most primitive" (op. cit., p. 33). The principle applies also to stag-parties: "Stag parties may be attended by highly cultivated individuals who, nevertheless, have the tendency to pass the time by telling off-color jokes" (ibid.).

10
THANKS TO THE HOSTS

Many parties do not bring much pleasure to the guests and leave the hosts with a sense of failure. The failure cannot always be traced to specific mistakes, especially in the case of modern gatherings which seem to instill in the participants a sense of failure, or at least of inadequacy. But failure can also be the consequence of the hosts' inadequate perspective; the hosts may have a conception of their role which is not consonant with the guests' psychological need for identity support. As we have said repeatedly, this need is mostly unconscious in the guests, and as a consequence, it is not perceived by the hosts. The result is dissatisfaction for both, since the disappointed guests cannot reward the hosts with praise if they did not experience pleasure themselves.

After years of studying parties and what constitutes their success, in 1960 David Riesman and his collaborators wrote:

> . . . we cannot help but feel that generally, in the population to which we had access, the role of host is a neglected one—a role taken too much for granted, and often underplayed to such extent that the party remains diffuse, without the élan and sense of excitement which marks a truly festive occasion.[1]

Eighteen years later, Patricia Curtis wrote in the *Ladies Home Journal* magazine:

> A young couple I know (let's call them the Browns) invited me to a party they gave recently to launch the holiday season. When I arrived

at their front door, I could hear the sounds of festivities inside, but nobody answered the doorbell for the longest time. Finally, a guest let me in, and waved me in the direction of the bedroom where coats were piled. She wandered off, and I sidled up to a couple near the bar. We talked politely until the conversation withered from lack of common ground. After a few pleasant but unrewarding talks with other guests, some of whom were as much at loose ends as I was, I politely made an excuse and went home.[2]

We can identify with these sentiments because we too have experienced the same discomfort.

In this chapter, we will try to find detailed explanations to this choir of complaints. A general hypothesis to explain various dissatisfactions is that hosts of modern parties are acting according to an outdated role model. This role model was inherited from a time when most parties were composed of previously acquainted family, clan, or clique members. These traditional "family parties" were and still are organized to celebrate existing social ties, and the task of the hosts is limited to bringing their guests together. At best they need some skills to guide the social orchestra, but often the gathering takes care of itself. Unlike traditional parties which celebrate existing bonds, modern parties do not celebrate the unity of the past but rather aim at building some unity among mostly unacquainted people. At the beginning of the party, this unity is not a given fact; it is a reality slowly built through conversational exchanges. When the guests arrive, practically nothing yet has been achieved. It is the role of the hosts of a modern party to permit their guests to interact and grant each other identity support. More than a benevolent orchestra conductor, they have become social brokers.

Confirmation of the hypothesis that many hosts are playing an outdated role model can be found in the fact that the complaints recorded above are not directed against hosts who have organized a "family party" but against the hosts of the modern receptions where many, if not most, of the guests meet for the first time.

This is not to say that the two roles—that of host of family parties and that of host of modern parties—are entirely different. The traditional duties of the hosts have not disappeared, but new duties have appeared. As far as the old ones are concerned, they have been in part redefined to fit the format of the modern party.

In this chapter, we will first review the traditional expectations governing the host role; then we will study the new duties which the modern gatherings demand of the hosts.

The way in which the guests are invited to family versus modern gatherings already reveals the difference between the two. In the case of what we call the family party, the guests are somehow "convocated," rather than invited. The hosts, in calling them to their house, are not so much doing them a favor as fulfilling their responsibility toward the group. Conversely, by attending the family reunion, the "guests" are satisfying some kind of tribal duty rather than doing the hosts a favor. Consequently the hosts are less afraid than in other cases that their invitations will be refused; the denial is not directed toward the hosts themselves, but rather toward the whole family. On the other hand, the members of the family are supposed to be as eager to attend the party as they are to organize it. A refusal on the part of a guest will be acceptable to the family only if it stems from some kind of physical impossibility. In expressing or sending their regrets, the family members will address themselves not really to the hosts but to the whole group: "Tell everybody how much I regret not being able to come."

The situation is different in the case of a modern party, which does not celebrate already existing ties between the prospective guests. The guests who actually attend the party, not knowing who was invited, will not even notice those who did not come and in most cases, do not care. They will not be offended by their absence. The acceptance or the refusal of the invitation will be directed to the hosts alone. And while no family member could be suspected of staying away from the family party for reasons of personal choice or preference, the guest who does not choose to attend a modern party may well be suspected of preferring a more rewarding activity or party. The guest will then try hard to disguise the refusal under the appearance of some necessity, for instance, a prior engagement: "If I had known your invitation was coming, I would not have accepted . . ." and so on, ". . . but, now, unfortunately it is too late to disengage myself." The excuse is plausible, it might even be true. The hosts will try to persuade themselves that it is true.

The different relationship between the hosts and their guests in the two types of parties has immediate consequences for the timing and the formulation of the invitations. In the case of the modern party, the hosts will do everything to preserve the plausibility of the possible excuse presented by their guests; doing so, they protect them and themselves from embarrassment. They avoid sending their invitations too much in advance, at a time when no one is likely to be already engaged, thereby depriving their guests of the good excuse of a prior engagement. Of course, they will not send them at the last minute, when most people may have already another engagement, but they will respect the notification time which is customary (according to nation, social class, or region) so that their guests could plausibly have received and accepted another invitation. The guest's "regrets" will then be credited to the previous invitation and will not be considered an insult.

For a similar reason, the hosts of a modern party avoid inviting their guests by telephone, because this does not really leave the invited individual the possibility of balancing the pros and cons of accepting the invitation. If we accept it, we preclude the possibility of using our time differently, for instance, we could not accept another invitation which has not yet arrived but is expected. If we refuse, we may be left stranded at home if the other invitation does not come. The individual who must give an answer on the telephone must, then, on the spur of the moment, use some well-worn tactics like: "Well . . . I don't know . . . I first must ask Jerry (the husband) or Susan (the wife) whether we are free on this date." This, of course, fools only those who want to be fooled. But the intelligent hosts will remain embarrassed, wishing they had sent a written invitation.

These problems do not exist in the case of a family reunion, as we said, because the hosts are not so much inviting the participants, as signaling the members of the clan that they will meet. Of course, if the organizers want to give them a chance to come, they will apprise them early enough of the coming party, but this is due to practicality and not to etiquette. Family reunions actually may be announced months in advance, since all members are supposed to be so eager to participate that they would not consider attending another festivity. And there is no problem in inviting them by telephone: "You say you might not be able to come? Well, you know the place and the date, we hope you can make it. If not, too bad!" The "too bad" means "too bad for you" even more than "too bad for the family."

The hosts avoid inviting their guests at the last minute. This seldom happens in the case of a family reunion, since all the members are usually signaled much in advance of the event and there is no fixed number to reach. But in the case of the modern party, when individuals are invited at the last minute, they may get the impression they were on the "substitutes list." Last minute invitations are sent only if there is a plausible motive for doing so. For instance, the hosts say that they have to arrange a dinner for their second cousin who arrived unexpectedly yesterday from Texas. But there is the case where actually the hosts need someone to replace a guest who has suddenly become ill, or when they need to "de-fuse" a party which otherwise would comprise thirteen guests.[3] To remedy the situation, the hosts call on a very good friend, Betty, and explain both why she had not been originally invited and why she is now needed.

We heard of a woman who, because she must often organize rather formal dinners, is accustomed to phone a friend at the last minute. One of those who have obliged her in these last minute substitutions was a little hesitant about doing it anymore: "Last time I was there, I was introduced to the crowd in these—approximate—words: 'Ms. Jones does not really fit in our party, but since Ms. Smith could not come, she was nice enough to accept and complete our table.'"

Today's hosts are expected to prepare different party settings depending upon whether they are hosting a family reunion or a modern party. In the first case the guests are invited to what can doubly be called a private party. It is private not only because it is organized by a private citizen, but also because all the family or clique members share idiosyncratic memories, customs, and secrets, which serve to separate them from the outside world. What is said and done by them during the party often is not for public knowledge. There are no objections, then, if the rooms where the party is held contain many signs of the private occupation, hobbies, and pet activities of the members' family; grandfather's pipe lies on the desk, daddy's favorite crosswords are on the TV console, grandma's knitting work has been left on a seat. Baby may sleep in the crib. Everybody is comforted by being immersed in the warmth of the family's customs and traditions once again. Even the smells of the old furniture or blankets are welcome, or that of grandpa's old suits, and the familiar aromas coming from the kitchen promise well known culinary delights. Doubtless the house has been put in order and cleaned; but it did not need to become depersonalized.

Quite different is the setting prepared for the modern party. In this case the hosts are not gathering the family but a representative sample of the world. They eliminate from the receiving room what is too idiosyncratic, personal, or familial. The stress is on more universally agreed-upon messages, or symbols. Magazines, except for a literary or scientific journal, have been put into a drawer. The same is true of pipes, needlework, or correspondence. Typewriters and sewing machines are hidden in the closet. The receiving room takes on a worldly look, underscored by meticulous cleanliness and flowers from the florist. Instead of the usual earthenware or plastic glasses, the finest china and crystal are exhibited. Possibly silverware takes the place of the daily stainless steel service and linen is preferred to cotton or paper napkins. All this, of course, is relative to the nation's culture, to the social class or the income of the host. But at every level of the social ladder, a contrast will be found between the warm and *gemütliche* family reunion and the colder, more formal, more worldly, and anonymous reception organized to be a representation of the world.

Again, similar differences will be expected in the food and drinks the hosts offer their guests. In both cases the hosts want to please them with good and even festive delicacies. But they will not serve the same food at a family gathering that they would serve at a worldly affair. For the family party, the hosts explore the family traditions and offer the ethnic dishes and drinks which remind them of their mutual ties. This will be the time for an Irish stew with a good ale, or a *polenta* and Valpolicella, or *Knödel* and Liebfraumilch. Traditional dinners are abundant and aim at filling the stomach as well as raising the spirits of the guests. By contrast the food and drinks at a modern gathering are not meant to feed the guests but are designed to create an atmosphere of worldly refinement. The food is delicate, even exotic in character. It is also presented with distinction. Fashion, and not tradition, decides what should be served. There was a time when one would find mostly mixed drinks, caviar, and smoked salmon at cocktail parties. Today one is often served wine and small quiches or hot cheese sandwiches. What matters to the hosts is to demonstrate that they are informed of what is done in the world.[4]

Do the hosts of modern parties organize common activities of various kinds for the pleasure of their guests? What about card games, charades, projective painting, palm reading, graphological interpretation, square and folk dancing, social dancing, and so on? Our ancestors would not have thought to invite guests to their home without one of these activities. They would often, too, ask someone to sing, play the piano, the flute, or the violin. The party games and the attached prizes or penalties were part of social living. Authors describing popular customs, such as Charles Dickens,[5] have preserved for posterity the memory of these amusements. Today they have become the exception. Why? Possibly because the enormous leisure industry provides us with all kinds of recreational activities and competitions which our ancestors had to organize themselves privately. They did not have the resources of recorded music, movies, televised plays, concerts, and debates. They had no discothèques and night clubs (until recently public dance places were held in low esteem). Parties were the normal place to listen or to perform. The upper classes as well as the middle class, to a large extent, had larger houses. They had gardens, too. The peasants had access to the courtyards of the farms for dancing. Modern hosts may still organize parties centered around card games, but they would define them as such and invite only those whom they know like to play. If the house is large enough, the hosts may suggest a card game in one room and designate another room for social dancing. Few hosts, however, compel everybody to engage in these or other activities. The main reason is that these activities are in tune with the climate of family reunions while they do not fulfill any function in modern gatherings. They were needed to inject some excitement into family parties, which otherwise would have been quite boring. The guests knew each other and could not engage in the hard but exciting game of identity negotiation. But since man then, as today, was a competitive animal, competitions were organized to give everyone the opportunity to impress others. By contrast, the guests at a modern reception have enough challenge in discovering each other. There is seldom enough time during a party for this game, let alone charades.[6] Most modern hosts have enough sense of the requisites of a modern party for abstaining to impose games and competitions on their guests.

The hosts' interventions, on the other hand, may be needed for another task, that of seating their guests at the dinner table, if their gathering is a dinner party. When the family group was gathered around a dinner table, the rule presiding over the seating arrangement was that of rank. The rank order was determined mostly by age, if the "family party" was actually a gathering of the members of the same family. In the case of aristocratic, diplomatic or official parties, the rank order was mostly a combination of title and age. The hosts, of course, would also consider mutual compatibility, but this was not their main criterion. Family dinners may still follow the social custom

226 / The Pleasure of Your Company

of seating the participants by age, but within wide categories of age, freedom of seating would probably prevail. Several tables may be arranged, each for an age group. As far as aristocratic, diplomatic, or official dinner parties are concerned, they have not disappeared and still follow more or less the above mentioned criteria, but these parties are now outnumbered by more democratic parties, in which it would be difficult to find any official or agreed upon rank order among the guests. This absence of official differences and titles has persuaded many hosts that the best decision, for them, is to abstain from any prearranged seating. It may be easier, but it leads to many pitfalls. Enid Nemy justly observed:

> The devil-may-care, live dangerously, hostess allows guests to take any chair that doesn't already have a body in it. This nonchalance also allows the lady (or gentleman, as the case may be) to imagine that everything will work itself out, and it does, in much the same manner as a football scrimmage eventually sorts itself out. No matter that football players wear padding and rarely rely on four-inch heels and chunky rings to speed their way to their destination.
>
> About 50 percent of the guests at these parties end up scratched and bruised, and rarely is it worth it. Henry A. Kissinger is already surrounded, Farah is nowhere to be seen, the person on your right looks suspiciously like your spouse, and you could have stayed home and eaten the expired cottage cheese.[7]

At a family dinner, everyone has so much in common with the other guests that the free seating will not have too negative consequences. But at a modern party where so many people are unacquainted, and are of heterogeneous background or areas of expertise, the hosts are the only people who can match them in a felicitous way. In a free seating situation it seldom happens that the final seating reflects the compatibilities, affinities and mutual attraction of the guests. For the one or two who do sit next to whom they wish, the majority ends up with someone who is a much worse partner than the choice the hosts could have made. Possibly they have been harpooned during the preceding drinks by a bore who sticks to them and follows them tenaciously to the table. Maybe, as Nemy suggests, just before the sitting, one had a word with his or her spouse (Do you know who that is standing there? At what time should we go? If I were you, I would not eat the mayonnaise, and so on") and in the absence of other acquaintances standing nearby, will eventually sit with him or her. This, however, was not the purpose of the party. It could also be that either of the spouses had spotted a very attractive individual and would have liked to sit next to that person, but not knowing him or her well, did not dare to do so: "What shall I talk to him or her about? And how is it going to be interpreted?"

If the hosts have invited a special guest, whose conversation could capture the whole table, they usually place them or her in a central position, in such a way that the dialogue does not shut off any members at the table from participating. For this purpose, the placement which seats each of the hosts not at the two ends of the table but in the centers is preferred. The guest of honor is seated to the right side of one of the hosts (or hostess). He or she is in full view of the whole table and the dialogue that develops among him or her and the hosts, especially with the host (or hostess) located on the other side of the table, will be easily heard by everybody.

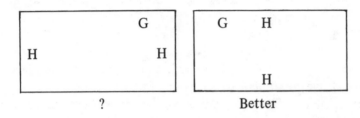

This specific placement is not needed if the hosts do not foresee a general conversation. The placement of the other guests takes into consideration their age, their mutual interests, their level of educational sophistication, and their more or less secret desires. Once they have established their list, the hosts mentally write next to the name of each guest the names of the other guests they think would be welcome to each one. No doubt there are a few dilemmas and the hosts decide for the best. There is no perfect placement. The guests, even if they enjoy the company of their neighbors, may regret that they have not the possibility of also speaking to handsome David or to interesting Pamela. In most cases they must only show a little patience; occasion to speak to their favorite partner will be given after dinner when the guests withdraw into the drawing room and take coffee and liqueurs. The situation will then be freer and they will be allowed to approach whom they want. However, they may hesitate to enjoy this freedom, for various reasons reviewed in a previous chapter.[8] They might have liked being "compelled" by the hosts to sit next to their attractive choice. Also, at times, dinner is not followed by any free interaction. It was the case at a party I attended a few years ago. Anabella, a famous gentlewoman, was passing through the city. She had hired the services of a professional party organizer, let us call him Mr. Asconi, and required him to gather a few people to entertain her. The dinner party of sixteen persons was held in a restaurant and it was clear that once dinner would be over everybody would go home. In other words, guests would have interacted only with their table neighbors. In the middle of the dinner Mr. Asconi asked six people to shift seats, which provided an entirely new pattern. To each, the astute Asconi murmured that so and so would like so much to converse with him or her. It worked well, in part because the guests were not well acquainted and were happy at the opportunity of discovering new people. We are not sure the method would work in all circumstances. As said above, it may prove better either to shorten the time spent at table and permit a longer free interaction afterwards, or, if the guest list is short, to organize a buffet dinner with a freer sitting structure. By freer we do not suggest that people sit exactly where they please. We mean that following the hosts' suggestion, they might sit at a place they will later leave to someone else when they go again to the buffet to refill their plates. The new seating will also be suggested by the hosts who will help their guests make the transfers. To give the guests more opportunity to stand up and shift seats, the hosts can have the food come in "installments." Following the example of Mr. Asconi, they can then communicate to their guest—Paul helping himself at the buffet, the desire of a specific individual to speak with him. To console Paul's previous partner Jane, the hosts may approach her and sit with her, letting her believe that the whole shifting had been engineered to permit the hosts to converse with her.

All these interventions are possible only if the buffet dinner is limited to a small group. If, on the contrary, the party brings together several dozen guests to be seated at as many different tables, there is no other solution than to post placement charts, in various places, permitting all guests rapidly to find their seat. If some of the guests are missing, last-minute skillful rearrangements will allow all the tables to be complete, with no empty seats.[9]

Having seated their guests, the hosts may think that now they can demonstrate their sociable talents by presiding over a fascinating general conversation. They will give the floor to each guest in turn, skillfully silencing the narcissistic monologist and encouraging the interesting but too modest storyteller. However, before embarking upon this venture, they may reflect upon the kind of people they have around them. Did they really come to listen to others' speeches? Is the short speaking time allocated to each of them a sufficient compensation for so much listening? And given the "pluralization" of the world, does each of them have anything to contribute that could be of interest to everybody else? It seems that general conversation better fits family gatherings where everybody is interested in what the other members of the family do and is curious to hear what is new in their lives. As we said in the previous chapter, in a modern gathering there is little common ground and all guests want to engage in their own identity negotiation. It is a fact that, if we except those seated dinners organized around a celebrity and where everyone is anxious to listen to him or her, in modern dinner parties the guests speak in duos, sometimes in trios. We have observed that even when the guests are seated at tables of four, the most likely structure will be the division of the four into two duos, with a possible change of partner at some point. Consequently, the hosts who try to impose a general conversation may swim against the current and meet with little success. However, in the case of a small party where the guests, without being relatives, are sufficiently acquainted with each other, the hosts may think that a general conversation might be welcome. This supposes that they can think of a common theme which will elicit interactions with most, if not all, the guests. The hosts will monitor the exchange, insuring that the level of conversation remains accessible to all, volunteering the supplementary information that those with less expertise in the subject might need to understand. They try to maintain a pleasant tone, possibly by interjecting a joke if some tension develops between two guests. If someone tends to speak a little too much, the hosts will first acknowledge what the speaker just said and then make an allusion to some area where another guest has better expertise, suggesting a shift of speaker. David Riesman writes: "The host serves by a kind of unobtrusive coaching to elicit what is unique and yet socially connective in each of his guests as well as in himself."[10]

The chairing or the coaching of the group does not mean that the hosts steal the show. Their self-effacement is not a withdrawal from their task, however. Without their interventions the "general conversation" will turn either into a monologue or into a dialogue between two guests, excluding everyone else. It might even turn into a fight. And if, by chance, someone has indulged in too many martinis and becomes insulting, the hosts do not hesitate to ease the guest into the bedroom, the bathroom or even to the street, after having called a taxi. I still remember a very painful experience which I was condemned to sit through along with the other guests because of the total ineffectuality of the shy host. Charles, during the dinner, had been invited by the host to speak of his ethnological research in a country of Latin America. The host was hoping an interesting dialogue would develop between Charles and another guest, Pedro, a Latin-American. Resenting, however, the "effrontery" and "pretense" of a British national lecturing the group on his views of a Latin American people, Pedro angrily ridiculed Charles's narrations and interpretations instead of discussing them. Everyone was embarrassed, hoping that the host would do something. Instead, he was silent. Only after half an hour of this fight did one of the guests take the responsibilities of the negligent host upon himself and bring a halt to so unpleasant an encounter. Everyone was angry at Pedro, but also at the host, who had been unable to manage the situation.[11]

This last observation leads us to discuss a question often raised: After the hosts have prearranged the party, established their guest list, sent their invitations, prepared the setting of the party, the food and the drinks, should the hosts let their party unfold by itself or go on intervening once they have greeted their guests? There is little doubt that the guests often expect some intervention from their hosts. They are the only resource in the case of a guest being sick, drunk, or aggressive. The problem is not really whether they should or should not intervene but what kind of intervention is expected of them. Many hosts limit their intervention to the crisis situation just mentioned, but do not think they have anything to do to guide their party toward success. Since games and general conversations are most of the time out of the question, they just wait for the party to end. One can find them standing by the door, greeting those who arrive and bidding farewell to those who go. One can at times see them serving food or drinks.[12] They are persuaded that the rest will take care of itself. This would have been the case in a family party, where no one needs any help in interacting with others. But a modern party is a completely different game and many hosts have not perceived the difference. We shall concentrate here on what intervention is expected of the hosts in the most challenging case, that of a relatively large, standing reception in which many of the guests are unacquainted.

Before we come to the details of their expected interventions, a word is necessary about the number and the quality of the people that the hosts of a modern party will invite.

The number of the guests should be large enough to permit each of them to encounter several compatible partners. It seems that 25 or 30 is a minimum to secure this result.[13] Fewer people condemns guests to chat, for the whole party, with the only individual who shares one of their pet topics: be it helicopters or duck hunting. On the contrary, with a larger crowd the chance of finding a good match increases. When determining the number of guests to invite, another aspect to consider is the size of the receiving room(s). Density may be low at a selective dinner party. A dinner party is more appealing when the guests are not crowded, that is, when the room is not densely filled. The arranged seating will tell everyone that the low density is not a sign that many had refused the invitation but that the hosts wanted to limit their invitations to a few select individuals. But at a large reception, to which likely many people were invited, a low density may communicate a feeling of failure: Only a few bothered to come; the mood of the party is henceforth depressed. A packed room, on the contrary, conveys the idea that everyone wanted to participate in this important event. This, in turn, creates general excitement. Density, however, is bearable only if kept within reasonable limits. At some gatherings, it becomes simply impossible to move through the crowd. And this precludes the shifting of partners. Besides the physical limitations, there is also a psychological reason for inviting not too large a crowd of guests: no one likes to be lost in an enormous, anonymous crowd. Beyond a certain number—50 or 60 people—the party looks so unselective that the guests no longer feel that they were chosen on the basis of their outstanding qualities. In addition, the unselective aspect of the crowd makes it much more difficult for the guests to approach new people. Why should these strangers be more accessible in the party than, say, in the middle of a crowd in Central Park? Finally, when a party is too large, even the hosts are unable to entertain many of their estranged guests.

Experienced hosts prefer to organize several parties if they are obligated to a great number of people. It permits them to restrict the groups to a reasonable size and to match mutually compatible people. In effect, seldom do all the people known to particular hosts fit together. Even if the guest list of a large reception can accommodate more variation among the guests than a small dinner party, nevertheless, a "statistical" compatibility of the guests is desired. While the guests cannot expect that they will have interests and backgrounds similar to everyone else, they hope that they will be compatible with a large fraction of the guests.

There may also be problems with the personalities of some of the guests. Some do not fare well in large gatherings, especially the shy ones who need perpetual help and prodding. Without it, they remain alone or stuck with the same individual. There should be some compatibility of social power, too. What matters here is not similarity of wealth or political power but equal capability in attracting the other guests. Some people are wealthy but incapable of any kind of conversation. A man whom I knew was very rich and friendly, but had not read a book since he had left high school, owned no books in his house, never traveled, never visited a theater or a concert hall, and even avoided reading a newspaper. It was impossible to find him any partner. On the contrary, other people have a low income, but this does not deprive them of being highly interesting partners in conversation; they are young artists or composers, beginners in all fields, or they have acquired an enormous expertise in politics, in the arts or the sciences. These traits make very desirable guests.

At this point one should observe that certain idiosyncratic traits like the tendency to talk too much (which is unwelcome when a general conversation is expected[14]) are not so damaging in a standing reception, since the guests, at least in theory, are able to shift partners. This specific problem often requires the help of the hosts. But before we discuss specific cases requiring the hosts' intervention, let us first discuss the most needed and often most overlooked or poorly accomplished of the hosts' duties: that of introducing their guests to each other. In family parties or in traditional aristocratic or upper-class parties, introductions were either unnecessary or consisted mostly in telling the names of the guests to refresh everyone's memory. Individuals' names were enough to remind the audience who the people were, what their positions or histories were. If, by chance, the individuals themselves were not known to the audience, at least their family names were in everyone's mind and these were enough to start a conversation with them, made of pertinent questions about their relatives and memories of common ancestors. By contrast, in a modern gathering, if we except parties regrouping the town upper crust, the names of individuals or of their families do not mean anything to the other persons in the gathering and are of no help in starting a conversation. It is then the task of the hosts of a modern party, first, to know enough about each of their guests and, second, to introduce them to each other by mentioning any common interest they may share; be it occupation, hobbies, common travel, or similar artistic or political preferences. Hosts who do not remember one of their guests' names are very easy to forgive, if at the same time, they can tell that this person is a fervent admirer of Matisse or Paganini, a black belt judoka, or a regular visitor of the Metropolitan Museum. If the other guest shares any of these multiple interests with that person, both will easily sail off on an exciting conversation. In the absence of the right type of introduction, they may beat around the bush for fifteen minutes before getting bored with each other.[15]

The introduction ritual is not a task to fulfill only at the beginning of a party or each time a new guest arrives. It is an ongoing process. Especially in large receptions, the hosts do not always have the time to introduce the arriving newcomers to every single guest already in the house. This may become possible during the party, if one of the guests—known to the hosts to be little acquainted with the rest of the crowd—is spotted alone or interacting with the same person or couple:

> Once you've introduced your guests, don't abandon them. One superb hostess I know is constantly aware of everything that is going on in the room, without seeming to be. No guest ever sits or stands alone for more than a minute or two. She is at this person's side quickly, chatting, easing him or her smoothly into another group.[16]

We have just explained why parties of over 50 or 60 guests are difficult to manage. However, there are cases when the occasion demands organizing a very large gathering, for example, a famous person is in town for only one night and all those who have a title to meet that person must be invited. The same can also be said of large consular receptions or national holiday celebrations at the embassy. These very large parties will bring to the participants the pleasure of being one of the select "few" (everything is relative!) who were invited to enjoy a common festive mood. Could the participants also hope to enjoy each other's company? Normally, that is, given the way most of these receptions are organized, the answer is no! What seems an impossible task—how could the hosts take care of 100, 200 and sometimes even more guests?—could become possible with a little organization. After all, the science of modern organization has solved problems much more formidable than that of animating and monitoring a gathering of a few hundred guests! This can be done if the organizers were to select a few co-hosts, well acquainted with large numbers of the crowd, who could take charge of the arriving guests after they have been greeted by the hosts, and introduce them to some of the previously arrived participants. There is no reason why, after the main flow of guests has arrived, they could not go on with their sociable interventions if they perceived this would be welcome. They could relieve embarrassed dyads and after having indulged in a little chat with an isolated individual or couple, match them with other individuals or dyads. Recently, at a large reception in a cultural center in New York, one of the co-hosts could be seen tirelessly introducing people to one another. However, this is done very seldom, even when the hosts' interventions are badly needed. The most obvious case crying for help is that of the guest who stands alone, glass in hand, waiting to be introduced to other guests. Less readily perceptible are the pairs of guests stuck together. At a party last year, we spotted a couple that was standing in the middle of the livingroom, isolated from the rest of the gathering. They were not really facing each other, and each of them was looking around for relief. But nobody was close enough to either of them to be eased into their sinking interaction. Neither of the two dared to abandon the other companion, either because neither wanted to embarrass the other or because neither one knew exactly where to go afterwards—except approach another group and beg to be admitted. Their situation was all the more disturbing in that they were in full view of everyone else and could not attempt some kind of silent and sneaky maneuver. The hosts, very busy with the food and drinks, did not perceive the trouble which would have had no end if a couple of guests had not finally approached and rescued the hopeless pair. Of course, the hosts are not expected to intervene all the time and interrupt a happily sailing duo. However, external signs of good conversation do not always mean that the interaction is going well. Quite often two persons who have nothing left to tell each other go on speaking of banalities, because they do not know how to end the engagement. They may even give many signs of vivid interest in what they respectively say, so that no one can suspect their embarrassment. However, if one carefully observes their eyes, one will see that both or at least one of them looks insistently around in search of some relief. This is the signal that could trigger intervention by one of the hosts. If one of the hosts has misinterpreted the signs and intrudes into a well-functioning duo, he or she will be consoled by the thought that the consequence of breaking into a well-functioning duo are less serious than that of leaving two individuals in their mutual torment. If the pair like each other and wish to remain together, they will show it by sticking to their previous topic of conversation or by ignoring the possibility offered by the host of making a civil departure. If they truly like each other, they can always resume their conversation later. In other cases, the intervention of the hosts will have the effect of sending an attractive guest who has been monopolized for a long time by one person back into the general throng, and the other guests will be glad to have the opportunity to enjoy the conversation of the performer, secretary of commerce, explorer, composer, or general manager.

During the party the hosts mentally return to their guest list and recall those marked with an asterisk: those who need special attention—the newly arrived in town, the younger couples not yet well-introduced, the older, less attractive people, the foreigner, and the shy ones who must be prompted to interact.

At a reception last year, one could see a couple, a man and a woman, who, instead of looking at each other while talking, were standing side-by-side and looking together at the other guests. It was evidently a (married) couple, ready for interaction with others, but who had not yet realized that possibility. In talking to them I learned that they had just arrived in the city and did not know anyone at the party. The hosts had not spotted the embarrassed side-by-side position, which is not the usual way for a well-functioning pair to stand. At that time the hosts were busy showing the last acquisition in their collection of silver sailing boats to a small group of intimate friends.

All this supposes that the hosts do not let themselves be monopolized by one of their guests. They must keep their attention on all of them. This does not prevent them from giving each of them a short but very personalized moment of attention. It is true that some guests have a tendency to attach themselves to the hosts and monopolize their time, but before explaining to them that they have something else to do, the hosts give them a few seconds of total attention. Speaking of a different order of social relations, where, however, a useful parallel exists, I still remember the radically different approach of two of my university professors when I was knocking at the doors of their offices trying to talk to them. One would immediately tell me: "I am sorry, I am busy now. Come another time, or another day." The other would always express his pleasure at seeing me and after a couple of friendly words would continue: "Well, we must absolutely find a moment to talk. Let us see . . . , can you come on such a day, at such a time?" The final result was the same; the talk was postponed. Actually the second professor had gained time, because the first would soon feel guilty and be compelled to spend a lot of time excusing himself. Many hosts act like the second professor, that is, they give full attention to everyone and then regretfully excuse themselves, which flatters the guest. If the hosts have carefully prepared the party and meditated over the guest list, they won't have any problem in finding something very personal to tell each of their guests and will avoid the irritation caused by repeating to each guest the same compliments, in the same tone, with the same words and smiles.[17]

Of course, and as suggested above, personalized treatment does not imply partiality or the granting of special favors to one guest while others are ignored. I remember a large (too large, actually) reception where the hosts, after having greeted their guests at the door, spent the rest of the evening with the same small group of old friends. They were joking and laughing aloud, while the rest of the partygoers were chaotically zigzagging across the room. Several guests, alone and looking for companionship, passed by the hosts' clique. The hosts vaguely looked at them and resumed their joyous conversation with friends. The case is extreme, but some milder forms can easily be found at all kinds of modern parties.

The hosts never intervene with more visibility and noise than is strictly necessary. The guests should not see the party as an occasion for the hosts to flaunt their power. One wants them to guide it in an unobtrusive manner, with low voices, a minimum of words and gestures, and without offering explanations and justifications for what they do.[18] They are praised for being enough in control of the whole situation without showing their preoccupation or anxiety for what has happened, should happen, does not happen, and so on. And they should not make a big fuss while opening and serving a bottle of wine, as Pflaumen does in McCarthy's "The Genial Host":

. . . and then the wine was brought in, a Château Latour Rothschild.

This was Pflaumen's apogée. Having tapped on his glass to get the table's attention, he read aloud the Château and the year, and then uncorked the bottle himself, standing up to do it. Somebody at the end of the table, a man with a hearty voice, called "Look out, there, George Arliss may come out of that bottle!" Pflaumen, pouring a little into his own glass, laughed with the others, but he was not quite pleased—it was the sort of joke he was capable of making himself. "Give us a speech, about the wine," said one of the ladies obligingly, "the way they do at gourmet dinners." "Why," said Pflaumen, still standing at the head of the table with the bottle in his hand, "it's not one of the great Bordeaux. . . ." "I prefer the word 'claret,'" someone else put in, "it's so full of English history." "You mean," retorted Pflaumen, "English history is so full of *it*." He waited for the laugh, which came reluctantly—it was said that Pflaumen had "a pretty wit," but there was something chilling about it; he had never learned how to throw a line away. "Anyway," he went on, with a little laugh, so that no one should think he took all this too seriously, "it's a nice brisk wine, on the astringent side. I thought it would do well with the steak." "Perfect!" exclaimed a lady, though the glasses were still empty. "Of course I think it's silly," continued Pflaumen, starting to go round the table with the bottle, "to be too pedantic about what you drink with what. I'll take a good Burgundy with a broiler and a Rhine wine with a kidney chop any time I can get it." Murmurs of approval greeted this unconventional statement, and Pflaumen passed on down the line, carefully decanting the wine into each glass.[19]

M. E. W. Sherwood writes: "A fussy hostess who scolds the servants, wrinkles her brow or even forgets to listen to the man who is talking to her is the ruin of a dinner."[20]

Hosts will not be remembered kindly for the noise and volume of their interventions, but will be for the smooth unfolding of the party and the pleasure that the guests derived from being elegantly led by them toward new people, new experiences, and mutual recognitions.

There are various kinds of social gatherings. Each requires a different setting and suggests different types of intervention by the hosts. We have centered our attention on two specific types of gatherings: the traditional family party, where the hosts are practically absolved of responsibility once they have prepared food and drinks and brought their clan or clique together; and the modern gathering where the participants, largely unacquainted, come to check their identities by interacting with many different people. In this type of party the main duty of the hosts begins where the role of the family party hosts leaves off, that is, at the moment when their guests arrive, hoping to meet each other. As we said at the beginning of this chapter, less than social orchestra conductors, they are expected to play tireless social brokers.[21]

NOTES

1. David Riesman, Robert J. Potter, and Jeanne Watson, "The Vanishing Host," *Human Organization* 19 (1960), p. 17.

2. Patricia Curtis, "The Art of Staging Great Parties," in the *Ladies Home Journal* magazine (December 1978, p. 27). We recommend it as the shortest and densest piece of writing on how to stage a good party. Along the lines of the above quotation, Helen Lawrenson writes in the New York *Times* (October 10, 1979, Sec. C, p. 1): "When I can tell you what I had to eat, it is because for some reason something was wrong."

3. Simmel alludes to the institution of the *"quatorzièmes"* in nineteenth-century Paris. Some men, called "fourteenths" because they were ready to complete a table which otherwise would have been occupied by only thirteen guests, were waiting all dressed up in their apartment between five and nine p.m., ready for a possible assignment. Their names were listed in the equivalent of our yellow pages. See *The Sociology of Georg Simmel*, Kurt H. Wolff trans. (Glencoe, Ill.: The Free Press, 1950), p. 420.

4. Craig Claiborne wrote in the New York *Times*:

Over the years, I have had the occasion to ponder what might conceivably have been served to Samuel Johnson to have prompted his remark: "That was a good enough dinner, to be sure, but it was not a dinner to *ask* a man to."

Certainly not lobster in cream with tomatoes, tarragon and a dash of cognac. Perhaps it was something on the order of boiled mutton with brussels sprouts on the side. Or overcooked lamb with mashed turnips. Or perhaps the conversation and guests that evening had been wickedly dull.

Whatever the goad for his spleen on that occasion, I suspect that I share one thing with Dr. Johnson: I take my invitations to dinner seriously. This world offers too much of interest for me to think time well spent at an indifferent and carelessly composed meal in someone's home. Far better the alternative of a book and an omelet at my own home.

If I am asked (as I have been on numerous occasions) what are the perfect ingredients for a successful party, I think they are several, beginning with an occasion born of a desire to please. Beyond a host or hostess who genuinely cares about the pleasure of the guests come food, interestingly and conscientiously prepared; a consistency of atmosphere (no Dom Perignon out of plastic cups at the beach, please), and guests characterized by any interest at all so long as each possesses a sense of humor (Craig Claiborne, "The Pleasure of Your Company," New York *Times*, December 20, 1978, Sec. C, p. 3).

We read in M. E. W. Sherwood (*The Art of Entertaining* [New York: Dodd, Mead and Co., 1893], p. 76): "It is related of Lord Lyndhurst that when somebody asked him how to succeed in life, he answered, 'Give good wine.'" A French statesman should have answered, "Give good dinners." Talleyrand kept the most renowned table of his day, quite as much for political as hygienic reasons. At 80 years of age he still spent an hour every morning with his *chef*, discussing the dishes to be served at dinner. The preoccupation for good food is all the more necessary if the party is a large reception: "A 'party,' therefore, merely because of its emphasis on number, which excludes a common interaction of more refined and intellectual moods, must all the more strongly make use of these sensuous joys [food and drinks] that are shared by all with incomparably greater certainty" (Georg Simmel, op. cit., p. 113). To underscore the festive aspect of a party the presentation of the food and drinks as well as the comfort of the guests are of prime importance:

> And there is one other aspect of "entertaining" in various homes that I find particularly loathsome. If you would have me dine in peace and pleasure, if you would escape my muted and sometimes not-so-muted wrath, do not ask me to pose my dinner plate—be it Spode or paper— on my lap (Craig Claiborne, op. cit.).

5. Charles Dickens ("A Christmas Carol" in *Christmas Book* [New York: The University Society, Booklovers Edition, 1908], pp. 52–53) describes a party where young people after dinner indulge in music, forfeits, and a "game at blind-man's buff."

6. "The younger and less experienced hosts, particularly, were sometimes fearful of risking a party devoted exclusively to conversation, and would plan for some alternative. Thus, at one party where people wanted to talk, they were urged by the host to play bridge; at another, to paint 'projective paintings,' the materials for which had been provided; at still another, to play charades—and in each case it was obvious that the host had staked so much on his plan for the party that only a tactless guest could have refused his request. Often, guests who were reluctant to 'play games' when the proposal was first suggested would find themselves having a good time, once the game was underway. Others would regret having lost an opportunity for conversation" (David Riesman et al., op. cit., p. 23).

7. Enid Nemy: "Party Pitfall, Who Sits Where," New York *Times*, November 23, 1978, Sec. C, p. 14.

8. See Chapter 6, "The Choice of Partners."

9. At a large buffet dinner where the guests were left free to sit where they wished at one of the many tables, I had managed to sit next to a woman (on my left) with whom I knew I would have many common points of interest.

To my right were two empty seats. I had hardly started to converse with my neighbor, when the party organizer seated to my right a latecomer. The latter, having to his right the last empty seat, had only one companion, myself. I had to take care of him. He resisted any effort I made to start a triadic conversation with the woman at my left and myself. The topics of conversation he brought back, again and again—his difficult career and the injustices of faculty and student evaluations—and the tone of his voice—confidential and too low for my other neighbor to hear—condemned me to a boring and embarrassing evening, since I could no longer entertain my other neighbor. The solution was in the hands of the party organizers, who should have removed the empty seat and plate from the table and rearranged the seating so that everyone would have had two neighbors. If other latercomers had arrived, it would always have been possible to squeeze him or her between two people.

10. David Riesman, et al., op. cit., p. 27.

11. Two extreme cases of hosts escaping their responsibility are mentioned by David Riesman and his collaborators:

> At one party, . . . a hostess finding one of her guests holding forth in a domineering way—unsociably though not intrinsically uninteresting—found excuses to confine herself to the kitchen for the duration, unable either to endure or control what was happening. Another hostess, exhausted before her party began by the work of house cleaning and preparing food, left her guests and went for a walk when she discovered that the party had grown beyond anticipated size (with guests bringing other guests), that she could not influence its course, and that, in any event, she had already "paid her way!" (op. cit., p. 25).

12. In her already quoted article in the *Ladies Home Journal* magazine, Patricia Curtis writes:

> You should of course give your guests something good to eat, and plenty of it. But that is not what makes a social event memorable. When I think back on the parties I enjoyed most, it's the pleasure I found in the other people that come to mind; I can't even remember what we ate (op. cit., p. 27).

13. David Riesman, et. al., write in a footnote to the already quoted article:

> Our party reports show what many hostesses intuitively know: that thirteen—or any number between ten and twenty—is indeed an unlucky number, too large, save in the most skillful hands to sustain excitement in a single conversation, and too small to provide the background noise and multifarious choice of partners which are given by a large stand-up cocktail party or buffet (op. cit., p. 24, note 14).

14. M. E. W. Sherwood wrote in her *Art of Entertaining*:

In making up a dinner with a view to its intellectual components avoid those tedious talkers, who, having a theme, a system, or a fad to air, always contrive to drag the conversation around their view, with the intention of concentrating the whole attention upon themselves. One such man, called appropriately the Bore Constrictor of conversation in a certain city, really drove people away from every house to which he was invited . . . (M. E. W. Sherwood, op. cit., p. 75).

15. See Chapter 7.
16. Patricia Curtis, op. cit., p. 27.
17. ". . . if a gentleman comes to your house and you tell him with warmth and interest that you 'are glad to see him,' he will be pleased with the attention, and will probably thank you; but if he hears you say the same thing to twenty other people, he will not only perceive that your courtesy was worth nothing, but he will feel some resentment at having been imposed upon" (*The Canons of Good Breeding: or the Handbook of the Man of Fashion* [Philadelphia: Lee and Blanchard, 1839], p. 87; quoted by Erving Goffman, *The Presentation of Self in Everyday Life* [New York: Doubleday, 1959], pp. 59–51).

18. It is not easy, as David Riesman and collaborators observed, to find the line between unpleasant interventionism and ingenuous laissez faire: "Our observations have intensified our conviction that much sociability is needlessly frustrating, falling between the two stools of over-solicitous and anxious fussing and an unworkable ingenuousness" (David Riesman, et al., op. cit., p. 19).

19. Mary McCarthy, "The Genial Host," *The Company She Keeps* (New York: Simon and Schuster, 1942), pp. 147–148.

20. M. E. W. Sherwood, op. cit., p. 29.

21. The expression (broker) has been used by David Riesman and collaborators in the article mentioned above (David Riesman, op. cit., p. 22).

11
BLUNDERS, OFFENSES, AND REMEDIES

Even in the well-structured world of professional and technical activities, performances often do not meet the expected standards; blunders and mistakes are common. In the less structured world of sociability, one is even more likely to act in a way that others will find improper, strange, or offensive. This is not so much the case in family gatherings where the participants, knowing each other, have also acquired a very clear picture of the situation, and an exact knowledge of the limits they should not cross, the opinions that should or should not be expressed, and the manners that are expected. But blunders and mistakes are more likely to happen in the modern gatherings where the social reality is so vaguely structured, that we seem to stumble blindfolded about an unfamiliar room. Blunders are not only more likely to happen in modern gatherings, but they are more damaging because there the accent is on the promotion of one's ideal-self. This greater likelihood of blunders in modern gatherings and their greater damaging consequences will be the first topic in this chapter. Given that mistakes are more likely to happen and will be more damaging, participants of a modern gathering are particularly tense—as we said in Chapter 5. As a consequence, they use more defensive tactics and are especially prudent in showing their cards. They have also developed specific remedial strategies; these, on the other hand, are easier to use because of the amorphous state of the situation. The second theme of the chapter, then, will be the tactics used by the participants of modern gatherings to prevent embarrassment and blunders, and to remedy them when they have occurred.

242

Third, we will turn to mistakes that are seemingly impossible to remedy and consequently much more damaging, the errors and blunders that their perpetrator is unaware of having committed. And here again, these unconscious mistakes are more likely to be found in modern gatherings because the absence of a sense of community and structure prevents the normal mechanisms of social control from operating.

The mistakes reviewed in this chapter are not the intentional acts of aggression that sometimes even the traditional gentleman, and today's gentlewoman as well, may commit in a social gathering. What we contemplate here are the unintentional flaws that mar our performances. Some of them are only self-damaging, as when we spill some food on our clothes or mispronounce a famous name; others are mutually damaging, that is, the blunder offends others as well. The distinction should not be pushed too far, however, because our self-damaging mistakes also create some kind of disruption in the gathering. Both types of mistakes can happen in any kind of gathering. But in a modern gathering they are more likely to happen for two reasons. First, in a modern gathering the rule of the game is to present an idealized image of oneself and not to enact the routine performances of well-known daily roles. This necessarily implies taking risks, that is, the probability that one will make mistakes. Moreover, modern gatherings regroup people whose values, norms, roles, teams, political preferences, and sexual tendencies are largely unknown. Everything we say lands on a mine field and we never know whether or not it will trigger an explosion.

For example, James is a good talker and many listeners are grouped around him. He lets himself get carried away by the Chablis and the admiration of the audience. He is describing, in vivid terms, the plight of a young man left with two young children after he was abandoned by his wife—and in the group there is a woman in exactly the same circumstances as the wife he described; he then recounts a plane accident—the father of one of the guests died three months ago in the same accident. Frederick complains about young people, who do not study anymore but look for fun and take drugs—his neighbor, June, had accompanied her son to the precinct when he was booked for possession of cocaine two days before. And Paul orates on why people want to kill themselves, especially "those who have everything to be happy"—and, in the group of listeners there is, unbeknown to him, a young woman who has attempted suicide four times.

In all these examples, the speakers have acted as if they knew the mapping of the situation when they did not. Others are more prudent. But the fear of the unknown leads them to utter many trivialities. In order, then, to avoid the dilemma of keeping silent or making insipid statements, participants of a modern gathering avoid the uncertain situation of a general conversation and take refuge in duos and trios where, after a little exploration, the personality and role–identities of each partner can become sufficiently delineated to permit substantive conversation and bolder performances. Of course, the limitation of the number of partners does not totally preclude mistakes. The opening bids never provide a perfect picture of our companions or of their precise levels of competence.

While Andrew earns his living as a clerk in a bank, his real passion lies with archaeology. He developed this interest the previous summer in Greece when he met a group of young divers who were busy lifting the treasures from a sunken Greek ship. He was given the opportunity to dive to the bottom of the sea and helped spot a couple of amphoras. Back in Dallas, he bought three books on archaeology and read them at night. He thought of himself as a specialist in the branch. His partners at social gatherings were impressed by his new identity and his enthusiasm, until one day he talked with an anthropologist, also interested in Greece who mentioned that the Minoan civilization influenced Mycenaean architecture. Wanting to show his knowledge, our self-appointed archaeologist said, "Oh, yes, Messina must be so beautiful. I know it was founded by the Greeks. I hope to go there one day."

"No, not Messina, but Mycenae . . . anyhow I understand you are interested in old things, aren't you?"

"Yes," and Andrew then realized that there are people in the world who know a little more about archaeology than he did.

This and similar mistakes mentioned in this or in previous chapters would not have been so readily committed in a family gathering where everyone has acquired a clearer picture of the identity, competence and opinions of the various participants.

The impact of the mistakes is also very different in a family gathering than in a modern gathering. In the former type of party, what the participants seek is to enjoy both to be together again and to consolidate their common ties. In such gatherings people are not afraid to act silly or to engage in some deviant activity. It increases the general fun. The manager who dresses at work in a strict three-piece suit, and never moves her hands when she speaks may, at the office party, indulge in one too many glasses of punch and, having taken off her jacket, may start a rowdy rock dance with one of the employees. Her steps may be slightly awkward but everyone applauds rather than objects. Much more would be necessary to tarnish her well-established image among them. The same is true if, at the end of the tribal dinner, Uncle Joe stands up and sings an old Irish tune. His voice may be raspy and out of tune, but again, who cares? He is contributing to everyone's joy and he does not pretend to demonstrate his talents as a singer. If Cousin Jane breaks a glass or if Tony makes an off-color joke, grandpa will cover up their faux pas by telling one of his good-natured stories. The faux pas themselves are easily forgotten. Everybody's personality is known in its entirety and a small mishap does not damage it.

The case of the modern party is totally different, where the participants are largely unknown to each other. The only impression that each participant will gather of the other participants is based upon their performances in the party. If these performances fail, the performer loses face. Ervin Goffman was correct when he wrote: "the impression of reality fostered by a performance is a delicate, fragile thing that can be shattered by minor mishaps."[1]

There is another reason why mishaps are so damaging in a modern gathering. The performances there are supposed to present to others the most impressive aspect of each participant. All the guests are expected to show their best sides, since nobody compels them to perform a role they do not know—as may be the case at work sometimes. We would forgive a performer who, for the sake of saving a play, agrees at the last minute to improvise a hardly known role. But if the role is the best part in the performer's repertoire, one will deny that person any indulgence: One single flaw is a catastrophe. While at work or in a family gathering, people are acting in a relaxed way; in a modern party they are evidently tensely staging their best show. Their very tension makes their mistakes look all the more ridiculous: They were trying so hard and look what happened!

June drinks her coffee with what she thinks is utmost good taste. She holds the cup with only two fingers, the others, especially the little one, beating the air with imagined elegance. All of a sudden, as she sips from her cup. she must cough and as she does, sputters coffee on her spotlessly white evening dress.

Isidoro—first secretary at his nation's embassy in an African country (his first job abroad)—has been invited by a rich, local planter to a dinner with dignitaries and other diplomats. At dessert, among other fruits mangoes are offered. He takes one. It is his first experience with the slippery and treacherous fruit. First he has rather good results at peeling the mango without soiling his cuffs. He is heartened by this first success. As he thinks he has solidly pinned down the peeled mango on his plate with the fork, he attacks it with his knife but the incorrigible fruit escapes, taking its flight up into the cleavage of the hostess.

Stephen, at a cocktail party, has met the dean of the Manhattan School of Journalism. An apprentice writer, Stephen tries to impress the famous scholar with an impromptu story of a young woman and her baby alone in the big city. She had to beg for her food. One day she entered a local produce shop and looked for the manager who was in the rear of the store. She asked him to give her some of his spoiled fruit. The manager reacted angrily and started to chase her toward the door. "As she ran," he continued, "she pissed on a seal." Before the narrator could correct his last phrase ("I mean she slipped on a peel"), the famous professor had burst into loud laughter.

Per se these are such minor mishaps that nobody should worry about them. But what makes them so damaging is the very effort that the perpetrators were making to stage flawless performances, as if their whole lives were depending on the perfection of the show. Maybe their lives were not depending on it, but their "face" was.

The damaging effect of these mistakes is deeply feared—even if unconsciously—and this explains not only the tension in the participants, but also their formality, their stiffness, their frozen behavior as if they were walking on eggs. They know they are "play-acting," "in representation." They constantly monitor their activities and gestures, and avoid taking too many risks.

These fears lead the most prudent of them to use defensive tactics of various kinds, like disclaimers, very slow disclosure of themselves, or, on the contrary, immediate and preventive uncovering of a possibly very sensitive element of their identity. We have already described disclaimers and the slow mutual disclosure of one's identity at the beginning of an interaction in Chapter 8. In a family gathering there is no use for disclaiming identities that our partners would not attribute to us anyway and there is no need for uncovering—slowly or rapidly—our identity. But in a modern party both can be very usefully employed to avoid making a fool of ourselves, or to suppress a side of ourselves which might be incompatible with our partner's personality. A third defensive technique has not yet been described. We call it *preventive information*. Even more than the two techniques previously mentioned, it is directly related to the unstructured situation of a modern gathering. It is used by the individuals who are aware of belonging to an "odd" category—odd at least given the general context of the gathering. Rather than conceal the characteristic which makes them vulnerable, they immediately disclose it. This avoids their being embarrassed by what others may say about the sensitive category. This would be the case of a German in the midst of Jews, a Jew in a majority of Arabs, an atheist among fundamental Baptists, an Irish Catholic among Calvinists, or a liberal in a very conservative circle, and so on.

In spite of all the precautions, mistakes occur. When they do occur, the perpetrator is more or less anxious to avoid the consequences. In a family gathering the mistakes do not dramatically change the idea that people have of the culprit. The necessity for repair is less pressing than in the modern party, where the image of an individual hinges on the present performance. From time immemorial, people have invented formulas to restore their damaged images. Some of them, however, do not work equally well everywhere. Paradoxically, many of the repair techniques work better in a modern gathering than in a family gathering, because they consist of reshaping one's self-image in a way that makes the blunder look inoffensive or forgivable. This is clearly possible only if the audience is ignorant of the "real" personality of the perpetrator and can—at least temporarily—accept the new definition he or she tries to present to them.

We shall describe first the techniques that work in any kind of gathering, and later those that are more specifically adapted to the modern gathering.

Among the classical remedies to blunders, one can list redimensioning and reinterpretation, which are mostly used to repair the self-damaging blunders, and assertive civil inattention and apology to repair mutually damaging mistakes.

Redimensioning consists in diverting the attention from the secondary and unimportant area where the mistake was committed and concentrating the attention on what the speaker thinks is more important: A man could not remember the name of the place where his story had first occurred. "It was in South America . . . maybe in San Salvador" (second blunder). Before his listeners could object, he added: "Well, the essential point of the story is not where it happened, but what happened there, whether it was in Antofagasta or Riobamba is the same. . . ." Redimensioning can be even shorter. The author of the mistake, as he realizes it, by showing sovereign indifference to his blunder, demonstrates that he is not disturbed by a minor flaw: his self-image is so well established that it could not suffer from it: "Did I say that? Really? Well, what was I saying? Oh yes, the troubadour was singing. . . ." This tactic works well in a modern gathering where the perpetrator can convince his nonrelatives that he truly made an out-of-character oversight or blunder, whereas in the family gathering the reaction might be: "Here, look, good old Joe did it again!"

Reinterpretation is somehow similar. It consists in diverting the attention of the audience from the blunder by rerunning part of a statement or story to make it acceptable to the audience. If a storyteller, whom we will call Joe, has alluded negatively to someone who has misbehaved and discovers in his audience an individual who has acted in a similar fashion, Joe may try to absolve the criticized person by placing responsibility for the wrong behavior on someone else. James has been telling the story of a man who has been abandoned by his wife and left alone to take care of their three children. James suddenly realizes that one of his two partners is a woman in a very similar situation. Before she can protest, he adds: "This is at least the way the story has been presented to me. But . . . who knows? It may be the husband who made life so miserable for her that she had to escape."

We call *assertive civil inattention* a way of asserting, in an exaggerated manner, that one has not seen or heard something that one actually did see or hear. This is done to protect oneself as well as the other party. This technique operates especially well when one has been caught "backstage," as Ervin Goffman puts it,[2] that is, in a place or situation where one should not have been.

Once at a reception, Maurice, an acquaintance of mine, was sent to the second floor in search of a bathroom. He opened the first door; it was a closet. The second door was not the bathroom either, but a bedroom and on the bed the oldest daughter of the family was lying naked in the arms of one of the guests. Maurice precipitously closed the door.

Later, during the evening, the young woman approached him:

"I wonder," she said, "whether it was you I saw at the door of my bedroom?"

"In the bedroom?" answered Maurice. "Which bedroom? I don't understand."

There are cases in which people have not invented any remedy other than a strong apology. They hope that their partners will accept it with civil courtesy.[3] This courteous acceptance is in their best interest, since one day they may be in need of a similar understanding. Apologies, however, are not easy to make; they are supposed to be proportionate to the offense. Too short a formula is unconvincing. If one breaks a highly valuable piece of china, interjecting a rapid "sorry" in the midst of a conversation will not do. But if the mishap is really of limited importance, an overflow of excuses will only underscore the offense. Susan made a really inoffensive allusion to Italian women overindulging in pasta and having to face problems with their figures. She then realized that George's mother was Italian—a very slender woman actually. Susan then exploded in apologies: "Oh I am so sorry! How foolish of me! I should have known! I had no intention of offending you! Some of my best friends are Italians! Actually I think these old plump ladies are quite cute. I hope you will forgive me! I was mostly speaking of the Italian women of the past, and of the peasant women actually. . . . ." The extended apology only makes things worse.

This leads us to mention one of the most often used remedies: low profile. It works in any kind of gathering, but much better in a fragmented gathering where few people know each other and where, if the blunder has been committed in a duo or a trio, there is little probability that it will be telegraphed around to the whole gathering. Sometimes low profile works even in a large gathering, because when the mishap occurs nobody or only a few people may have noticed it. The basic principle is: "Your overloaded boat might make it to the shore, but do not make waves!" For example, Jack suddenly realizes that his fly is open. Instead of apologizing, he quickly moves out of sight and does the repair job, coming back without any allusion to the reason for his departure. Francesca, the hostess, discovers in the middle of a conversation that Johnny's dirty sock is lying under the armchair. She rapidly looks around to see if anyone noticed the cause of her disturbed face and at some point when the guests' attention is elsewhere, she rapidly whisks the object out of sight. A hostess hopes that few people, if any, have noticed that the butler has started serving the wrong guest or has dropped a piece of meat on the floor. All of them try to repair the situation without making any noise: "... I have observed in the course of my life," writes Antonie Brentano in her diary, "that if one knows how to keep quiet when a mishap occurs, the guests do not notice it, while if the hostess makes a move, then the attention of everybody is awakened."[4]

The remaining tactics to be analyzed work particularly well in modern gatherings: cosmicization, focusing, joining in, and revolving the stage. All four are based upon the assumption that the perpetrators of the mistakes, being relatively unknown to the audience, can try to redefine their identities, or their roles in a situation, or even the situation itself, without risking resistance from the audience. On the contrary, in a family gathering someone might interject: "come on. . . ."

Cosmicization is an effort to assign the cause of the error to some cosmic, uncontrollable destiny, which extends the problem beyond its particular application to the individuals at hand.[5]

For example, if Jack cannot or does not want to eat something, he usually blames it on some allergy. "The worst thing is that I adore kidneys!" Attributing his refusal to an allergy rather than to the taste of kidneys, he claims he is not responsible. What can you do about an allergy? Of course, it works only with strangers; relatives would know that Jack is not affected by any such condition.

Focusing one's image is another technique frequently used to explain away ignorance. It could have been used by Andrew, the newly declared archaeologist: "Well I must state here that my competence is limited to underwater research and I practiced it only in the Mediterranean." Similarly, an historian explains that his expertise is limited to eighteenth-century England or to the First Chinese Dynasty. The music lover prudently declares that she has only a hint of what atonal music is and the cardiologist does not like to speak about skin diseases.

The third technique we have observed is *joining in*. When narrating some misadventure in an ironic fashion, people may discover that someone in their audience has been struck by the same misfortune. In that case, the narrators make themselves victims or at least very close friends of the victim of the accident. For example, we once heard a man mentioning the DC–10 accident in Chicago, mostly to express his contempt for the airplane builders who want to make a fast buck, and so forth. When he realized that someone among his listeners had lost a close relative, he himself remembered suddenly that his old pal, his best friend in the world, died also in the accident. If the technique is used with some sincerity, the embarrassed or offended party may want to demonstrate in some way that he or she accepts the effort to bring things to order. But here again the remedial strategy works only when we are speaking with strangers who, not knowing the history and the precise attributes of our personalities, can accept our own definitions and redefinitions.

The last and most sophisticated way of victoriously fighting the bad impressions created by an improper behavior or by a show of ignorance consists in turning the flaw into an asset by suggesting a change in the situation. We call this technique *revolving the stage.* This, again, is possible only in the unstructured situation of a modern gathering where the speakers or perpetrators are temporarily given the privilege of defining the situation. As we shall see, the change of setting may in turn result in a reversal of roles between the performers and their audiences.

In revolving the stage, the authors of the mistakes or blunders do not deny committing them, but by changing the setting, that is, by suggesting a different context and perspective, they may make their faux pas appear respectable, if not even a great feat. Take the actor who is dressed on the stage in a bathing suit. The setting is a dining room with a radiator in one corner. Ridiculous. But revolve the stage and a beach with ocean and palm trees appears. Perfectly normal. Robert, 24, back from a long stay in Africa is invited to dinner by the Upperhills. While participating in the discussion, he becomes conscious that his table manners appear strange. He sticks his knife in his mouth, picks food from his plate with his fingers, and rests his elbows on the table. "Please, you must excuse me; after two years spent with the Peace Corps in the bush I've forgotten myself." Suddenly everybody imagines him- or herself somewhere in the jungle and that it is the beautiful clothes and the elegant manners which have become odd, while the ill-mannered young man is taking on the part of a hero. The impact may even be too strong and we have noticed people who, in that case, reestablish some balance. Robert may add: "But now I'm going back to school and hope to get my Ph.D. in psychology, and I must readjust to American manners." The stage has become familiar again and everyone feels at ease.

A similar technique (stage revolution and reversal of roles) was used by a friend of mine. Both of us were studying at the University of Chicago during the 1950s. We had been invited to dinner by Anselm Strauss, the well-known social psychologist. Other professors were also present. In our honor, stories of travels through Europe and sojourns in Paris were told. Paris was then perceived by Americans essentially as "Gay Paree" and the conversation turned to Maurice Chevallier, Brigitte Bardot, and most of all, the Folies Bergères, the Casino de Paris and other "girlie" shows. Not being born in Paris, I was somehow excused from contributing to the conversation. But my friend, a true Parisian, was a little embarrassed. How could he tell our hosts that few Parisian natives visit these places? What about revolving the stage? My friend mentioned his having been far too busy with his studies at the university and so occupied with the innumerable opportunities offered in Paris for learning (museums, Comédie française, operas, concerts) that he had had little time for these other indulgences. Our friends smiled with some embarrassment. "Well," said one of them, "of course a true Parisian probably does not patronize those places. They are for the tourists. Take Chicago, for instance. Do we ever go to see the burlesque shows near the Loop?" The next day after his lecture, Anselm Strauss pointed out to me the technique used by my friend: He said that by shifting the attention from the nude shows to the university, the museums, and the serious theater, my friend freed himself from the part of the ignorant, timorous young man and became a true Parisian, a serious university student. The other guests were degraded from the role of world-wise experts to that of goggle-eyed tourists.

The change of setting—and the change of role which follows—is actually an invitation to change the value system to be used in evaluating the performance. Each situation must be judged by the specific standards corresponding to what is to be accomplished. On the beach one hopes to exercise and relax; in a restaurant one looks for the satisfaction of eating well; at a nude show one is expected to get some sexual titillation; in a museum one tries to acquaint oneself with the civilization and art of the past, and if one is in the Peace Corps in Africa, one endeavors to help the poor and further economic development. In the example of my friend's inexperience with frivolous Parisian shows, his remark was an invitation to shift from the values of fun and sensuality to those of education, responsibility and success. His invitation to raise the conversation to a higher level could only be managed because he was dealing with strangers who did not know him and his real value system. In a family gathering, his pretense at morality and duty would have only elicited: "Come on, don't tell us that you never have some fun!"

As a conclusion to this study of remedial techniques, we would like to observe again that while in modern gatherings mistakes, blunders and offenses are more likely to happen, people have found ways to remedy them that work better there than in family gatherings.

The mistakes we have described so far are of the conscious type. Sooner or later the perpetrator becomes aware of having committed them, and consequently can work at repairing the damage. Much more damaging are the mistakes that the perpetrator remains unaware of having committed. Some people continue month after month, year after year, making the same mistakes, offending the same or new people, accumulating gaffes, without ever being made aware of it. Everyone gossips about it, but they never know.

When he finds himself in a triad, Frederick has the habit of speaking only to the more attractive of his two partners and of ignoring the third party entirely.

Albert is known to intrude into existing dyads, and without any consideration for the topic his two companions were discussing, introduces his own subject of conversation.

Judith is invited to a dinner party. She rejoices at the idea. Two days before the party, she receives another invitation which is more compelling. She simply forgets about the previous one.

In all these cases and an infinity of others, the perpetrators, while being aware of their behavior, are unconscious of breaking any principle of civility. This is the way they behave and they find it all right. Needless to say, they are not ready to change their ways.

In other cases, paradoxically, the deviants know the rules but are unaware of breaking them. Something is wrong (exceptionally or habitually) in their attire; he speaks endlessly; she often attacks the team of the other guests; he has bad breath, poor body posture or a facial tic; she does not listen to what others say; he often looks absent-minded, angry, or bored. If all these people knew how they appeared, they would probably rush to make the necessary repairs. The problem is that they do not know.

How is it possible that individuals can repeatedly indulge in a form of behavior that the group considers wrong and remain unaware of it? Is there not in all societies and groups a mechanism called social control which aims at redressing the "wrong" ways? Do social gatherings constitute a different type of social interaction?

Probably, yes. In other social activities the common task is very clearly defined and is divided into several precise roles which must be fulfilled by various individuals chosen because of their specific aptitudes. What is expected of them is not primarily inventiveness but an ability to exactly fulfill their tasks. If they commit a mistake, immediate feedback will follow: "You are not yet familiar with the filing system? Please learn it by tomorrow." Or: "Do you know what you are supposed to do? OK. Then do it, please." The employees do not rejoice in the rebuff, but they see the merit of the case. Quite often, the employees do not fully identify with their occupational roles and do not take the correction personally.

Quite different is the situation in a party. It is true that family gatherings are regulated by rather strict social control. Knowing each other, the participants do not hesitate to correct each other—within limits that previous experience has taught them to respect. Quite often they feel that out of duty to their family team they must inform each other of their mistakes, since the honor of the team or the family is at stake. But in a modern gathering, unless a team member is present and can witness the mistake, none of the unacquainted participants feels entitled to correct the others, since they are not responsible for their welfare. On the contrary the various guests are expected to give encouragement to the performer and ignore mistakes that do not directly endanger their own welfare. Mistakes and blunders are the normal consequences of the nature of modern sociability. People try and miss. They will try again and possibly be more successful. A bridge master said once that a good bridge player is not the one who never makes any mistakes, but one who makes fewer mistakes. We could say the same of the famous gentleman. He is not the one who never (involuntarily, of course) inflicts pain, but the one who does it seldom. Participants in modern gatherings are flattered if their companions try to impress them. But the attempt to impress others implies the risk of making mistakes. The jugglers who always attempt more and more difficult stunts in order to impress their audience are bound to miss once or twice. They get the applause anyway, as do the guests, when they try hard enough, and accept their failure with good grace. They may console themselves with the thought that the modern world is wide and quite compartmentalized. While the mistakes we commit in a family gathering may remain part of our record for a long time, the mistakes committed in a modern gathering will seldom reverberate beyond the gathering. If we have lost our reputation before one specific audience, we can think of the many opportunities we will have in the future to meet new people who have never heard of our past adventures and will be ready, hopefully, to perform with us the always new and un-finished play of identity negotiation.

NOTES

1. Erving Goffman, *The Presentation of Self in Everyday Life* (Garden City: Doubleday, 1959), p. 56.

2. Ibid., pp. 123–135.

3. See Erving Goffman, *Relations in Public: Microstudies of the Public Order* (New York: Basic Books, 1971), pp. 95–187 and *Interaction Ritual Essays in Face-to-Face Behavior* (Chicago: Aldine Publishing Co., 1967), pp. 19–23, 97–112. Goffman distinguishes four steps in a remedial interchange which follows a mistake or offense: (1) the offender is challenged by the other participants: You made a mistake; (2) the offender comes to remedy his or her mistake; (3) the others show acceptance of the remedy; (4) the forgiven person shows gratitude (pp. 20–22).

4. *Goethe's Briefwechsel mit Antonie Brentano*, ed. by Rudolf Jung (Weimar: Herman Bölhaus Nachfolger, 1896), vol. III of *Schriften des freien Deutschen Hochstiftes*, p. 11.

5. The strategy of "cosmicization" is used in a preventive way by administrators to avoid having to face difficult problems: When presented with such a problem by an inferior, they acknowledge the importance of the issue but point to the fact that many other and larger groups or units of society, if not the entire world itself, are confronted with the insoluble problem.

12
CONCLUSION

Modern social gatherings are unfinished symphonies. Unlike traditional parties—family parties and particularly formal dinner parties—modern gatherings are largely unstructured; they have no clear scenario, no fixed beginning and conclusion. Moreover, while it is true that they fulfill many functions like any other gathering, such as culture building and maintenance,[1] modern gatherings never really achieve what they are mostly intended to do. Identity negotiation is an endless pursuit, first because the modern ideal self is an open reality, permanently in search of a clearer definition or of a new definition, and second, because the performances through which individuals attempt to define and present themselves are always tentative and never bring to their authors the complete confirmation of their identities. When, in a social gathering, these performances win approval, the encouragement may help the performers to develop the still unfinished reality. Unfortunately this progress does not achieve peace and security in their minds. For while they know that the next time they display their newly discovered potentialities (in an optimal encounter) they may experience support, they are more aware of the indifference or even rebuffs they may receive. There is even more: the guests of a modern party are supposed to represent the "world," but they constitute only a small sample of this extremely undefined reality, and the success obtained within this imperfect microcosm must be endlessly renegotiated within always new and better samples of the evanescent world. What constitutes the world changes also in the eyes of the upwardly mobile individual, and the world of yesterday may soon look to them like a small village crowd. In all this nothing is really permanent except the unfinished character of modern sociability. Every encounter needs to be confirmed or corrected by a new encounter. The successes which individuals may obtain in these modern gatherings are partial and temporary victories. What is not temporary, however, is the permanent sense of failure. The upwardly mobile, ambitious individuals know that there is always someone higher up, not in their leagues, who, if the occasion were granted, would deny his or her support. The sense of failure is built in to the game of modern gatherings. This sense of failure, then, is not always and essentially the consequence of poor management on the part of the hosts or an inadequate guest list. It is inherent to modern society and as a consequence is inherent to modern sociability. While we may derive total satisfaction from a warm and exciting family gathering in which the ties with our relatives or colleagues are revived, modern sociability never quenches the guests' thirst for recognition and the more they drink of it the more urgent grows their thirst.

This open, unfinished character of modern sociability makes it congruent with the society within which it develops. It is congruent with modern social structure, with the cultural expectations of our post-capitalist society and with the personality of modern humans.

As every other institution, social gatherings cannot be understood if they are not situated within the larger social context. Not that all institutions are linked to each other by rigid mechanical couplings; in every period of history, one can find remnants of the past as well as imported models that succeed in defying the general trends. Interdependence of the various social subsystems does not prevent some elasticity. The human mind always keeps the possibility of managing some contradictions within the global system. The survival of groups like the Amish or the Mennonites, the present resistance of a few hippie communes, the stubbornness of cooperatives of production in a capitalistic world show that congruence and interdependence are not synonymous with deterministic linkage. However, the deviant groups or patterns cannot be maintained without stress.[2] Those who cannot manage such stress tend to adopt models of behavior and foster institutions that are more in line with the other social subsystems. Exceptions and variations may be interesting to study but they are not typical or representative of the *Zeitgeist*; they are not what the French call "signs of the time." On the contrary, in each period of human history, specific institutions of behavioral patterns appear which are in syntony with the larger social complex.

The family gatherings are congruent with a communal society which thrives by reaffirming its unity. These family gatherings still satisfy a present-day necessity, inasmuch as today's society still contains primary ties in the family, the neighborhood, the church, the place of work, and so on. The aristocratic gatherings, with their formal structure, reflected a hierarchical society. Only the nobility was invited, and every aspect of the gathering evolved according to the individual's rank. There was a clear scenario and the hosts presided over an elaborate succession of events. The conversation among the participants was not a means to enhance the status of individuals—which had been determined at birth—but of reaffirming the values and cultural patterns of the aristocratic order. These gatherings were formal and even ceremonious.

Modern gatherings are congruent with a society which has lost its sense of a common destiny and established order. They are congruent with an open socio-economic system, with a culture dominated by the success ethic and with a competitive, often narcissistic, "other-directed" personality (to use Riesman's coinage).[3]

Modern gatherings are congruent with the open structure of society. By this we do not mean the political subsystem which has its clear limits, its well known mapping, and its rather fixed operational definitions, but the socioeconomic system which is largely abandoned to the blind expansion of its various individual components. The only standard which presides over the economic game is survival; it consists in doing as well or better than one's competitors. The type of goods to be fabricated or sold, their quality, and their prices are fixed by what the market (that is, by what others) permit or command. To use again Riesman's expression, it is the triumph of other-directedness. Similarly, the modern gathering offers to individuals a place, a marketplace, where they can exchange with others—supposedly representing the world—the performances of their selves. But as in the economic market, individuals are faced with thousands of possible self-definitions and nobody tells them what identity they should present to others in the same way that nobody tells the business owner what he or she should try to sell. The only rule is success. And success will manifest itself only after the individual has tried. Those who try may win but they can also lose. They lose face and all the work undertaken to make a good show, similar to the business owner whose investments can be wiped away overnight by a shift in the market.

Modern gatherings are congruent also with the cultural system, especially with its ethical component, the ethic of achievement and success. The Catholic medieval and baroque ethic was so preoccupied with salvation after death that it had no specific message for the inspiration of daily activities. The only rule was the avoidance of sin. On the other hand, the temporal order and its hierarchy were conceived as shaped by Providence. The public festivities and the aristocratic sociability were celebrations of the God-given organization of the world. They could be fully enjoyed. If by chance some sinful activities were indulged in during the festive enjoyment, God was ready, through the sacraments, to cleanse a soul whose only mistake had been to over-enjoy His "admirable creation." By contrast, the Protestant ethic of the seventeenth and eighteenth centuries was not conducive to much socializing. Socializing was considered a waste of time. Humans had to work. So wanted God. Or, rather, humans persuaded themselves that the successful consequences of their work were signs of God's blessings.[4] The religious foundation of the work ethic slowly disappeared as religion in the nineteenth century was assigned new functions.[5] But work itself kept some kind of divine coloring, until at least, the capitalistic system was so solidly established that it could go on operating by the strength of its functionality and no longer by divine command. A further step was made with the development of very large corporations which themselves seem to perdure by some kind of inertia: The individuals' efforts are futile and unrelated to the overall success of these enormous machines. Extremely few in these large corporations are the individuals who can acquire the sense of the efficacy of their efforts. The rewards individuals seek are no longer the success of their business in the marketplace, but their own success within the large businesses. They are not that of creating a product or of dominating a unit of production, but monetary success. Their ethic is not that of work but of success, not that of producing but that of consuming, for both the pleasure of the goods that are consumed and of the prestige which accompanies their acquisition. Sociability today is no longer in contradiction with the prevalent ethic, as was the case when work was the *leitmotiv*; modern sociability is directly in congress with the success ethic, with its accent on prestigious consumption, self-promotion, and play.

Modern sociability is also in tune with the type of personality which has originated within the context of the industrial society. Modern individuals are not the religious creatures toiling for their eternal salvation, channeling their aggressiveness into religious virtuosity, and rejoicing in religious fiestas and pageants. Nor are they the knights, dreaming of military ventures and, after their victories, indulging in the earthly pleasures of eating and making love. They are no longer the economic *condottieri* who work the whole week and on Sunday rest not only in the righteousness of being the Lord's servants, but also in the pride they derive from the signs of divine election. Modern humans are rather the shrewd combiners who have succeeded by all means including connections, academic degrees, swindle, and fraud, to reach positions of power and wealth. Their frantic efforts are seldom directed at developing their best inner capabilities or becoming creative individuals. What they want is success and in their quest for success they anxiously look at the messages that others send them. Success after all is essentially relative to the judgment of others. Modern gatherings, by offering to participants encounters with a representative sample of the world, permit them to discover not so much who they are in the absolute of their inner capabilities, but more who they are in the eyes of others; in other words, modern gatherings permit the other-directed individuals to establish and confirm their ideal selves as others perceive them. But given the uncertainty of their identities, given the tentative character of the performances through which their identities are presented, and given the imperfect representation of the world found at all gatherings, the game of identity negotiation is an endless and endlessly unfinished enterprise.

NOTES

1. On the various functions of social gatherings, see Chapter 1: "Why Do We Organize and Attend Social Gatherings?"

2. I am indebted to William Michelson (*Man and His Urban Environment, A Sociological Approach* [Reading, Mass.: Addison Wesley Publ. Co., 1977]) for the concept of congruence and its implications. Michelson himself derives his reflections from Talcott Parsons, "An Outline of the Social System," in Parsons, Edward Shils, Kaspar K. Naegele, and Jesse R. Pitts, eds., *Theories of Society* (New York: The Free Press of Glencoe, 1961), pp. 30–79.

3. On the concept of other-directedness, see David Riesman, *The Lonely Crowd* (New Haven, Yale University Press, 1950).

4. On all this I adopt the main argumentation of Max Weber in his *Protestant Ethic and the Spirit of Capitalism* (New York: Charles Scribner's Sons, 1930).

5. On religious change in the nineteenth century, see: Linda K. Pritchard, "Religious Change in Nineteenth Century America," in C. Y. Glock and R. N. Bellah, *The New Religious Consciousness* (Berkeley, Calif.: The University of California Press, 1976), pp. 297–330.

BIBLIOGRAPHY

Baritz, Loren, *The American Left*, New York: Basic Books, 1971.

Bavelas, A., "Communication patterns in task-oriented groups," in Leonard Broom and Philip Selnick, *Sociology*, Evanston, Ill.: Row & Peterson, 1955.

Bell, Daniel, *The Coming of Post-Industrial Society*, New York: Basic Books, 1973.

Bell, Daniel, *The Cultural Contradictions of Capitalism*, New York: Basic Books, 1976.

Bennetts, Leslie, "Beauty Is Found to Attract Some Unfair Advantages," New York *Times*, March 10, 1978.

Berger, Peter, *Invitation to Sociology*, Garden City: Doubleday, 1963.

Berger, Peter, *The Sacred Canopy*, Garden City: Doubleday, 1967.

Berger, Peter, Brigitte Berger, and Hansfried Kellner, *The Homeless Mind*, New York: Random House, 1977.

Berne Eric, *Games People Play*, New York: Grove Press, 1964.

Berscheid, Ellen and Elaine Walster, *Interpersonal Attraction*, Reading, Mass.: Addison Wesley, 1978.

Blau, Peter, *Exchange and Power in Social Life*, New York: John Wiley and Sons, 1964.

Blumer, H. G., *Symbolic Interactionism: Perspective and Method*, New York: Free Press, 1967.

Blumer, H. G., "Action Vs. Interaction," *Society* 9 (April 1972), pp. 50-53.

Burckhardt, Jacob, *The Civilization of the Renaissance in Italy*, New York: Macmillan, 1921.

Caillois, Roger, *Man and the Sacred*, Glencoe, Ill.: The Free Press, 1959.

Chadwick-Jones, John, *Social Exchange Theory, Its Structure and Influence in Social Psychology*, New York, London: The Academic Press, 1976.

Clore, Gerald L. and Donn Byrne, "A Reinforcment-Affect Model of Attraction," in Ted L. Huston, *Foundations of Interpersonal Attraction*, New York: Academic Press, 1974.

Coleman, James, *The Adolescent Society*, Glencoe, Ill.: The Free Press, 1961.

Cooley, Charles, *Human Nature and The Social Order*, New York: Scribner's, 1922.

Coser, Lewis A., and B. Rosenberg, *Sociological Theory*, New York: Macmillan, 1975.

Derber, Charles, *The Pursuit of Attention: Power and Individualism in Everyday Life*, Boston: G. K. Hall, 1979.

Dermer, Marshall and Darrell L. Thiel, "When Beauty May Fail," *Journal of Personality and Social Psychology*, 1975, 31, no. 6, pp. 1168–1176.

Durkheim, Emile, *The Suicide*, Glencoe, Ill.: The Free Press, 1951.

Durkheim, Emile, *The Elementary Forms of the Religious Life*, New York: Collier Books, 1961.

Elias, Norbert, *The Civilizing Process*, New York: Urizen Books, 1978.

Fass, Paula, *The Damned and the Beautiful: American Youth in the 1920's*, Oxford: Oxford University Press, 1977.

Freud, Sigmund, *Collected Papers*, London: The Hogarth Press, 1953.

Fromm, Erich, *Escape From Freedom*, New York: Rinehart and Co., 1941.

Geniesse, "The Perfect Guest," New York *Times*, Nov. 23, 1978, section C, p. 8.

Gerth, Hans and C. Wright Mills, *Character and Social Structure: The Psychology of Social Institutions*, New York: Harcourt, Brace & World, 1953.

Glock, Charles Y. and Robert N. Bellah, *The New Religious Consciousness*, Berkeley, Calif.: The University of California Press, 1976.

Goffman, Erving, *Presentation of Self in Everyday Life*, Garden City, N.Y.: Doubleday, 1959.

Goffman, Erving, *Behavior in Public Places*, New York: The Free Press, 1963.

Goldberg, Philip A., Marc Gottesdiener, and Paul R. Abramson, "Another Put Down of Women?: Perceived Attractiveness as a Function of Support for the Feminist Movement," *Journal of Personality and Social Psychology*, 1975, vol. 32, pp. 113-116.

Gouldner, Alvin W., *The Coming Crisis of Western Sociology*, New York: Basic Books, 1970.

Greenwald, A. G., T. C. Brock, and T. M. Ostrom (eds.), *Psychological Foundations of Attitudes*, New York: Academic Press, 1968.

Hall, Edward T., *The Silent Language*, New York: Doubleday, 1959.

Hickman, C. A. and Manford H. Kuhn, *Individuals, Groups, and Economic Behavior*, New York: Rinehart and Winston, 1956.

Homans, George, "Human Behavior as Exchange," *American Journal of Sociology*, 1958, 63: pp. 597-606.

Huizinga, J., *Homo Ludens*, New York: Roy Publishers, 1950.

Huston, Ted. L., *Foundations of Interpersonal Attraction*, New York: Academic Press, 1974.

Israel, J. and H. Tajfel (eds.), *The Context of Social Psychology: A Critical Assessment*, London and New York: Academic Press, 1972.

James, William, *Psychology: The Briefer Course*, New York: Harper, 1961.

Keniston, Kenneth, *The Uncommitted, Alienated Youth in American Society*, New York: Dell, 1965.

Lévi-Strauss, Claude, "The Concept of Reciprocity," in Lewis A. Coser and B. Rosenberg, *Sociological Theory*, New York: Macmillan, 1957.

Lewis, Oscar, "Folk-urban Continuum and Urbanization," in John Walton and Donald Carns, *Cities in Change*, Boston: Allyn and Bacon, 1973, pp. 90-100.

Lyman, S. M. and M. B. Scott, *A Sociology of the Absurd*, New York: Appleton-Century-Crofts, 1970.

McCall, George J. and J. L. Simmons, *Identities and Interactions*, New York: The Free Press, 1978.

McCarthy, Mary, "The Genial Host" in *The Company She Keeps*, New York: Simon and Schuster, 1942.

McClelland, David C., *The Achieving Society*, Princeton, N.J.: D. Van Nostrand, 1961.

Manis, Jerome G. and Bernard N. Meltzer, *Symbolic Interaction, A Reader in Social Psychology*, Boston: Allyn and Bacon, 1978.

Mauss, Marcel, *The Gift*, Glencoe, Ill.: The Free Press, 1954.

Mead, George Herbert, *Mind, Self, and Society*, Chicago: University of Chicago Press, 1934.

Meltzer, Bernard N., "Mead's Social Psychology," in *The Sociological Psychology of George Herbert Mead*, Center for Sociological Research, Western Michigan University, 1964, pp. 10–31.

Meltzer, Bernard N., John Petras and Larry T. Reynold, *Symbolic Interactionism: Genesis, Varieties, and Criticism*, London: Routledge and Kegan Paul Ltd., 1975.

Michelson, William, *Man and His Urban Environment: A Sociological Approach*, Reading, Mass.: Addison Wesley Publishing, 1977.

Moreno, J. L., *Who Shall Survive?* Washington, D.C.: Nervous and Mental Diseases Monography, no. 58, 1934.

Murstein, B. I., "Physical Attractiveness and Marital Choice," *Journal of Personality and Social Psychology*, 1972, vol. 22.

Nisbet, Robert, *Quest for Community*, New York: Oxford University Press, 1955.

Park, Robert E., "Human Nature and Collective Behavior," *American Journal of Sociology*, 1927, vol. 32, p. 739.

Parsons, Talcott, "An Outline of the Social System," in Talcott Parsons, Edward Shills, Kaspar K. Naegele, and Jesse R. Pitts (eds.), *Theories of Society*, New York: The Free Press, pp. 30-79.

Pin, Emile, *Les classes sociales*, Paris: Spes, 1963.

Post, Emily, *Etiquette*, New York: Funk and Wagnalls, 1937.

Reich, Charles, *The Greening of America*, New York: Bantam Books, 1970.

Riesman, David, *The Lonely Crowd*, New Haven: Yale University Press, 1950.

Riesman David, Robert J. Potter, and Jeanne Watson, "The Vanishing Host," *Human Organization* 19, 1960.

Riesman, David and Jeanne Watson, "The Sociability Project: A Chronicle of Frustration and Achievement," in Philip E. Hammond (ed.), *Sociologists at Work*, New York: Basic Books, 1964.

Rogers, Carl, *Client-centered Therapy*, Boston: Houghton Mifflin, 1951.

Schlesinger, Arthur, *Learning How to Behave*, New York: Macmillan, 1946.

Sherwood, M. E. W., *The Art of Entertaining*, New York: Dodd, Mead & Co., 1893.

Silverman, I., "Physical Attractiveness and Courtship," in *Sexual Behavior*, September 1971, pp. 22-25.

Simmel, Georg, *The Sociology of George Simmel*, Kurt Wolff trans., Glencoe, Ill.: The Free Press, 1950.

Singelman, Peter, "Exchange as Symbolic Interactionism: Convergences between Two Theoretical Perspectives," *American Sociological Review* 37 (August 1972), pp. 414-424.

Singer, Jerome L., *Daydreaming*, New York: Random House, 1966.

Strauss, Anselm, *Mirrors and Masks*, Glencoe, Ill.: The Free Press, 1959.

Sullivan, Harry Stack, *The Collected Works of H. S. Sullivan*, New York: W. W. Norton, 1964.

Tennis, G. and J. Dabbs, Jr., "Judging Physical Attractiveness," *Journal of Personality and Social Psychology*, 1975, vol. 31, pp. 513–516.

Thibaut, John and Harold Kelley, *The Social Psychology of Groups*, New York: Wiley and Sons, 1959.

Thomas, William, I., *The Unadjusted Girl*, Boston: Little, Brown, 1923.

Thorne, Barrie, and Nancy Henley (eds.), *Language and Sex*, Rowley, Mass.: Newbury House Publishers, 1975.

Tönnies, Ferdinand, *Gemeinschaft und Gesellschaft*, Leipzig, 1887.

Touraine, Alain, "Situation du mouvement ouvrier," in *Arguments* Janvier,-février, 1959, pp. 7–15.

Touraine, Alain, "Classe sociale et statut socio-économique," in *Cahiers Internationaux de Sociologie*, Vol. XI, 1951, pp. 155–176.

Van Gennep, Arnold, *The Rites of Passage*, Chicago: The University of Chicago Press, 1960.

Waller, Willard, "The Rating and Dating Complex," *American Sociological Review* 2, 1937, p. 730.

Watson, Jeanne, "A Formal Analysis of Sociable Interaction," *Sociometry* 21 (Dec. 1958), pp. 269–280.

Weber, Max, *The Protestant Ethic and the Spirit of Capitalism*, New York: Charles Scribner's Sons, 1930.

Weinberg, Martin S., "Sexual Modesty, Social Meaning, and the Nudist Camp," *Social Problems* 12, no. 3 (Winter 1965), pp. 314–318.

Wrong, Dennis, "Some Problems in Defining Social Power," *American Journal of Sociology* 73 (May 1968), pp. 673–681.

Wylie, Ruth C., *The Self Concept: A Review of Methodological Considerations and Measuring Instruments*, Lincoln, Nebraska: University of Nebraska Press, 1974.

Zimmerman, Don H., and Candace West, "Sex-Roles, Interruptions and Silences in Conversation," in Barrie Thorne and Nancy Henley (eds.), *Language and Sex*, Rowley, Mass.: Newbury House Publishers, 1975.

SUBJECT INDEX

PERSONS INDEX

ABOUT THE AUTHORS

EMILE JEAN PIN, born in Lyons, France in 1921, is a professor of sociology and former chairman of the Department of Sociology at Vassar College. He holds graduate degrees in classics, philosophy, law and political science and a Ph.D. in sociology. For ten years he was the director of a social research center in Italy. He has taught in France, Italy, Latin America, Canada, and the United States. He has traveled extensively and has been a guest at the most varied types of parties. He has published several books and many articles, notably in the area of sociology of religion and on the subject of social classes.

JAMIE TURNDORF, C.S.W., received her A.B. from Vassar College where she concentrated on the study of American culture. She subsequently received her M.S.W. at Adelphi University. Currently she practices psychotherapy privately and at Craig House Hospital in New York State. Ms. Turndorf has extensive training and experience in the field of dramatic arts. She has performed off-off Broadway, and for the past ten years she has been preparing for an operatic debut.